Ireland's
World Cup 2002

Mick McCarthy

Ireland's World Cup 2002

with Cathal Dervan

SIMON & SCHUSTER
TOWNHOUSE

First published in Great Britain and Ireland by Simon & Schuster/TownHouse, 2002
An imprint of Simon & Schuster UK Ltd and TownHouse and CountryHouse Ltd, Dublin

Simon & Schuster UK is a Viacom company

1 3 5 7 9 10 8 6 4 2

Simon & Schuster UK Ltd
Africa House
64–78 Kingsway
London WC2B 6AH

www.simonsays.co.uk

Simon & Schuster Australia
Sydney

TownHouse and CountryHouse Ltd
Trinity House
Charleston Road
Ranelagh
Dublin 6
Ireland

A CIP catalogue record for this book
is available from the British Library

ISBN 1-903650-48-8

Typeset in Times by M Rules
Printed and bound in Great Britain
by The Bath Press, Bath

Dedicated to the memory of Charlie McCarthy,
loving father and proud Irishman.

Contents

Acknowledgements ix
Foreword xi

Part I: Qualifying

1. 1999 3
2. 2000 15
3. March–June 2001 49
4. August–December 2001 79
5. February–April 2002 111

Part II: The World Cup Finals

6. 13–17 May, Sunderland and Dublin 133
7. 18–23 May, Saipan 151
8. 24–30 May, Izumo 181
9. 31 May–1 June, Niigata 219
10. 2–11 June, Chiba and Yokohama 233
11. 12–17 June, Seoul 281

Afterword 307
Appendix 311

Acknowledgements

To Fiona, Anna, Katie and Michael and to Liz, Cillian, Lia and Ciaran just for being here.

To Treasa at Townhouse and Amanda and Rachael at Simon & Schuster UK for being there when we needed them.

To Jenny for crisp and clear editing.

To Liam, Clare and all at Watermarque for their support.

And finally, to the players and staff and fans for a great World Cup.

Foreword

The call from Eoin Hand came out of the blue. It was the middle of May in 1984 and I was coming to the end of my first season with Manchester City in the old First Division after a record-breaking transfer from my native Barnsley. Eoin was then the manager of the Republic of Ireland's football team and he asked two simple questions on the phone that afternoon. Would I like to declare for my father Charlie's native land? Would I like to play for his Republic of Ireland team?

Would I what? I was twenty-five years old and it seemed that international football had passed me by. Then Eoin handed me my Republic of Ireland debut in a Dublin friendly against Poland and kick-started a fifty-seven-game career that saw me captain my country and lead the Irish team out for the quarter-finals of the 1990 World Cup in Rome's Olympic Stadium.

When Eoin made that call, he landed me right in it. My eldest brother John was getting married that summer and I was down for best man duties. I explained to Eoin about my brother's wedding and asked him to wait before he went public on my Irish call-up. He thought I was turning him down but I only wanted the chance to tell John personally that I would not be able to stand by his side at the altar, and to tell my wife Fiona that she would be going to yet another family wedding on her own. I got a bit of stick for that, but it was worth it. Eoin's phone call that day opened up the world to me and I have enjoyed almost every minute of my time with Ireland ever since.

I discovered a sense of belonging the first time I pulled on that green shirt, a pride in my nationality that has never diminished in the eighteen years since. There have been good times and bad times, on and off the pitch. There have been days when I have danced with elation, and nights when I have cried with frustration, days and nights I would never swap with anyone. I have had experiences I never even dreamed of.

Growing up in an Anglo-Irish family in the Barnsley suburb of Worsborough Bridge I was as aware of my Irish heritage as I was of my Yorkshire roots. My father Charlie, like so many Irishmen before him, was forced to leave Tallow in County Waterford in search of employment. He found love in Barnsley and married my mother Josie. Together they brought four children into the world – John, Kevin, Michael and Catherine – and ensured we were as proud of Barnsley as we were of Ireland.

My father's pride in all things Irish was passed on to me from an early age when I would watch him play hurling in Yorkshire, many miles from his birthplace. Yet it was only when I wore the shirt of his native land that I discovered what being Irish is all about. I cannot tell you how proud he was to see his son win that first cap in 1984. And I can never quantify how proud I was to lead the Republic into the World Cup quarter-finals after Jack Charlton handed me the captaincy en route to the 1990 finals.

Never for a second of any of those fifty-seven caps was I presumptuous enough to believe I would manage my country one day. Yet just six years after those finals, I succeeded Big Jack as Irish manager. I have been honoured to follow in Jack's footsteps and I would like to think I have brought the commitment and dedication that was evident in my playing career into my job as Irish manager.

Reaching the World Cup finals as captain of the Irish team was the pinnacle of my playing career but my pride in that achievement has been surpassed by the pride in reaching the finals again as manager. This book is the story of that amazing journey, its highs and lows.

Football is a team game and this book is as much a team's story as my own, a story of a team's journey told through the eyes of their manager. It is about me and my personal experiences down a World

Cup road but it is also about the players who play for Ireland and the backroom staff who do their best to ensure that the Irish team play to their full potential. You know the players, the central characters in the story of the Irish football team. It is as important to know who's who behind the scenes as well.

Probably the one you know best is physio Mick Byrne, my Mr Motivator and as important off the pitch as the players are on it. I have known Mick since I first stepped off the plane to play for Ireland back in 1984. He has been at my side in all my time as player and manager since then and he is always there for the current members of the Irish squad. He means the world to me. He has played as big a part as anyone in our success down the years.

Ian Evans, better known as Taff, is my right-hand man. I often joke that in God I trust, everything else I leave to Taff. I have known him since we played together at Barnsley and have nothing but faith and respect for his abilities as a coach, mentor and friend. Taff was my assistant at Millwall but when the Irish job came along he urged me to take it, knowing how much it meant to me. That was typical of the man, he was happy to give up on our working relationship if it meant I could become the manager of my country. Thankfully, he has been with me almost since day one of my time with Ireland.

Packie Bonner is another who has been with me since my first game in charge, a Lansdowne Road defeat to Russia in March 1996. Packie and I soldiered together on the field for Eoin Hand and Jack Charlton and for Celtic. He will always be remembered as the Irish goalkeeper who saved a penalty from Timofte in the shoot-out that decided the last sixteen game against Romania at the 1990 finals and sent us through to the game against Italy. These days Packie is my goalkeeping coach, but he is much more than that, he is a man I would trust with my life.

Alongside Mick, Ciaran Murray, our chartered physiotherapist, and Martin Walsh, the honorary medical officer, ensure the fitness and health of the players in our charge. Joe Walsh and Johnny Fallon look after the equipment and all the Umbro gear, Tony Hickey ensures our security is never an issue. And Eddie Corcoran and travel agent Ray Treacy make sure that the logistics are spot on whenever and wherever we are based.

These men are my family whenever the Irish team plays, at home or abroad. They are the men who keep the show rolling and the team on the road. Without all these guys, my job would be a lot harder. For all their hard work and dedication I say a big thank you. I am grateful. The players and the manager are the ones whose responsibility it is to get the results. Those players have never let you – or me – down in their quest for success.

International football is still, believe me, the pinnacle for any player. In the build-up to the 2002 qualifiers in Japan and South Korea, there were many who questioned the future of the game at international level. The money now on offer to the top stars, some claim, will dilute the importance of the national jersey. Not to my mind. When I look at the pride and the passion that the Irish players parade every time they pull on that shirt, I know that international football has a real future.

In this account of our World Cup adventure, I refer to those players as 'my team' but that is simply a term of endearment for this group of people whom I have come to consider as my friends and brothers in arms over the years. In reality it is not my team, it is the Irish team, the team that plays for Ireland and for every Irish man, woman and child across the globe. As such, we have a responsibility to play as well as we can for our country, to work as hard as we can for the Republic. We must fly the flag with pride. I believe we did that this summer in Japan and Korea.

I hope you enjoy the story of that journey – and I thank you for your support.

Mick McCarthy
Republic of Ireland manager
Dublin, August 2002

Ireland's
World Cup 2002

PART I

Qualifying

ONE

1999

Strange as it may seem, the journey to the World Cup finals began in the final twelve seconds of a European Championship disaster. The deep wound inflicted by a late equaliser in the Macedonian capital on an October night in 1999, and the subsequent play-off loss to Turkey, acted as an inspiration to us all, players and management alike, in the World Cup qualification bid that followed.

SATURDAY 9th OCTOBER, SKOPJE

European Championship Qualifier

Macedonia v Republic of Ireland

I stand on the edge of a football pitch in the capital of Macedonia. Ireland are standing on the edge of the 2000 European Championship finals. We are 1–0 up and twelve seconds away from qualification. All we have to do is survive one last corner and I can finally say I have made it as an international manager. Hang on for twelve seconds and I can finally emulate Jack Charlton and qualify for a major finals.

As if.

I am frozen in time as that corner kick is taken. The ball flies off Goran Staverevsks and ends up in the back of Alan Kelly's net. We are so close to making the breakthrough in Skopje, and yet so far away.

I know I am good enough to lead the Irish team out in Holland or Belgium at the Euro 2000 finals. I know my team is good enough to play with the big boys. I had faith when the draw was made, even when some pundit back home suggested we would do well to finish fourth to Croatia, Yugoslavia and Macedonia.

Going to Skopje, in need of the win to see us home and dry, I told anyone who would listen that we deserved to make it through that final hurdle. Yes, we had problems in midfield, Roy Keane was out injured, but we were good enough to prove his absence would not be fatal.

And we almost do it. We make it through the ninety minutes, we protect an early Niall Quinn goal until the fourth official's board goes up and a Spanish referee called Fernandez Marin subjects us to another four minutes in purgatory.

Those four minutes are in stark contrast to the ninety that have gone before. Macedonia conceded to Big Niall in the seventeenth minute and never looked like making a retaliatory strike. We missed a chance to make it two and kill the game but we looked solid, if not spectacular, throughout and I am comfortable on the sideline. I feel we can hang on but there are danger signs as we approach the dying minutes.

Hristov, the one-time Barnsley striker, and Bekiri both go close. Alan Kelly is equal to the challenge, denying first Hristov then Bekiri with a great save that results in the final and fatal corner. One kick and one header later and we are off the top of the group and into the play-offs at best.

Who do I blame? No one really. Not the players who have just given their all and were worn out on their feet after ninety-four minutes. It is one of those things. Goran Staverevsks was in the right place at the right time for Macedonia.

Do I blame myself? No. There was nothing I could do in those final twelve seconds to change the path of history. I had done as much as I could sending that team out there, making the changes I felt needed to be made in the course of a game we dominated but never killed.

We are forced to endure Macedonian celebrations that suggest they have won the European Championships. The reaction of their players is a disgrace. Half their bench want to attack me, the other half want to mock me. I have no idea what I did to upset them, though some of the lads reckon they were annoyed by a late Alan McLoughlin tackle.

Down on the pitch, I want to tear my hair out. The match is over but the group has yet to be decided. We have to wait on the final result from Zagreb where Croatia and the Yugoslavs are still playing. Their second-half has been delayed and our misery is prolonged. Across the Balkans, Yugoslavia, down to ten men, are hanging on dearly to a 2–2 draw. It will be enough, if it ends this way, to see them pip us as group winners and go straight to the finals. We will then face the play-offs yet again, face a re-run of the Euro '96 loss to Holland at Anfield in 1995 and the World Cup '98 play-off defeat in Brussels two years later.

If Croatia score they will win the group, Yugoslavia will go into the play-offs and we will end up with nothing. There is still time and there is still hope, however forlorn. There are tears and torment as we wait in the dark and dank Skopje dressing-room. I look at Mattie Holland, introduced as an eighty-fifth-minute substitute for Mark Kennedy, and I wonder what he is going through. It is his debut, his first cap, on the night it all goes wrong. He must wonder if he will ever feature again for Ireland as reality sinks in.

The word comes through in broken English. Yugoslavia have held out and are through to the finals. The Republic are into the play-offs along with England, Scotland, Denmark, Turkey, Slovakia, Ukraine and Israel.

I have to lift the spirits. If that dressing-room atmosphere carries through into the play-offs we will be dead and buried before a ball is kicked. I tell the players to get their faces off the floor, to lift their heads high. They have lost the battle but we can still win the war. Leaving that concrete stadium from another age, we have to believe that Ireland can beat anyone in those play-offs a few weeks from now.

Macedonia haunts me. I know that I will always have to live with the memory. We screwed up in Skopje. People still talk about recriminations for that eventful night, so let's get some facts straight.

I did not – and do not – blame Keith O'Neill, a second-half substitute for Robbie Keane in that game, for the defeat. Yes, he slipped as that corner came in but that was not the reason why the ball ended up in the back of Alan Kelly's net. I wasn't even aware that he had gone down in the box until someone pointed it out to me afterwards. He was not the player who should have picked up Staverevsks, the loose man, at the corner-kick, there were defenders there to do that job. Suggestions that O'Neill has been banished to international exile because of what happened that night are as wide of the mark as I wish that Staverevsks header had been. Keith's failure to make any further impact at international level is down to Keith, not to anything that happened in Macedonia.

His lack of progress hurts me more than people will ever know, more than he will ever realise. I gave him his debut when he was only a kid at Norwich. Very early in my reign as Irish manager, I put him upfront with David Connolly in a strikeforce that I believed would serve Ireland well for many years to come. They delivered to begin with; people spoke of Keith and David bringing about a premature end to the international careers of Niall Quinn and Tony Cascarino. They raved, as I did, about Keith's power and pace and David's ability to stick the ball in the back of the net. They were even offering odds on the possibility of either of them finally breaking Frank Stapleton's international goalscoring record in the Irish shirt. Sadly, Keith has never lived up to that potential. Injuries have not helped his cause, nor has his lack of progress at club level, despite big-money moves to Middlesbrough and Coventry.

I have picked Keith for Irish squads since Macedonia, but he has always been injured when the call to travel came. I know that he feels that he has fallen out of favour with me but that is not the case at all. Only one criterion comes into play when I pick the international squad – form. If Keith ever regains the form of his youth, I will be quite happy to bring him back and I will celebrate his return to international football with more gusto than most, maybe even Keith himself.

I have often been asked why I took Mark Kennedy off with five minutes to go, after one of his better games for Ireland. He was, in my opinion, a spent force at that stage of the match. He had run himself into the ground and we needed fresh legs as Macedonia applied the late pressure that would eventually lead to their goal. Matt Holland was the only option on the bench. I threw him in at the deep end and I have always meant to ask him if the experience left any scars.

My other abiding memory of Macedonia is the feeling of guilt that followed me around for many months to come. I had just signed a new contract to stay on as manager before the game and I did wonder if I had just cheated the FAI and their faith in me. I knew I was the right man to lead Ireland forward but the Skopje result did none of us any favours.

A couple of days before the game the FAI, through chief executive Bernard O'Byrne and president Pat Quigley, had announced that they were about to sign a new two-year deal to keep me as Ireland manager, no matter what happened in Skopje. Their faith was welcome, considering the fact that our European Championship destiny was still in the lap of the gods. Bernard and Pat both put forward the theory that continuity was important to this Irish team. They argued that I had rebuilt the side, that I had introduced the likes of Keith, David, Robbie Keane, Ian Harte, Shay Given and Damien Duff to senior international football and built a new team around Roy Keane. The FAI knew I needed time to see the job through, collectively we needed time to allow the team to mature into the force I knew it could become on the world stage.

When I applied for the Irish job in 1996 I was not the favourite to get it. There were other candidates who were better qualified and more experienced, I have always accepted that. Some of them got as far as the interview and backed out, others didn't even throw their hats into the ring, despite all the speculation linking them with the job. I was a relatively new manager of Millwall back then, that job coming my way more through circumstance than planning. I was the former Ireland captain but that was about it as far as my credentials for the Republic job went on the surface.

Naturally, I saw things differently. The one fact that I made clear at my interview was that I felt I could become the best man for the job. When I left for Macedonia with a new contract in my back pocket, however, that was not a very universal point of view.

Strikers are judged by the number of goals they score and managers are judged on results and results alone. It is the oldest lesson in football and it can also be the cruellest. That night in Skopje, as the European Championship bid lay dying in the mud, there were precious few people, I suspect, who were glad that I had signed that contract.

At the press conference that followed the game, I was asked if I would quit. No. Would they get their fresh meat? No. Were there any positives to be taken from this debacle at all? Of course there were. We had beaten Yugoslavia and Croatia in Dublin. We had come within three minutes of a draw, the only time I ever played for a draw, in Zagreb. We had lost to a lucky Yugoslavia goal in Belgrade. We were within twelve seconds of the European finals in Skopje.

And we have the play-offs to come.

MACEDONIA 1, REPUBLIC OF IRELAND 1

SATURDAY 13th NOVEMBER, LANSDOWNE ROAD

European Championship Play-off

Republic of Ireland v Turkey

There are certain things you take for granted as the Republic of Ireland's football manager, none of them of your own making. For a start, there is always an injury headache before any international game. And there is always a disaster or a war or a crisis waiting around the corner. The home leg of this play-off does not disappoint on either score.

As ever, my squad is ravaged by injury. Defenders Steve Staunton, Gary Kelly and Ian Harte and midfielders Mark Kennedy and Mattie Holland are all ruled out at various times in the build-up to the game, and suspension keeps Charlton captain Mark Kinsella out of contention too. No change there then.

The absence of Steve and Ian necessitates a move for Denis Irwin to left-back once he manages to shrug off his own injury problems. Defender Kenny Cunningham and strikers Tony Cascarino and Niall Quinn also carry knocks through the week so my mood swings by the day.

I am so short of defenders that I suggest we will look to win the game 7–6 at one stage. I also call in Curtis Fleming, Jeff Kenna and Jason McAteer a couple of days before the match. Curtis gladly abandons a four-day break in Malaga with his club Middlesbrough and swaps it for a few days in his native Dublin and a trip to Turkey. It's no surprise. He's a great guy, Curtis, a lovely fellow.

As we camp down in the luxurious surroundings of Kilkea Castle in Athy, Co. Kildare, for a few days, Turkey decide to base themselves at the Portmarnock Links golf hotel. They were advised to stay on the Southside, closer to their training ground at Belfield, but they opted instead for Portmarnock. Naturally, they are none too impressed with the drive through Dublin's notorious traffic jams and begin to moan, practically as soon as they arrive.

The whole affair casts an ugly backdrop to the match. There are even bizarre claims that 15,000 Irish fans gathered on the beach at Portmarnock on the night before the game and made so much noise that the Turkish players were unable to sleep. We have to concentrate on the football and ignore these stories. My squad is so stretched by injury that I will settle for any lead going to Bursa.

And then another crisis looms as we warm up on the Lansdowne Road pitch. Niall Quinn's neck is troubling him. There is no way Niall can play and Tony Cascarino, only just back from a knee injury, is thrown in at the last minute.

As the game begins, it is obvious that the Turks are only interested in taking something back home for the return leg as coach Mustapha Denizli leaves Hakan Suker as a lone striker and crams the midfield. He has a great little player called Sergen in the middle of the field, a midfield general who causes all sorts of problems for Roy Keane and Lee Carsley.

It is the goalkeeper Rustu who proves to be Turkey's hero on the night however. He serves early notice of his intentions when he turns a Kevin Kilbane drive over the bar in only the first minute then proceeds to frustrate Roy, Robbie and Kenny Cunningham. His best save arrives in the thirty-ninth minute when he somehow keeps out a Cas effort that looked certain to see him equal Frank Stapleton's Irish scoring record of twenty goals.

Hakan Unsal and Ercan have a couple of half efforts for the Turks but nothing too serious. At half-time they throw Arif Erdem on to partner Hakan Suker upfront and they are certainly more adventurous on the resumption. We find it difficult to break them down and threaten Rustu. As the game progresses, they grow in confidence with Unsal and Arif trying their luck.

We need a goal to take to Turkey but there is little sign of it arriving until Robbie Keane pulls one out of the fire in the eightieth minute with a quite superb strike. Is it the breakthrough?

No, moments later the ball strikes Lee Carsley on the hand in our box, the referee points to the spot and Tyafur Havutcu scores for Turkey. To add insult to injury, Robbie picks up a yellow card for cheek and is ruled out of the return leg.

At the press conference afterwards, their coach has a go at our hospitality and our fans. Still seething over the result, I am not impressed. Irish supporters are loyal to us, certainly, but they are also courteous, supportive and respectful of other nations when they come here. I have never seen fans like them anywhere in the world. If he's talking about the same people I am, he is sorely mistaken.

If he's priming me for what to expect in Bursa, I am not bothered. We've had everything to contend with in this European Championship with the Balkan crisis constantly affecting fixtures. If they can throw anything else at us, then bring it on. My dad Charlie used to tell me about the fighting Irish spirit and I think the Turks will discover it for themselves.

In football terms, I know we can bounce back from this disappointment. We have a few sore limbs and a few broken hearts inside. Some wounds opened in Skopje are still raw but we will battle on and we can come through this test. I'm sure we can.

Republic of Ireland 1, Turkey 1

SATURDAY 18th NOVEMBER, BURSA

European Championship Play-off

Turkey v Republic of Ireland

Not for the first time, the hype fails to live up to the reality. We were told to expect a 'Welcome to Hell' arrival in Bursa after an eight-hour trek by plane, ferry and road. Instead, the locals greet us with flowers and a hospitality that is almost Irish.

There is a catch however. Mindful of their own training ground experiences in Dublin, the Turks first want us to train miles out of town, then send us to the local Velodrome. The pitch is shocking, dusty and threadbare and far from acceptable. I am annoyed but we have no choice but to put up and shut up. They claim it is the best pitch around and we have little time to argue our case. It is just nice to see that every nation upholds the FIFA Fair Play rule.

As ever, we travel with injury problems. Alan Kelly is out and his brother Gary joins Dean Kiely, a sixty-fifth minute debutante at the home game, in the squad after a late call-up. Niall's neck problem is still bothering him while Gary Breen, Kenny, Stephen Carr and Lee Carsley all carry bumps and bruises to Bursa.

I know this is going to be the toughest test yet. Thanks to the away goal the Turks scored in Dublin, we have to score here to stay alive in this competition. It will not be easy. Turkey will have fanatical support behind them in the Attaturk Stadium and we will have our work cut out to silence them. The conditions don't help, the pitch is bumpy and the wind lively as the game begins.

Disaster strikes after just five minutes when Stephen Carr twists on an ankle and is unable to continue, Jeff Kenna replaces him. We adjust admirably. Aware of the need to be positive, we dominate the first-half. Roy Keane looks happy to have Mark Kinsella back beside him and snaps at the home side's midfield continually. Kevin Kilbane is off to a stormer down the left and runs the nervy Turks ragged.

Once again, Rustu is the villain as far as we are concerned. He saves from a Keano drive on fourteen minutes then wins a fortunate free-out after appearing to haul David Connolly down outside the box. It should have been an Irish free-kick. And a red card could easily have been the result of their entanglement but Rustu survives until an aerial collision with Kevin forces him off before the break.

Coming up to the interval, Turkey finally create something when a Sukur header clips the top of the crossbar from a Sergen Yalcin free-kick. Dean Kiely then comes to the rescue, advancing quickly to deny Suker before Rory Delap hacks the rebound to safety.

Come half-time, the message is to carry on as we are. I know there is no point going gung-ho and leaving ourselves open at the back but also realise that the longer we go without a goal, the more we will need to throw men forward. Turkey, too, accept the need to up the ante on the resumption. Within five minutes of the restart Okan twice goes close with Sergen also just off target.

Play switches ends with increasing regularity as the clock counts down. Arif hits the crossbar with a header. Mark Kinsella and Niall go close at the other end. Dean makes a world-class save from Sergen.

Damien Duff and Cas enter the fray in a bid to get the goal that will take us through. A minute from time we go close when Kenny's cross catches the wind and substitute 'keeper Egin tips it over the bar. It is heartbreaking on the bench. Four minutes of added time expire as we look for a penalty and Roy has a goal-bound shot blocked.

French referee Gilles Veissiere blows the final whistle and the dream is over, strangled in Skopje and embalmed now in Bursa.

It gets ugly at the end. Cas is assaulted by a Turk who dashes from their dug-out as Tony leaves the pitch. He is jostled by riot police as Irish players try to protect their team-mate. It is all so horrible, so undignified. Tony is punched by one of their players as he tries to defend himself. Then he is sent-off by the referee! I do not expect my players to have to fight their way off the pitch after an international football match. It is disgraceful, the final insult in a European Championship campaign that ultimately causes so much pain.

My players can hold their heads up. We march on with our chins up and chests out as proud Irishmen. Those players gave their all in this campaign but fortune turned its back on us. To miss out on the away goals rule is a sickener.

I am going to change my middle name to lucky by deed poll in Dublin next week. Mick Lucky McCarthy, that's me.

After the game there is much talk of retirement. I had talked Tony Cascarino out of such a move two years earlier, when we lost to Belgium in the World Cup play-off. Tonight, there is no changing his mind. He has served Ireland well for many years now and we will miss him.

Denis Irwin wants to quit as well. I ask him to go away and think about it; a knee-jerk reaction tonight is not the best way to take such a decision. But he wants to spend more time with his family and I understand that perfectly. The demands on his time are excessive from Manchester United, the top club in England, never mind his country. Denis has just played one of his best ever games for Ireland. I do not want him to quit but I will accept it if he feels it is the right thing to do, and he does.

People reckon there is a problem between Denis and me but they are wrong. We did have words a couple of years back when I picked Jeff Kenna ahead of him for a friendly against Argentina at Lansdowne Road. He wasn't happy about it but Jeff was the man in possession at right-back at the time. Denis came to see me and I explained my reasons for picking Jeff ahead of him. I also explained that the best way to react was to prove to me that he should be in the team. He did just that. He was excellent when he came on that night and he has been brilliant for Ireland and United ever since. I know he could do a job for me for a couple of years to come but we have serious strength now on both flanks and Denis believes it's the right time to go. Good luck to him. I owe him a lot.

Niall Quinn is another with retirement thoughts in his head. Leaving Bursa in these circumstances, he says it may be time to go. I disagree. With Tony gone and Denis going, I need Niall around for the World Cup campaign, on and off the field. He is still a handful for any defence, even at thirty-three, and he has so much influence on the youngsters in this squad. They need him to guide them on the road that leads to Japan and Korea. I need him to get us there. He agrees, thankfully, to stay on for as long as the World Cup adventure lasts.

Now we're talking.

TURKEY 0, REPUBLIC OF IRELAND 0
(*Aggregate score, 1–1. Turkey win on away goal rule.*)

TWO

2000

The draw for the World Cup qualifiers puts Ireland in with Holland, Portugal, Estonia, Cyprus and Andorra, so many call this the Group of Death. I ask the FAI to get at least one of the big guns for the first game and we end up away to Holland in September and Portugal in October! First come a series of friendlies, and the US Cup, vital preparation for the World Cup tests ahead.

WEDNESDAY 23rd FEBRUARY, LANSDOWNE ROAD

Friendly International

Republic of Ireland v Czech Republic

Friendlies are meaningless when you win them and of national importance when you lose them. Or so it seems, judging by the reaction and the column inches devoted to them.

For me, they offer the chance to work with the players on a daily basis for a while. From a purely selfish point of view, that is the biggest bonus because it is the one element of club management that I really miss. I love the freedom that the international job gives me, don't get me wrong. I have a lifestyle now that will be very hard to emulate when I go back to the asylum, my pet name for the world of club football. But I do miss the training ground banter, the day-to-day involvement that goes with a league job. That's why friendlies are eagerly anticipated in the McCarthy household. They offer me a chance to get my hands dirty again and I relish the likes of this Czech Republic game.

The routine for these friendly weeks when we play at home on a Wednesday night is straightforward. The players arrive in Dublin on Sunday night and we train on Monday, morning and afternoon if the need arises. Monday night is movie night, those who want to can attend the pictures, those who don't can stay back in the hotel and relax. Tuesday sees the training session at Lansdowne followed by a press conference and, sometimes, the team announcement. On Wednesday morning we go for a stroll in Malahide followed by lunch back at the airport hotel and a sleep in the afternoon before the coach trip across town to Lansdowne.

This friendly is more important than usual. It is the first time the Irish squad has come together since the end of our European Championship involvement. We need to regroup and start again. I need to convince the players that I am up for a new year and a new challenge and I need to see more of the same from them.

There are always withdrawals at this time of year. Players are heavily into the club season by now and wear and tear always becomes a factor before this sort of game. Whenever I name a friendly squad, I know there will be withdrawals through injury. It is a fact of life for every international manager. We don't play a competitive game again until September so the clubs have to be respected on these occasions. They pay the players' wages after all.

As I have grown in this job, I have come to accept the needs of club managers a little more. There are times when they require first call on their players, times when it is my right to have the strongest side available to me. This is definitely a case of the former.

Alan McLoughlin has followed Cas and Denis into retirement and he too will be missed. I always regarded Alan as a better player than the press gave him credit for, always reckoned he never got the number of caps that should have come his way. He knows there are younger legs on the way through now and he is realistic enough to move aside and let someone else have his seat on the aeroplane. I admire that honesty in Macca.

Who will come in? These fixtures are the perfect opportunity to blood new players. The best example of that came when the Olomouc friendly against the Czechs, back in March 1998, saw Robbie Keane, Damien Duff, Alan Maybury, Lee Carsley, Graham Kavanagh, Gareth Farrelly and Rory Delap all make their first appearances for Ireland.

This time, I want to give the Leeds United midfielder Stephen McPhail his first cap but injury has ruled him out. Instead it is Sunderland's Paul Butler who gets his chance, in at centre-back with Gary Kelly and his nephew Ian Harte at full-back.

Paul, who also qualified for Wales, has a baptism of fire. Jan Koeller, the striker he is marking, scores both first-half goals as the beaten Euro '96 finalists build up a 2–1 lead. A Karel Rada own goal, after the first Koeller goal, opens up our account and uncle sets up nephew when Kells crosses for Hartey to score the equaliser just before the break.

Half-time sees Paul Butler replaced by Phil Babb and I throw Jason McAteer on for Mark Kennedy. Inspired substitutions, if I may say so, as we push forward and Robbie Keane goes on to score a late winner.

It is a good start to a difficult year ahead. We have wiped the Skopje cobwebs away, if not the scars, and we have beaten one of the top sides in Europe. It is good to be back at work.

Republic of Ireland 3, Czech Republic 2

WEDNESDAY 26th APRIL, LANSDOWNE ROAD

Friendly International

Republic of Ireland v Greece

Debut time again. Roy Keane is out, a pulled hamstring in a Manchester United game denying us his services against a side in England's World Cup group. He rings to tell me that he won't make the trip but he's adamant that he wants to go to America in the summer for the US Cup, the booby prize for those teams not in the Euro finals.

Stephen McPhail misses the boat again. Injury is delaying his international debut and I am sure it is as frustrating for him as it is for me. Instead five others take their bow. Steve Finnan, Richard Dunne, Barry Quinn, Alan Mahon and Gary Doherty will all remember this night. So will the Greek star Vassilios Lakis, scorer of the only goal of a fairly scrappy contest.

Mark Kinsella, Kinse as we know him, gets the man of the match award but Stevie Finnan must have run him close. I like Steve a lot on this performance.

Republic of Ireland 0, Greece 1

TUESDAY 30th MAY, LANSDOWNE ROAD

Friendly International

Republic of Ireland v Scotland

I can laugh at it now. The day before the game I am asked how good Scotland are. Well, they were good enough to take a 0-0 draw away from Holland a month earlier and Craig Brown, an old buddy of mine, got incredible stick for not winning the match. I found that hard to believe. In fact, I say, I would give my right arm for a scoreless draw away in Amsterdam this September.

Craig's team then go and rub my nose in it, of course. They prove what a good side they are with a win in Dublin that justifies my belief in their ability. They are easily the best of the three teams we have played so far this year. They even allowed us an early goal when a Mark Kennedy effort hits Craig Burley on its way to the net!

Stephen McPhail finally gets to make his debut, as does the Watford striker Dominic Foley. McPhail looks comfortable on the ball but the middle of the field belongs to the Scots.

The other story of the night concerns the return of Terry Phelan to international duty. I played with Terry in the early nineties and injury gives him another chance here. So does the fact that Kevin Kilbane is needed further upfield after starting the game at left-back.

Barry Ferguson and Neil McCann are booed all night, because they play for Glasgow Rangers, and not Celtic, but theirs is the last laugh. McCann is involved in the build-up to Hutchison's sixteenth-minute equaliser and Ferguson grabs the winner after half an hour. Even the boo boys have seen enough to shut up by the time the referee blows the final whistle.

REPUBLIC OF IRELAND 1, SCOTLAND 2

SUNDAY 4th JUNE, CHICAGO

US Cup

Republic of Ireland v Mexico

I do admit to mistakes every now and again; I have got things wrong in the past. I only ever once tried to play for a draw and Davor Suker made me pay with a very late winner in Zagreb in the Euro 2000 qualifiers. This time it's a change in formation that trips me up.

Mexico are under strength due to club commitments at home and we are missing a host of seasoned internationals, including Roy Keane. Injury has forced him out but I'm not too concerned about it. I don't need to drag Roy across America to know how good a player he is and what he can do for my team. He will be there when we need him in September.

Keane's absence also gives me the chance to dangle a Dutch carrot in front of a few other wannabe World Cup stars. I stress to them that the US Cup is important to us. I see it as the start of our bid to qualify for Japan and I want them to treat it as such. That explains my desire to look at some new players and even try a new system out today. I am going to play 4–3–3 and see how we get on. I want to have two wide men supporting Robbie Keane up front and see if it is an option for the future.

Mistake. Big mistake. I suffer, not in silence, as we go two down to goals from Daniel Osorno and Sanchez inside fifty-four crazy minutes. Believe me, only the brilliance of Dean Kiely in goal kept it down to two. We need structure in the middle of the park and balance upfront. End of 4–3–3.

Normal service is restored after the second goal and the players respond magnificently. Goals from Richard Dunne and Dominic Foley pull us level and I am pleased as punch. We have got out of jail tonight. More importantly, the players showed the spirit necessary to perform that rescue act. That meant more to me than the draw. They dug deep to get back into the game and produced real character when it mattered. That's just what we need for the World Cup campaign.

Republic of Ireland 2, Mexico 2

TUESDAY 6th JUNE, BOSTON

US Cup

Republic of Ireland v USA

A most bizarre night at the Foxboro Stadium outside Boston, home to the New England Revolution. Tonight the game is ruined by incessant rain. Anywhere else and I don't think the match would have been played, so heavy was the downpour.

We respond to the conditions with a goal, scored in the thirty-first minute of actual play by Dominic Foley. Considering he was supposed to be on holiday with his girlfriend right now, I am delighted that the trip is working out so well for the Cork youngster. Stephen McPhail is also making the most of his chance, his pass for Dominic's goal was exquisite. In the middle of the field, Mattie Holland really looked the part.

The less said about the American equaliser the better. Ante Razov was at least five yards offside when he scored but the referee and the linesman allow the goal to stand. Welcome to the US Cup.

Even the gods know it was a wrong call. They get their revenge when the lights go out almost straight after the goal. By the time play resumes, our anger has subsided and we end the night with another draw.

Republic of Ireland 1, USA 1

SUNDAY 11th JUNE, NEW JERSEY

US Cup

Republic of Ireland v South Africa

New York is the fun element of the trip for the players. They were billeted in out-of-town hotels in both Chicago and Boston but Manhattan and Fitzpatrick's is the call for the trip to the Big Apple. They also have twenty-four hours off to enjoy the sights and the sounds and all the attractions of the city that never sleeps. They do just that and more judging by their response to the first real training session before the South African game but I am not worried.

One of the main reasons for going Stateside was to galvanise and unite the squad ahead of the World Cup qualifiers. When Jason asks if I can get a club job and bring them all together in the Premiership, I know things are going according to plan.

Giants Stadium is the ground where Ireland beat Italy in the 1994 World Cup – happy days. I have also, as it happens, been involved in some crazy games here. My last Irish cap was won on this ground against Portugal back in 1993 and I was sent off here as manager in 1996, along with Niall Quinn, against Mexico in another US Cup, my first tournament in charge of Ireland.

Our chances of winning this tournament are remote after the two opening draws and America kill them on this same pitch when they beat Mexico to lift the trophy before our game.

The Africans take the lead through Shaun Bartlett in the seventeenth minute and just before the break Stephen McPhail equalises direct from a corner. This game is significant for one fact and one fact only, as Niall Quinn equals Frank Stapleton's twenty-goal Irish record. I have never been happier for any player, especially considering I was told by a journalist that he had retired through injury when we played out in Iceland in the '98 World Cup qualifiers. I then had to talk him out of retirement after the play-off defeat in Turkey last year so I take a lot of pleasure out of this goal. Niall is a great guy and I know he will get the record in his own right before he retires.

REPUBLIC OF IRELAND 2, SOUTH AFRICA 1

SATURDAY 2nd SEPTEMBER, AMSTERDAM

World Cup Group Two Qualifier

Holland v Republic of Ireland

Nothing is ever easy when you're Mick McCarthy and the manager of the Republic of Ireland international football team. In the past, we have lived through everything from scud missiles to the threat of carpet bombs in our attempts to qualify for World Cups and European Championships so little should surprise me. This trip promises to be just as difficult and it lives up to that promise.

Half the country thinks I am mad to take on Holland, Euro 2000 semi-finalists, in their own backyard in our first 2002 World Cup qualifier. Not me, I believe this is the right time to face the Dutch in Amsterdam. When the FAI sent Bernard O'Byrne to the fixtures meeting for this game, I told him to get me Holland or Portugal away in the first game and he obliged. My thinking is simple. After the Euro 2000 finals, Frank Rijkaard stepped aside as coach and playmaker Denis Bergkamp retired. And if there is a right time to take on one of the big teams then this is it, straight after a major finals when they are on their way down from a big high and half their squad is feeling the effects of their summer exertions. It has worked for us in the past, we caught Croatia cold in Dublin two years ago on their first competitive outing after the 1998 World Cup finals. The Dutch European Championship campaign was impressive but I do not expect them to start this campaign at anything approaching the same intensity.

Louis van Gaal, successful with Barcelona and Ajax as a club coach, is the new Holland supremo and I know it will take him time to adjust to international football. No matter how experienced you are in the club game, you cannot just step up to the world stage and take to it immediately. It took me time to adjust to the demands at this level. When I got the job the FAI gave me a two-year contract and I always felt that was balanced in their favour. It was clever on their part, a safe option for them if things didn't work out. Any new boss needs time to get to know his players and their ways and the squad need time to adjust to new methods as well. It does not happen overnight but very few national associations are prepared to give you time. I knew I needed more than two years and I firmly believe the development of my Irish team proves that.

Thankfully, the FAI have been good to me ever since that first contract. They have realised that we are moving in the right direction, that results and performances are improving all the time and we are now very close to a side that can qualify for the major tournaments. The Merrion Square officials deserve credit for their patience. They have seen the progress made and realised that it has taken time and patience, on everyone's part. The continuity factor has been a bonus as far as the players are concerned and they have responded to me over the last four years.

This is, by and large, my squad now. They know exactly how I want to play the game and the majority of them have come to international football during my time in charge. We have grown up together and we are ready now for the big challenge. Qualification for the 2002 World Cup is everything, starting with this game in Holland.

A full six days before the game, controversy lands on our doorstep. The drill for the week leading up to the game was meant to be simple. The players were told to arrive in Dublin anytime on the Monday, ahead of our scheduled get together for training on the Tuesday morning. Their time on Monday was their own, they were free to do anything they wanted so long as they reported for training on Tuesday morning.

Traditionally, the players go out for a drink on their first night together in a week-long trip. I have no problem with that. I have done it myself in the past and one of the great things about this Irish squad is the spirit of unity. Nights out help build that bond. This time is different, of course.

Monday gets off to a bad start when I announce that Roy Keane, who played for United twenty-four hours previously, will be late joining the squad. He has a back problem that needs treatment at Old Trafford and wants to stay at home for an extra day, at least. I am happy to agree to that but some of the media think otherwise. They stir the rift stories again without any foundation.

That night, I go out with my wife Fiona to celebrate her birthday with some close friends and I am none too pleased when the phone rings early on Tuesday morning. My assistant Ian Evans, more commonly known as Taff, is on the other end of the line. He tells me he has some bad news. Roy and Robbie Keane were both involved in games on the Sunday and I jump to the conclusion that the early call must be about their fitness and availability. I am relieved, at least temporarily, when he says it has nothing to do with them.

He reveals that two of my players, Mark Kennedy and Phil Babb, are in a Garda cell, arrested after a prank on Harcourt Street, in Dublin's city centre, that got out of hand late last night. I am stunned. There is only one rule when the players go out – act responsibly. They have broken that rule with a silly prank that ended with them jumping up and down on the bonnet of a car, a Ban Garda's car. They were out of order and they were caught, and I can't complain about that.

Phil and Mark are fairly sheepish by the time I see them brought into court. The drink has worn off and reality has well and truly sunk in. They are remanded on bail to appear before the judge again in November and we take them back to the hotel.

Sparky is almost in tears as he asks me if his international career is over. They know they have messed right up and I feel for them as we drive them back, I really do. It could have been me. In fact, I would argue that most people have engaged in silly pranks under the influence in their time. They got caught doing something stupid and they are paying a very heavy price.

I ask the two lads if they want to attend the daily press conference. My advice to them is to face the music now, admit to the prank and get the hounding out of the way. It is their decision, I do not want to be seen as a headmaster dragging the kids up in front of class but I do feel it is in their best interests to face the media there and then. They agree, not that their co-operation wins them many favours with the media pack. Some of the column inches devoted to Babbsy and Sparky over this story are over the top. They have made a mistake, they have admitted their guilt and they will be punished in the court of law and by their employers.

I have my own punishment to hand down later that day. In effect, I have no option but to send the two players home and suspend them from international duty until I have a chance to review the case with the FAI. I cannot appear to condone their behaviour by taking them to Holland with us. They are role models for many young Irish fans and they did not behave as such on Monday night.

I make it clear to both of them that they can play for Ireland again, if their performances justify the call-up. Sparky has since got back into the squad whilst Babbsy has seen others move ahead of him in the queue. He can still play for Ireland, if his club form merits it.

The Harcourt Street furore drags on into Wednesday when Roy finally arrives from Manchester and is asked his opinion on the subject. It was my decision to send them home so when Roy suggests it is harsh, some of the media jump on that one as well. I suppose it's an easy target for them.

In an effort to put the incident behind us, I bring the squad together to discuss it when we finally arrive on the training ground in Holland on the Thursday night. I explain to the players that the behaviour of Sparky and Babbsy was unacceptable and that anyone trying anything similar will also find themselves in trouble. I also ask that anyone who has a problem with my decision open their mouth now or forever hold their peace. There are no dissenters and finally we are able to concentrate on the game and the challenge ahead.

These are the days we live for in football. There isn't a player in the world who wouldn't feel motivated by the challenge of taking on Holland in the impressive Amsterdam Arena. I am as excited as the Irish players ahead of the game. We will never get a better chance to play the Dutch with van Gaal forced to pick his team without the services of Jaap Stam, Edgar Davids, Marc Overmars, Jimmy Floyd Hasslebank, Zenden and Arthur Numan. They have to experiment with Phillippe Cocu in for the retired Bergkamp and we will have a right go at them and exploit their weakness.

It would be easy to come here and defend. Instead, we intend to pick them off, to pass the ball through them, to play them at their own game and see how they cope with that. I want a result tonight. I want to take something from Holland and Portugal away and then finish them off at Lansdowne. That is the way we must approach this group if we are going to qualify for Japan and Korea. It is imperative that we take something out of the Arena tonight.

It is an easy Irish team to pick. Tony Cascarino, Alan McLoughlin and Denis Irwin have all retired since we last started a qualifying tournament. Kenny Cunningham is injured and Babbsy and Sparky are both back in England. I know the way I want to play the game. I want to go 4–4–1–1, with Robbie playing just behind Niall and our wide men pushing forward to support those two when we press. We need to negate the Dutch habit of putting a player in the hole, Cocu now instead of Bergkamp, and give them a taste of their own medicine.

That was the plan outlined to the players when we trained on the pitch on Friday night, after which I told them the team that will start our World Cup campaign. Alan Kelly is in goal with Dean Kiely on the bench. Alan is the player on form with Blackburn and Ireland in recent months while Dean was outstanding in the Euro play-offs against Turkey. Shay Given must sit in the stand for this one but I make it clear to the three players that I will rotate the sub keeper for this tournament.

Stevie Carr from Spurs gets in ahead of Gary Kelly at right-back.

He has outstanding ability and great potential and I know he will become one of the best defenders in the world over the course of this qualifying campaign.

Ian Harte will fill the left-back shirt now that Denis has retired, Ian's first competitive start in two years for Ireland.

Gary Breen, one of the successes of the summer tour to America, will play at centre-back. Alongside him I go for Richard Dunne, even though Steve Staunton is also available. I have been thinking this one through for some time now and actually rang Richard at Everton last week to see how he was feeling. I told him there was a chance he could play instead of Kenny, and ahead of Stan, and to ensure he was lean and sharp in training when he got to Dublin. He hasn't let me down and I know he will do the job tonight. Richard can be anything he wants to be in this game. He has great under-rated pace and mobility and he is so strong in the air. Like all young players, he can make mistakes but I have real faith in him ahead of the biggest game of his life.

The right side of midfield is something of a contentious position. The media believe Gary Kelly should play there and he has done a great job for me in the role previously. Jason McAteer is struggling at club level but he is a natural midfield player and I really like the energy he brings to the game. I go with him, even though it will raise a few eyebrows.

There is no contest in the middle of the field. Roy Keane, who has been taunted by Michael Reiziger through the press in the build-up to this game, is the best central midfield player in Europe while Mark Kinsella has really developed as his partner. Kevin Kilblane gets the nod outside them with Robbie and Niall upfront.

It is a massive game for Robbie. Since we were in the States, he has signed for Inter Milan from Coventry and I know half the world is looking to see how he copes with the move. He actually rang me for advice on the transfer during the summer. I was back in Fitzpatrick's in Manhattan on holiday when he called and my advice was to go for it. Even if Robbie only lasts a year in Italy he will learn from the experience and his financial future will be secure. There are no down sides to the move as far as I am concerned, he cannot come back from Italy a failure. He will be a better player for Ireland because of his time on the Continent and that shows early on tonight.

We start at pace. The game is only seven minutes old when Kevin crosses from the left and Quinny flashes a header off the post. We are moving with confidence, playing the ball through the middle and taking the game to the Dutch. They look bemused by it all as Hartey's free-kick dips over the bar at the end of another Irish assault.

Our reward comes in the twenty-first minute and is a thing of beauty. About nineteen Irish passes are strung together before Stevie Carr puts Jason clear down the right and his perfect cross is met late by the head of Robbie Keane. The ball is in the net before 'keeper Edwin van der Sar can react and the 5,000 or so Irish fans are on their feet. So am I. We have just taken the lead away to Holland, a lead we thoroughly deserve.

It gets better. Quinny and Kevin both go close to a second before the Dutch launch their only real threat of the first-half in the forty-first minute. They look to have a real chance when Paul Bosvelt connects but Richard Dunne blocks the shot with ease, cool as a cucumber at the back despite one hefty challenge on Patrick Kluivert that is penalised with a dangerous free-kick.

At half-time the dressing-room is a happy place. We are in control of this game, we are playing all the football and the important thing now is not to panic.

Van Gaal puts Clarence Seedorf, Robbie's room-mate at Inter, on to try and stifle Roy Keane. It's no use. As Keano drives us forward, we continue to control the tempo of the game. Another Kilbane cross tees Quinny up for a missed header before a sublime second goal arrives in the sixty-fifth minute. Again, we work the ball out of defence via Roy, Stevie Carr and Robbie. He flicks it for Niall and Jason is onto Quinny's touch as we had told him to do all week in training. He moves inside, hits it with his left foot and is already celebrating by the time van der Sar sees the ball cross the line. Two up and cruising. Or are we?

For some reason, we drop back when that second goal goes in. We get deeper and deeper and deeper, and pay the price when Ronald de Boer crosses for substitute Jeffrey Talan to head home at the far post in the seventy-first minute. It is a stupid goal to give away. We should have stopped the cross as it came in and then we should have cleared it.

Now the Dutch have the bit between their teeth. Kevin almost silences them when he goes close from the kick-off but again we drop twenty yards deeper than we were for the first hour.

I take Niall off and send David Connolly on. Quinny is dying on his feet after running himself into the ground and my hope is that David will prove his point to the Dutch. He is out in the cold at Feyenoord here and this would be the perfect time to remind them what he can do. He doesn't. Instead the Dutch continue to press as we replace Jason with Gary Kelly and Kevin with Steve Staunton.

Their equaliser has good fortune written all over it, Giovanni van Bronckhorst's eighty-third minute shot deflecting off the helpless Mark Kinsella and past Alan Kelly. For a second I am distraught. We have been hit hard by the gods towards the end of a game we could have won.

And it's not over yet. Right on the death, Kluivert cocks his foot as he goes in search of the winner. I fear the worst but Richard Dunne moves across the angles and steals the ball off his toe. Brilliant. Seconds later the whistle goes and I am delirious again. I throw my water bottle into the air and punch the heavens. We could have won, but we have a point from Holland and we'd have taken that this morning.

Doctors differ and patients die. Straight after the game, I am out on the pitch, slapping the players on the back and congratulating them on a job well done. Then we go to the supporters, to thank them for being here and to show that the result means as much to us as it does to them this far from home.

Not everyone feels the same way. Roy Keane is straight off the pitch, aggrieved that we have thrown away a two-goal lead against the European semi-finalists on their own pitch. In the mixed zone where the players talk to the press afterwards, he makes it clear that we have to learn to win games like this.

I was just the same as Roy after games with Ireland, particularly in Italy back in 1990. When we finally lost in Rome in the quarter-finals, I was straight off the pitch and up the tunnel. I was fighting with Jack, with myself, with anyone who'd fight with me. I was angry we had lost, angry with the referee and angry that it was all over. I never went back on that pitch, never saluted those fans, never got to enjoy what we had achieved in making it to the last eight of the World Cup. That is one of the big regrets of my playing career.

I wasn't happy with the way we surrendered a two-goal advantage in Amsterdam, far from it. I know we got too deep in the game, I know we withdrew into our own half when we were two goals up. We should have pushed on after Jason's goal, we should have pushed people onto them and stopped them shooting. But just look at the quality of the opposition. Look at the way they threw men forward when they went two goals down.

Roy is right to say we should have won the game and right to suggest we have to learn how to win games in these situations. But don't for a second think there wasn't a lot to be proud of in Amsterdam. As a manager, I have to look at the bigger picture and when you hear Louis van Gaal suggest that we were toying with his team in the first-half, you just know we did something right.

There was so much of that performance that was positive. We outplayed the Dutch for sixty-five minutes, we passed the ball through the masters of the art. We were solid in defence and masterful in the middle of the field. We took them on tactically and exposed real weakness in a side that finished in the top four in Europe. More than anything, we gave ourselves a real start to the qualifying campaign.

I'd have settled for a point before kick-off. I'd have been happy when the draw was made to come to Holland and get a 2–2 result. I make no apologies for that. As was said in the dressing-room afterwards, we set our stall out in Amsterdam tonight. We know we can go away from home and compete against the big nations now. And they know we can have a go at them as well. We drew a game we should have won and could have lost but there was far more positive than negative out there for me.

Richard Dunne was thrown in at the deep end and never put a foot wrong. His tackle on Kluivert at the end may ultimately prove to be the difference between qualifying and staying at home in two year's time when the World Cup goes to Japan and Korea.

Jason McAteer was right behind Richard in terms of effort and application. I picked him ahead of Gary because I wanted him to get forward, support the front men and try to nick a goal. The plan worked a treat and I am delighted for him that he is a hero again.

Roy and Kinse were excellent in the middle of the field. Holland kept changing their midfield to try and cope with them, which is a credit to our pairing.

Stevie Carr looked like the world-class player I know he is and Robbie capped his first World Cup game with a great goal.

I am positive as I fly to Estonia the next day and watch Portugal win 3-1. That puts them top of the group after a game that stresses just how hard it will be to get anything from Lisbon next month.

At least, we have a point in the bag now. There are some at home who suggested we would be lucky to get a point from the opening two games and that I would be lucky to have a job by the time we leave Portugal.

I wonder what they think now.

HOLLAND 2, REPUBLIC OF IRELAND 2

SATURDAY 7th OCTOBER, LISBON

World Cup Group Two Qualifier

Portugal v Republic of Ireland

One of the big regrets of my international career is that I never got to play at the Stadium of Light, home ground to the legendary Benfica. When Ireland last played there, in October 1995, I was a fan on the rain-sodden terraces as Jack's makeshift team were beaten 3–0 in the game that forced us into the Euro '96 play-offs and ultimately cost us qualification. Estadio da Luz, as an old friend Joao

Pinheiro knows it, is one of the great stadiums of world football, a massive bowl that is so atmospheric and so inviting.

I would love to play there on Saturday night and mark Luis Figo, the world's costliest player following his £37 million move from Barcelona to Real Madrid. In fact, I would almost swap management for an hour on the pitch against this great Portuguese team and players like Figo, Rui Costa, Joao Pinto and Sergio Conceicao. They are a better team than Holland, certainly a lot stronger than the Dutch team we drew with in Amsterdam last month. There is more flair about Portugal, they have more players with a trick or two up their sleeves, more individuals who are capable of winning a game on their own. They are also more resolute now than many a Portuguese team before them. That has always been a problem for their international sides, they have failed to match flair with steel and have been pushed aside rather too easily as a result. Not this team. They have a real leader at the back in Fernando Couto, aided and abetted by Jorge Costa, and in midfield Rui Costa, who will give us a real run for our money.

Added to that the element of surprise will also be missing from our game in the Stadium of Light. Portugal will have sent their scouts to the Amsterdam Arena for our opening match and they will know now that Ireland are no mugs in this qualification group.

Unfortunately, before we leave for Lisbon I have to get involved in more needless crisis management.

With Gary Kelly and Shay Given both ruled out through injury and not in a position toforce their way into the team, I decided to name the starting eleven on Tuesday afternoon after late call-ups for Curtis Fleming, Graham Kavanagh and Nicky Colgan.

Curtis has been called up late for my squads so often that he has a packed bag ready by the phone on the Monday of every international week. He jokes that he doesn't even bother to answer the phone any more, he just heads straight for Teeside Airport when it rings.

The team announcement on Tuesday turns out to be a big mistake. With no team to speculate on, the press have nothing to write about. So they turn a molehill into a mountain once again. And there are no prizes for guessing that Roy Keane and Mick McCarthy are once more the central characters in this drama. Roy picked up a dead leg playing for United in the Champions League against PSV last week and stays back in Manchester again for treatment on the Tuesday. The message that he will arrive in on Wednesday is left with the FAI in Merrion Square by someone from United but I don't get to hear about it until Tuesday night.

Mick Byrne, Keano's confidante within the squad, assures me that Roy will be in on Wednesday morning. That gives him plenty of time to be fully fit for the game. As long as he plays in Lisbon on Saturday night, I don't really care when Roy arrives in Dublin.

Sadly, there is a history of hysteria when it comes to Keane–McCarthy stories. I was never that bothered if he went to America or not back in 1996. He didn't go in the end and it became a big media story at the time. We have had a few chats to sort things out but it has all dragged on since then in the press. Anything that Roy says or does now is twisted to become a slight on me or his team-mates. It happened when he spoke honestly and openly about the need for Ireland to start winning games away from home after we lost that two-goal lead in Amsterdam. The press interpreted that as a jibe at me, so when Roy doesn't show up on the Tuesday in Dublin, the papers have a field day. He has gone AWOL again or he has snubbed Mick McCarthy, depending on which headline you read. By the time we leave for Lisbon on Thursday morning, one paper has decided to splash 'WAR' across its front page, over a story about my current relationship with Roy.

I am livid, absolutely furious. It really annoys me that an Irish newspaper would try to undermine our preparations for one of the biggest games the Ireland team will ever face. Have these people no national pride? Do they seriously understand how damaging that article is to me and to Roy Keane? I am still raging by the time we get off the plane in Lisbon and I address the media. I look for the guy who wrote the story but, of course, it is blamed on someone back in a Dublin office who doesn't even have the balls to face Roy or me with this ludicrous allegation.

Press criticism bothers me less and less as time goes on, I don't even read it anymore, but this headline really disturbs me. It seems as if someone with a grudge back in Dublin is trying to drive a wedge between me and my captain.

My response is to point people in the direction of Ireland's performances on the field. Anyone who suggests I have lost any of the players need only look at the way those players played for me in Amsterdam, Roy included. If you lose players, if they aren't bothered about you, if they don't respect you, then they won't play for you. Nobody can criticise the way my team performed in Holland so why someone would want to undermine our performance in Portugal is a mystery to me.

Despite the 'war' headline, I see no need for me to sit down with Roy before the game and even discuss this ridiculous story. That would only give it credence and I have no desire to do that.

As it happens, my relationship with Roy is fine right now as far as I am concerned, as it is with all my team. I am a footballers' man, I like footballers and people involved in the game. I respect players for their ability on the park and ultimately my only requirement of them is that they deliver when they play for my team. On that front, I can have no quibbles at all with Roy Keane. He is my best player and he is a key player for Ireland, not just in Lisbon on Saturday night but throughout this World Cup campaign. If we are to qualify for Japan and Korea then we need a fully fit and a fully focused Roy Keane in our side. What happens between us on a personal level is irrelevant. We may not go for a pint or exchange Christmas cards but that is immaterial so long as he gives his all in that green shirt, which he always does. He is a winner and I want him in my team. Full stop.

I know he gives the other players a rollicking when they do something wrong on the pitch and that is something that people often remark on when Roy plays for Ireland but they do appreciate it when he tells them they have done something right. One of the great thrills early on in my Irish career was when Liam Brady praised me for something during a game. You like to be accepted by great players.

Over the years it has frustrated Roy that Ireland are not Manchester United. They have resources that we can never dream of and he has the best of everything available to him there. Right now, he is a first-class professional at the pinnacle of his sport and I need him in my team.

Another player at the pinnacle of his profession is Luis Figo. He is the Portuguese Roy Keane, the very heartbeat of their team. He is a wonderful player, a wonderful human being judging by his demeanour on and off the field and the manner in which he plays the game. I voted for him the time he won FIFA World Player of the Year and I would gladly pay to watch him play.

But despite my respect for him as a player, I am not going to man-mark him unless he causes absolute mayhem in the Stadium of Light. I discuss this with the players on the training ground the day before the match and brief Curtis Fleming to be ready to do a job on Figo if he is running the show and we are running out of time. Curtis knows that his job is to stop Figo at all costs if it comes to it but I am confident we won't need to resort to those sort of tactics, I am not one for man-marking. We didn't do it when we played against Gheorghe Hagi of Romania a couple of years back and I always reckon it upsets us more than the opposition when we change our game plan. No, tonight we will play as we did in Amsterdam, stick Robbie behind Quinny and look to get Jason and Kevin Kilbane in support of those two when they are needed.

The journey from our idyllic hotel up a packed motorway from Cascais into Lisbon is mad. The traffic is crazy. There are Irish fans everywhere once we reach the vicinity of the ground and there is a real buzz as we make our way into the dressing-room before the game. I turn to Packie and, for the first time in a long time, I admit that I would love to play tonight.

The team talk is easy. Just do what we did in Holland, have no fear. If we can play the Dutch at their own game then we can take the match to Portugal as well.

It is a relief to sit in this dressing-room and watch the players get ready for the game. There is a feeling of unity within the group. Whoever was responsible for that 'war' headline has only brought us all closer together.

The game itself goes nowhere near as smoothly as things did in

Amsterdam. We are slow out of the blocks for some reason and Portugal make us pay. They have Joao Pinto in the hole behind lone striker Sa Pinto and he has a field day, trading little passes with Rui Costa and giving us the runaround.

Robbie has a half chance from a Quinny flick early on and Roy goes close with a shot that ricochets off Robbie but otherwise Portugal dominate the first-half. They have a couple of decent chances, Alan Kelly saves from Sa Pinto and Figo, and they look dangerous.

We have to do something. I need a sitter in midfield to contain Joao Pinto who is causing havoc. At half-time, I take Quinny off and put Mattie Holland in to bolster the midfield. His instructions are to sit tight, get close to Joao Pinto and allow Kevin and Jason to support Robbie when we break.

The switch seems to work until Portugal take the lead in the fifty-seventh minute as Rui Costa feeds Conceicao with a brilliant crossfield ball and he cuts inside Hartey before beating Alan in his right corner with the aid of a deflection off Richard Dunne. It is a killer goal and they almost make it two when Joao Pinto flashes the ball within inches of the goal thirteen minutes later.

Figo has switched wings to get away from Hartey and reminds us of his genius as he nutmegs Stevie Carr and then goes past Roy down in the far corner. Ouch.

Salvation arrives most unexpectedly in the shape of Mattie Holland after seventy-three minutes. For once, he ignores the instruction to sit tight, takes a pass from Roy and lets fly from twenty-five yards. It is a goal of some beauty as far as I am concerned. Portugal are stunned, they manage a couple of late efforts from Figo but to no avail.

Played two, drawn two. Played Holland and Portugal away and drawn both. Little wonder that I am ecstatic as the referee brings an end to the two minutes of stoppage time that dragged on for what seemed like two hours.

As the players leave the field, I throw my arm around Roy. War? What war?

We have made a good start to the Group Two qualifying campaign, but it is dangerous to read too much into that. Certainly, draws in Amsterdam and now Lisbon are something to celebrate but we must not get carried away. Both Holland and Portugal are quite capable of coming to Dublin next year and beating us. It would be a foolish man who refuses to acknowledge that possibility. By the same token, had we lost both games I would be looking to reverse those results when we host the two group favourites.

There are a number of things that I do take comfort from as we look to the start of our home games when Estonia come to Dublin in four days' time. We have now gone eight games unbeaten away from home and that is a habit that I am quite happy to develop. It is vital that we maintain our form on the road and start to pick up wins into the bargain.

The way the team has developed as a unit pleases me as well. For the match in Portugal I was able to name a team unchanged from the previous game for the first time in my four and a half plus years as Irish manager. Leaving Lisbon, I know that the same team will start again in the Estonia game. There is no need to change it, no way I could drop any of the players after the way they have performed over the last 180 minutes of football.

Alan Kelly is my number one on merit. His saves from Figo and Joao Pinto came at crucial times against Portugal and I am lucky to have three world-class 'keepers at my disposal.

Richard Dunne, untried at this level up to now, has been outstanding in the two games. He has taken the bait and risen to the challenge offered by the likes of Kluivert and Sa Pinto. Likewise, Mark Kinsella was excellent when we needed to roll up our sleeves in the middle of the field.

Quinny had every right to feel aggrieved when he was replaced at half-time in the Stadium of Light but that was purely a tactical decision. We were over-run in midfield and unable to get him any decent supply of ball at all. It will be different against Estonia when we will need to be much more positive for the full ninety minutes.

Mattie Holland's back is sore after all the slaps that came his way after his goal. He deserves his time in the spotlight, it was a great goal and badly needed. I have to admit that when I first saw Mattie play for Ipswich I wondered what all the fuss was about. Someone had written to me and told me about his Irish grandmother, and I went to see him play at Oxford one Saturday. I wasn't blown away by him that day and now I know exactly why. He is so conservative in everything that he does that he rarely stands out. He never lunges in, he's never under duress, he seldom has to make last-minute sliding tackles. He is Denis Irwin-esque if you know what I mean, in so much control that it is easy to lose sight of Mattie at club level.

At the time I still had Andy Townsend and Ray Houghton in the side so I thought I'd keep an eye on Mattie and introduce him slowly, through the B team. I spoke to his Ipswich boss George Burley who raved about him and then, when he made his B team debut against Dave Barry's National League side at the Carlisle Grounds in Bray, I finally got to see what he was about. He was brilliant that day out in Bray, head and shoulders above the other players from both sides. I knew then that he could come straight into the senior squad and do a job for us. Eventually, Mattie made his full debut as a sub out in Macedonia, in that draw in Skopje, and I am sure he must have wondered if he would ever feature again.

He had to wait until the US Cup last summer to get his real chance and he took advantage of the fact that Roy wasn't around. Mattie was a revelation in the States. The more I watched him out there, the more I realised he can cope with anything that's thrown at him. He can sit in the middle of the park, win the ball and pass it. He has great energy levels and great pace and the demands of the modern game are no problem for him.

I needed him to do a job against Portugal and he delivered. His brief was to stop them playing the ball through us and he did just that. To be honest, I never expected him to fire home the equaliser. I know he can strike the ball, but that one was just unstoppable.

On a personal level I am delighted, not just for me but for my family as well. They knew how much pressure I was under going to Holland and Portugal for the opening two games. Contract or no contract, the knives would have been out if we had lost those two games. My family knew that, they knew how much rubbish would come my way if we returned empty-handed. The men who write the headlines never look beyond their target, they never see the wife and the kids sitting at home in fear of the next instalment.

Maybe I should resign now, go out at the top and give the media something to really get worked up about. On second thoughts, no, only joking.

PORTUGAL 1, REPUBLIC OF IRELAND 1

WEDNESDAY 11th OCTOBER, LANSDOWNE ROAD

World Cup Group Two Qualifier

Republic of Ireland v Estonia

The boot is on the other foot now, we are favourites for our first home game of the World Cup qualifying series. It's a tag that sits uncomfortably on Irish football teams. We prefer the role of underdog, prefer to let the fighting spirit raise us to new levels. Being favourite is not something I like but it is something we are going to have to get used to in the coming months. This group will be decided by the results between Portugal, Holland and Ireland, I have no doubts on that score. What happens when the Portuguese and the Dutch come to Dublin will determine whether or not we go to the Far East in the summer of 2002.

Cyprus, Estonia and Andorra will not fancy themselves as real World Cup contenders in this company. They will, however, fancy an upset along the way. We have been victims of such banana skins in the past, Macedonia and Liechtenstein, under Jack, spring to mind as ready examples when we drew against teams we should have beaten, and we cannot afford to slip again. We must beat those three home and away to maximise the benefit of the draws in Amsterdam and Lisbon.

That should not be such a tall order if we seriously consider ourselves as World Cup qualifiers. Portugal have already shown the way with a 3–1 win against Estonia in Tallinn while Holland beat Cyprus 4–0 when we were in Lisbon. Those are the sort of results we must get to maintain our momentum.

Estonia are first up to the plate at Lansdowne and, to be honest, I'd settle for a scrappy 1–0 win if it ensured we finish the game with three points. That's not what we will play for, I want to get as many goals as possible on the board, but this is a time to get points in the bag.

Both Taff and I have been to see Estonia and I have also discussed them at length with Craig Brown, the Scotland manager. He has a lot of regard for Estonia. They are, in his opinion, the most dogged team he has come across in recent years and very hard to break down. They are physically big and powerful and have a world-class keeper in Derby County's Mart Poom. He will take some beating.

I have a couple of tapes of Estonia in action in this group and we study them briefly before the match. The important thing is that the players know their shape, who to pick up on corners and free-kicks and how they will approach the game. We have to force the pace of this game, the players know that. We must get width and we must get quality service up to Quinny who will have the benefit of Robbie directly beside him this time and not in the hole. The most important thing is not to concede an early goal. Teams like Estonia can dig in and make life impossible if they score early.

Richard Dunne and Mattie Holland picked up minor knocks against Portugal but the team is the same. Mattie certainly gave me some food for thought with his second-half performance against the Portuguese but there is no way he is going to displace Roy or Mark at this stage. At least if they are injured I know I have a ready-made replacement.

Lansdowne Road will be a boost to us. I stand over my competitive record as Irish manager with great pride and I am particularly proud of the fact that we have never lost a qualifier in Dublin. In fact, our overall competitive record is excellent. In the eighteen qualifying games we have played home and away in the Euro and World Cup groups, we have won ten, drawn four and lost four. We won every home qualifier for Euro 2000. We can keep that run going this time out.

A few days before the match, I sat Mark Kinsella down and told him it was time to start getting goals. As a side we create more chances than Ireland have done for some time but we put too much pressure on the strikers to convert them. We need the midfielders to get in with their share of goals as well. Mark, who was still scoreless after eighteen internationals, agreed.

The supporters are back in force at Lansdowne and it's almost like the old times with a full house again. They clearly see the results in Holland and Portugal as the start of something big. The players are anxious to deliver, they are calm but apprehensive before the game, knowing that the pressure is really on now. As a result, the early stages are a wee bit shaky as our wide men, Jason and Kevin, get the measure of their markers. Estonia, as predicted, prove to be stubborn opposition. What they lack in skill they make up for in effort and the first twenty minutes of the game prove nervy.

We produce a great chance early on when a rocket from Roy is pushed away by Poom, who then manages to scramble a Kevin Kilbane effort from the rebound onto the bar. Seconds later my heart is in my mouth as Terehhov turns a long ball into Indrek Zelinski, inside the box and with time on his hand. We are sleeping as he tees up the shot but Alan Kelly is equal to the challenge and the possibility of that dreaded early goal is dismissed.

It doesn't matter when, in the twenty-fifth minute, Hartey feeds a brilliant long ball forward and Quinny controls it perfectly inside the box. One touch is all he needs to steer it into Mark Kinsella's path and Kinse's close-range shot is always going into the corner of the net. So he does listen to me!

The goal settles us and puts Estonia on the back foot. They sit back and invite us onto them. Jason and Kevin make hay while the sun shines and Niall goes close to breaking the Irish goalscoring record. He has a great chance off a Jason cross just before half-time but Niall's header is just wide.

I opt for a change at the break. Duffer looked sensational when he went on as a late sub in Lisbon on Saturday night and I decide to give him the run of the wing for the second-half of this match. His ball skills are incredible and I know the Estonian defence, already stretched down both flanks, won't fancy the prospect of the Blackburn winger running at them at speed.

The second-half begins as the first ended. Roy and Mark have total control in the centre of the field and the killer goal duly arrives in the fifty-first minute. Quinny drifts to the near post to flick on a Hartey corner, Gary Breen stabs at it and Richard Dunne comes charging in at the far post to knock the ball, and anything else in the way, home from four yards. That's two goals in six internationals for the centre-half, not bad for a player in the Everton reserves, is it?

I'd have settled for a 1–0 before the game and we end with 2–0. Quinny was close to that record on at least another two occasions before the final whistle but there's no point being greedy.

The press conference after the match is one of those tetchy affairs that happen from time to time. I walk in with five points in the bag and I know that is a problem for some people in the rugby club pavilion to the side of the West Stand. They thought I'd be gone by now, they hoped we'd lose in Holland and Portugal and a fresh piece of meat would be sitting here now, talking about a win over Estonia as the first step on the road to a new promised land. Sorry boys, I'm still here. And I will be for some time to come.

We should be celebrating Ireland's start to the group. Instead, I can sense negativity and that irks me.

The first question – mission accomplished Mick? Yes. One-word answers, journalists are never happy with one-word answers.

Happy to have these three games out of the way? Well, not having to listen to the sort of bullshit I've had to listen to for the last two months, yes that makes me happy. That baffles them.

Let me explain. At the start of this Group Two campaign, I hoped for five points from these three games but that's me, the 'optimistic, confident, the-glass-is-always-half-full' me. Nobody else gave us a prayer, certainly not some of the people in this room. As they saw it, the away games in Holland and Portugal were perfect to set Mick McCarthy up for sacrifice. Amsterdam shut them up for a while until Roy was late in for the Portugal game and suddenly I'm at war with my best player. The draw in Lisbon ended that one. Now I am sitting at the top table in a Dublin press conference with five points in my World Cup bag, and I'm laughing, all the way to Christmas and beyond.

My players may finally get the credit they deserve now. They have soldiered with me for over four years, they have stomached the disappointments in Belgium and Macedonia and Turkey. They have come out smiling at the other end, better players, better men, a better team. And we are on the right road now. We have given ourselves a World Cup platform to build on, together. We are united in this quest to make it to Japan and Korea in twenty months' time.

So please, enjoy it.

REPUBLIC OF IRELAND 2, ESTONIA 0

WEDNESDAY 15th NOVEMBER, LANSDOWNE ROAD

Friendly International

Republic of Ireland v Finland

The build-up to the friendly against Finland is dominated by controversy involving my former striker, Tony Cascarino. In his excellent biography, Cas reveals his belief that he was a 'fake' Irishman when he played eighty-eight times for the Republic under Eoin Hand, Jack Charlton and Mick McCarthy.

I have to admit that I was astonished when I was first asked to comment on the claims contained in Tony's book. In all my time playing with Cas and then working with him as manager, he was one of the most wholehearted and committed international footballers I came across. There was certainly never any doubting his Irishness as far as I was concerned. He had an Irish passport, which is a help, but he also had a great bond with the shirt and a dedication to the cause. He wanted to play for Ireland in all the time I worked and played with him and that is the biggest consideration as far as I am concerned.

I get letters every week tipping me off about this player or that player with an Irish parent or grandparent. I always get them checked out, except for the letters from players who have already played international football with another country but fancy a go at the Irish team. That does happen, believe me. I am only interested in players who want to play for the country. Anyone who fancies an Irish cap as a career move can forget about it, we don't do career enhancing caps with Ireland.

Tony was never one of that brigade. His contribution over the eighty-eight games was immense, the role he played when I became manager was invaluable. I needed guys like Tony to bring the young players on and he delivered. Even before the last European qualifiers he wanted to retire but I persuaded him to stay on as the team matured and he obliged. It was only fitting that he was rewarded with the appearances record. My one regret for Cas was the manner in which his international career ended in the Euro play-off in Turkey last November. He deserved better than a punch in the face from a Turkish policeman and a red card on his Irish finale.

As it happens, his passport qualifications are fine and I am glad, very glad as we meet up in Dublin for this friendly and I bump into Tony, now a media pundit, in the course of the week.

The Finland game is a chance to look at a couple of new faces within the squad environment and build on the progress of the past three months. Fixtures like this are vital for the development of new players. I do not, as a rule, throw kids into championship football unless they have been blooded against the likes of Finland in a non-competitive environment.

It takes time for the kids to adjust to the set-up and the way we do things. It is intimidating for any young player to walk into a hotel and sit down for dinner beside the likes of Niall Quinn or Roy Keane, never mind train and play with them. I made my international debut at the relatively mature age of twenty-five and even then it took me at least ten games to become comfortable at this level. Some, like Robbie, come in and set the house on fire but they are the exception. Look at Kevin Kilbane who was thrown in at the deep end in Iceland a few years back and suffered because I asked too much of him too soon. It took him a while to find his feet at international level after that game but he is one of our most promising players now.

Kevin is coming good now and others will get the chance this week to show what they can do. Middlesbrough defender Jason Gavin is in the squad and is one of the players I am looking to over the next couple of years. Likewise, I want John O'Shea from Manchester United and Sunderland's Michael Reddy to train with us and become familiar with the senior squad in the build-up to the game. Dominic Foley, Steve Finnan and Mattie Holland are other players I will look to this week.

The problem for Dominic, and for Jason, Alan Kelly and Robbie at the moment, is a lack of first team football. Dominic is stuck in the reserves at Watford and he really needs to be playing regularly if he is to make a real claim for an Irish shirt. I'm amazed that Alan can't get a game at Blackburn. Whoever is keeping him out of the side must be some 'keeper judging by the way he has played in the three qualifiers to date. This is a concern for me, not going into this game but for the World Cup campaign ahead. By the time we go to Cyprus in March I want to see Alan, Jason and Robbie playing regular football.

I have spoken to Robbie about this issue. A new coach at Inter has limited his first-team opportunities and it is hard on the player. I was in the same position in my time at Lyons in France and I ended up back in England with Millwall because I needed first team football to protect my World Cup place in 1990. The bonus for Robbie is that he's young enough to battle through this at Inter. I was a thirty-something when I found myself in his boat and time was not on my side. Robbie is not going to lose his natural ability; that is not going to go away. He will come through this and the fact that he is in my team should help. Others may give up on Robbie but I won't.

I had wanted to start the match against Finland with the same side for a fourth successive match, a novelty in my time as manager. Unfortunately that remains a dream. Roy Keane pulls out of the game on the Saturday, a tight hamstring necessitating his presence in the Old Trafford treatment room for the week. Damien Duff is already out with a similar injury. Then Niall Quinn and Rory Delap fail to make it to Dublin for the match, Niall ruled out by a long-term back problem and Rory out with an Achilles tendon strain. That leaves me with twenty players when we report for training on the Monday, which is fine until Dean Kiely rings in sick with a shoulder problem. The joys of international management!

The first job is to appoint a captain for the game. Steve Staunton, Stan as we know him, is in the squad but is not guaranteed to start so I hand the armband to Mark Kinsella. It is an honour he deserves for his recent performances, his stature amongst his peers and his influence on the other players. A late developer at this level, Mark is already a great captain at Charlton and I know that leading his country will be a great experience for him. I've been there, done that, don't forget.

After all the injury withdrawals, I have another problem on my hands. Stevie Carr arrived at the training camp with a knee injury and we decide not to risk him in the game. Instead, I make five changes to the team. Gary Kelly will get his chance at right-back with Shay in goal, Steve Finnan will be in midfield along with Mattie and Dominic upfront with Robbie.

Steve's had to wait his time to make an impact at this level but he is playing well for Fulham and he does give me an option on the right. Like Jason, he can tuck in when he needs to and offers support to both the defence and the attack. I would have no hesitation in using him in a competitive game at this stage so I am interested to see how he does against the Finns. Likewise, I want to see as much as possible of Richard Dunne and Gary Breen as a central partnership going into this game. They have yet to put a foot wrong in the World Cup games but they need time to work on their understanding as a central pair and this fixture can only help. I don't expect the game to alter my selection for Cyprus too much. Continuity will be the key in March after the three qualifiers to date but this is a chance for someone to make a name for himself.

Match night is cold, so cold that even the second-half streaker keeps most of his clothes on. Only in Ireland . . . The result is never in any real doubt once we survive a very hairy opening twenty minutes. Shay Given is eager to take his chance in goal and makes a string of fine saves, most notably from Jari Litmanen, the lively Mikael Forssell and Jonas Kolkka.

Steve Finnan is my man of the match, though Mark Kinsella receives the official Eircom award. The Fulham player opens the scoring on fifteen minutes after a forty-yard pass from Kinse that splits the defence in two. Steve pushes the ball past 'keeper Jussi Jaaskelainen with his first touch and calmly finishes with his second. The goal is followed by a great performance from the Limerick born player, particularly when he switches to right-back for the second-half to accommodate Jason's return to midfield duty.

That goal was the settler we needed. Robbie, full of running, enjoys little luck in front of goal but he is trying his heart out, perhaps too much so. The goals will come again for him, but not tonight. Instead, Jason's cross makes the second for Kevin Kilbane as he breaks his international scoring duck with a header, of all things, early in the second-half. Right at the death we manufacture quite a brilliant third, Stan curling a long range free-kick home with that creative left foot of his.

A good night's work all round.

The easy win is followed by an easier press conference. Compliments from me are the order of the day all round, starting with Steve Finnan. He showed tonight that he is an intelligent footballer with energy, a good touch and the ability to put the foot in when required. Mark Kinsella was excellent as well. Dominic Foley needs first-team football to push on at this level but he knows that as well as I do. The same applies to Alan Kelly. He will be number one for the Cyprus match if he gets a game at club level. If not, then Shay made his mark on tonight's game. Kevin picked up where Mark left off last month and finally got amongst the goals for Ireland. I gave him a ribbing about his scoring ratio in training before the match and he took it on board. I expect to see more goals from him now that he's got the first.

Steve Staunton's goal raises a few comments and questions. Steve and I go back a long way and I would love to see Stan back in the Irish team, but he too must sort out his club situation.

Now, Christmas is calling and with five World Cup points in the bag, I can enjoy it.

REPUBLIC OF IRELAND 3, FINLAND 0

THREE

March–June 2001

It is make or break time for Ireland's World Cup chances. We must make home advantage count against Portugal in June and we must not slip on any of the potential banana skins offered by Cyprus (away), Andorra (home and away) and Estonia (home). The year gets off to a bad start when a February home friendly against Denmark is snowed off.

SATURDAY 24th MARCH, NICOSIA

World Cup Group Two Qualifier

Cyprus v Republic of Ireland

My father Charlie is dying, his cancer has caught up with him. I break away from the squad session in Dublin to go back home to Barnsley and say my goodbyes before we fly to Cyprus. I just want to tell him I love him one last time, say see you, goodnight and God bless. Dad is surprised to see me and asks me what I am doing there. He tells me to get back to work, to go to Cyprus and do my job, do Ireland proud.

I get the call early on the Thursday morning, four days after we said our goodbyes. It is not unexpected but it is still a smack in the gob. I knew coming out here that he was going to die but nothing can prepare you for the shock when it happens. I carry on in a daze, go to training, accept the condolences of players and staff who really have no idea what to say to me. I feel like crying all the time but I get on with my job. That's what my dad wanted me to do and I made him a promise.

I speak to Fiona and the kids and try to help them come to terms with their grief. We agree that I will fly home after the game on Saturday night and then rejoin the squad in Barcelona on Tuesday, ahead of the Andorra game.

The next day, I am in a position to publicly name the team. Alan Kelly loses out to Shay Given in goal, purely because Shay is playing first-team football and Alan is now third choice at Blackburn. It is a hard call on Alan. He was superb in the three qualifiers to date and has every right to feel aggrieved in this instance but goalkeeper is a position where you have to be playing. I have played outfield players before who were out of their club side but this is different, this is a specialised position. I have explained my reasons to him but since then he has also just discovered that his reported move to Manchester United, as cover for Fabien Barthez, is also a non-starter, I know he is not the happiest camper in Cyprus. Good pro that he is, Alan gets on with it.

Stephen Carr is injured so Gary Kelly will play at right-back.

The more difficult decision concerns centre-back. Kenny Cunningham is available again after injury for his first competitive game in eleven months. In his absence, Richard Dunne has formed a durable partnership with Gary Breen that was one of the key factors in our draws away to Holland and Portugal. This is actually the most difficult decision since I succeeded Jack. Loathe as I am to drop Richard, Kenny has been first choice, when available, in all my time as Irish boss. He is the old dog for the hard road as they say and Richard has been in and out of his club team of late. I go for experience and restore Kenny to the side.

Midfield picks itself, the only area of the team intact from the three qualifiers to date. Jason is also struggling at club level but he has never let me down in the past and all I want from him is a repeat of the games he produced in Amsterdam and Lisbon.

Quinny is again ruled out with his back injury, which is starting to cause me real concern. I need a fit Niall Quinn in this Irish squad, not just for the way he leads the line on the pitch but also for his knack of getting the best out of the youngsters off it. He has lurched from one injury crisis to another in recent years and that is a worry for me.

This time out, David Connolly gets the nod to partner Robbie, now of Leeds United, upfront. David is now back in the first-team picture at Feyenoord and scoring goals again at club level. Gary Doherty of Spurs is the only other real alternative open to me going into this game but I have watched Cyprus and I know their defenders would relish a clash with a big rugged centre-forward. Instead, I go for the little and little combination. We will run at them and see what they are made of.

Ronnie Whelan, my old Ireland team-mate, comes to see me in our Limassol hotel a couple of times during our week training in Cyprus. He manages Olympiakos, one of the big clubs out here now, and he is happy to pass on his insight. Ronnie has no trade secrets to give away but it is good to see him and have a pint with one of my old friends. Cyprus aren't a bad side in his estimation, but like me he feels their heads will drop if we can get our noses in front. They may have beaten Spain and Israel here in recent seasons but they can lose their impetus at times, as the late collapse against the Portuguese last autumn testifies.

I know that Portugal and Holland will both beat Cyprus home and away so it is vital that we pick the three points up here. There are no guarantees in football but this is the sort of game we have to win if we are serious about World Cup qualification.

The match sees Roy Keane win his fiftieth international cap and he wins it in some style. His midfield performance is the most dominant I have ever seen at international level from any player, for or against us. Keano doesn't just intimidate the Cypriots, he also drags Ireland to a new level in a game that had the potential to be an upset of Macedonian proportions. I feel sorry for the guy who is trying to man-mark him. Imagine being told in the dressing-room beforehand that your job for the night is to man-mark Roy Keane. I wouldn't fancy that.

In his position, Keane is currently the best in the world. Others may be able to pass the ball better or score more goals but, in the overall picture, there isn't a better central midfield player anywhere. He proves it over the ninety minutes tonight and throws two goals into the pot for good measure. I had said to him before the game to get into the box and get amongst the goals and he does just that.

Keane's first goal arrives on thirty-two minutes, a cool finish from twelve yards after good work by Kells and Kinse. Our crucial second goal arrives just four minutes from the break when Kevin is chopped down in the box by Georgios Theodotou and Hartey slams the penalty home.

The dressing-room is a more relaxed place at half-time thanks to that goal. I never expected an easy ride out here and Cyprus are not letting me down. Our two wide players are struggling to get past them so I make a change at the break, pushing Steve Finnan on for Jason and into right-back and switching Gary Kelly into midfield.

We look more settled as the game progresses, particularly after Shay makes one great save from Michael Constantinou. The icing on the cake arrives in the final ten minutes after two goal-line efforts from Constantinou are met by saving headers from Kells. A Kells shot takes a deflection to make it 3–0 in the eightieth minute before Keano links with Kinse to make it four.

The result is better than the performance, I am the first to admit that. We had more of the possession but we were never entirely comfortable, never as in control as that scoreline suggests. They stopped us getting crosses in and that is a worry but this is a good result. When is 4–0 not a good result?

Cypriot coach Stavros Papadopoulos is a gentleman. The day my father died, he sent a fax to our team hotel offering his condolences. It was a nice touch in a game where dignity and humanity are so often forgotten. At the post match press conference he talks Ireland up. We are, he says, perfectly capable of beating Portugal to the top spot in the group on the evidence he has seen so far.

The praise is welcome but I am not sure I can agree with the sentiment. Portugal are still the best team in the group. They have beaten Holland away already and the result of their home match with the Dutch in four days' time will go a long way towards telling us exactly what we have to do if we are to live up to Stavros's expectations. We have given ourselves an opportunity with three games on the road, one at home and eight points gained. My belief is that twenty-four points will see us through to Japan and Korea and we are still some way off that target.

Two subjects dominate the papers the day after the game, as I return to the UK to spend time with my family in the wake of my father's death. Roy has made some fairly hard-hitting comments about the FAI and travel and training arrangements for the Irish team in the course of a lengthy interview with the *Sunday Independent*. He has a right go at the state of the training pitch we normally use for home games at Clonshaugh in Dublin and also the fact that the players flew to Cyprus in economy class when FAI officials were up the front of the plane in business-class seats.

Now, I have to hold my hands up here and admit that I was sat in the first row of business class for the journey from Dublin to Cyprus. The players are the important ones in the group and Roy is right to say that. We should look after them in the best manner possible. He is entitled to his opinions and, as he is captain, we should listen to them. Perhaps he would be better served bringing these issues up with me and the FAI before running to the papers but I promise to take his comments on board and to act on them in conjunction with the FAI.

The other burning issue back home concerns Eircom Park and the end of the line for FAI plans to build a home for Irish football out in Tallaght, Robbie's hometown to the west of Dublin. I have been a big supporter of the Eircom Park idea since I was first brought back from a holiday in Florida to help launch it. Ever since I was a player I have advocated the need for a proper home for the Irish team, complete with the sort of training facilities that Roy is asking for. Football in Ireland has surely generated enough money since our breakthrough at Euro '88 to justify a stadium where we are the landlords and not the tenants of the Irish Rugby Football Union or even, in the future, the Gaelic Athletic Association or the government.

Lansdowne has been good to us over the years. I have enjoyed playing there and I have enjoyed sending my team out there as manager, knowing that the ground and, let's be fair, the pitch, give us a real advantage. But we are still borrowing the stadium and the pitch from the IRFU, we are relying on our landlords to do their best for us, as they always do. It is not their fault that the pitch is also required for rugby. That works to our advantage when foreign teams take a look at Lansdowne and don't fancy it, and I have certainly seen opposition teams go back into their shells after their first look at the pitch, but of course we want the best surface possible for Irish football.

There is a humility about the Irish football team, has been since Big Jack's days, that I never want to lose. But we must move with the times. We have some of the best players in the world now and they deserve world-class facilities when they play for Ireland. That is not going to happen now at Eircom Park, judging by the latest reports. The project appears to be dead.

Cyprus 0, Republic of Ireland 4

WEDNESDAY 28th MARCH, BARCELONA

World Cup Group Two Qualifier

Andorra v Republic of Ireland

I fly from family business in England on Tuesday and meet up with the squad in Barcelona, Andorra's choice of venue for their 'home' fixture. As usual, controversy has followed us to the Catalan capital, along with about 5,000 travelling fans. An anonymous fax has arrived in the FAI offices, and at FIFA, which questions the eligibility of six members of the Andorran squad under some sort of a dual nationality agreement with Spain. This may or may not allow them to play for Spain and Andorra but the fax is adamant that one of them, midfielder Marc Bernaus, played for the Spanish against Duffer in Brian Kerr's Ireland side at the World Youth Cup finals in Malaysia back in 1997.

I can do without distractions in the lead-up to the game but FIFA have to take the eligibility claim seriously and, as a result, go to town on both squads. They send a very stern official to look into the eligibility of both teams, Andorra and Ireland, on the day before the game. The overly officious FIFA man annoys our liaison officer Eddie Corcoran almost as soon as they meet.

We are not amused, particularly when he informs us, on Tuesday, that he wants to inspect the players and their passports at ten a.m. on the morning of the game. The request to get the players out of bed that early on the morning of a night game is ridiculous. I tell Eddie to tell him to forget it, we ain't seeing him until lunchtime on match day at the earliest. That is not good enough. So then he marches us all into a room on the Tuesday lunchtime and asks all the players to stand in a row holding their passports open so that he can compare the photographs with their faces! I kid you not, this guy, a top football official, asked Roy Keane to identify himself.

He is a hard case and he has a right go at me about calling him ridiculous. I think I have placated him but then he informs me that he wants us at the Mini Estadi a full two hours before kick-off on the Wednesday. He has to be joking. Our hotel is a five-minute walk from the Barcelona third-team stadium and there is no way we are going to leave for the ground until an hour and twenty minutes before kick-off. There is no need to be there any earlier than that.

The FIFA official, naturally, is unhappy when we arrive at our planned time, seventy-five minutes before the start of the game and three quarters of an hour after his deadline. Apparently, he reported us for a late arrival and we were fined by FIFA, even though I tried to tell him we had been held up by the fans outside the hotel.

As it happens, Bernaus is left out of the Andorra team and all their paperwork is in order. Another storm in a teacup.

Duffer is one of two changes to our team for the game. We need him in top form to patrol the right flank and get quality balls to Robbie and David Connolly. Jason is the man to lose out on the right wing and he half expected it after what he himself considers to be a below par performance on Saturday night. In fact, Jase was so disgusted with his game against the Cypriots that he reckoned he should change his surname to McAteerinos in honour of the fact that he was their best player on the night!

Mattie Holland is in the side, partnering Roy in the middle after a knee injury curtails Mark Kinsella's involvement.

The match looks likely to have echoes of Liechtenstein when the home team's defensive approach led to a scoreless draw that cost Ireland dearly in a Euro '96 qualifier. I am certain that Andorra will play a 1–9–1 formation as they have done throughout the group. They will just sit back, invite us on to them and see if we can break them down. We need a win tonight, more than anything else. I will settle for a 1–0 and gladly take the three points as well as the flak if that result comes our way.

The game is not pretty to begin with from an Irish point of view. As I predicted, Andorra are so happy to defend that there is as much chance of their goalkeeper getting caught offside as their sole forward. An early Robbie Keane header aside, we struggle to get through them in the first fifteen minutes. We pass the ball from side to side and in and out and never really throw one into the box. Robbie and David are getting little or no change from Andorra's very big defence and we need a trick or two to open them up.

Watching the tape of Andorra's match with Holland before the game, I reckoned we might need to get a target to aim at if we didn't open them up early on. I decided to make the change early if I needed to, taking Robbie or David off and letting Gary Doherty loose on them, to see how they deal with his aerial ability and power.

David is probably playing a bit better than Robbie but Robbie has a trick, an ability to do something out of the ordinary and unpredictable, and he has been my first-choice striker for quite some time now. It isn't happening for either of them but I opt to take David off, even though he is a far more natural centre-forward than Gary. I fancy Gary more as a centre-back to be honest. He is a little too manufactured as a striker for my liking, forced into the position through circumstance, but he is the closest thing I have to the injured Niall Quinn at the moment and I need that sort of strength upfront right now.

David has a face like thunder when he comes off after just twenty-six minutes and I can't blame him. It's not his fault that we have to barge the door down now rather than pick the lock. Nothing I can say or do now will help him at this moment and I don't have time to explain myself to him. We have had a few free-kicks, a couple of corners, a couple of efforts on target but no penetration. Their 'keeper Alfonso Sanchez looks comfortable and that is not a good omen.

The change works. Gary is only on the pitch for six minutes when he plays a good ball down the channel for Roy. Keano takes it into the box and though he doesn't seem to be offering a real threat, Sanchez decides to take him down. Penalty to Ireland and goal to the visitors as Hartey slams it home. It's not the prettiest of finishes but I'll take it.

I know Andorra won't score in this game, though Ildefons Lima tries a cheeky lob on Shay in the second-half that brings a smile to the referee's face. Instead, they sit back and allow Duffer to run at them for fun. He is a joy to watch as we control the remainder of the match, a couple of Robbie efforts going over and wide before two goals in the last fourteen minutes put the gloss on the scoreline. The first is a scrambled affair involving Gary Kelly, Roy and Robbie before Kevin steers it home from all of five yards. Then, three minutes later, Robbie, Duffer and Gary are all involved before Mattie makes enough room to score his second international goal.

I'd have settled for a 1–0, I am more than happy with 3–0. We made hard work of it but the result is all that counts.

David was not happy after the match, I would hate it if he was. But a manager cannot let sentiment get in the way of any decision. I like David Connolly a lot, as a player and as a man, but I had to take him off, no matter how long was gone on the clock. The result was more important than my relationship with any one player. That may sound cruel but sometimes you have to be cruel to be kind in this game. We talked about it and I assured him that his chance would come again. He is a natural centre-forward and too good a player not to make an impact in the future.

A bit like Robbie, David's career has seen more than its fair share of ups and downs, no more so than during his time in Holland. I was one of the people who told David to sign for Feyenoord a couple of years back, after he had burst onto the international scene with

Ireland and was the recipient of the kind of hype that has come Robbie's way since. I believed the move from Watford was too good for David to turn down at the time. He was going to one of the biggest clubs in Holland for seriously good money and he could only prosper in the Champions League environment that Feyenoord offered him.

Unfortunately, the move backfired when Leo Beenhakker was appointed manager soon after his arrival and made it clear that David was not part of his plans. He then fell out with the coach, was frozen out of the first team scene and was eventually sent down to the club's feeder team Excelsior, their reserve side if you like. That sort of treatment was enough to test any character but David, to his credit, stuck to his guns. He scored goals for Excelsior, lots of goals, and I discovered just how much they loved him when I went to see him out there. David's perseverance paid off and eventually he made it back to Feyenoord. His contract is up in the summer and I believe he will move back to England and back to a decent club.

He will also come good for Ireland again, despite all the stick that comes his way. His relationship with the media here has gone from supernatural highs to the lowest of the lows. He was their hero when he first came into the team but since they turned against him he has become reclusive towards them, so much so that I pulled him recently and told him that the surly approach is doing him no favours. David may not like the press but he is better off talking to them. You don't have to like someone to talk to them, as I well know.

Robbie is another player who could do with a confidence injection. If you measure confidence in goals and goal attempts then it's not happening for him right now. I told him coming off after the game that sometimes it happens for strikers and sometimes it doesn't. It is frustrating but he has to keep working away at it, keep doing it at club level. Despite his lack of goals, his contribution to the way Ireland play is, as always, first-class. Once he gets the goalscoring right at Leeds, that will transfer itself onto the international stage.

Thankfully the goals are coming from elsewhere. As we depart for the airport and a late-night charter flight back to Dublin, I am just glad to get out of Spain with another three points to add to our World Cup tally. I don't like games against the likes of Andorra, nobody does. You can't win friends in a fixture like this, all you can do is get the job done and get out of the place. We've done that in Cyprus and Barcelona over the last week. Two games, six points, seven goals and none conceded. Not a lot more I can ask for, to be fair.

As the bus pulls into the airport, we discover that Duffer has left his passport back in the hotel, where we had a quick meal after the match. I jump in a cab and go all the way back into town with him while the players check in and send their gear through. We find the passport down the back of a couch and race back to the airport and back to the best news of the week.

All night a number of people, including my good friend Joao Pinheiro, have been texting me the latest score from the Portugal–Holland game. At one stage, the Dutch are two goals to the good and cruising, not the result I want because a Holland win would bring them right back into contention for the group. When Joao tells me his team are being hammered on the pitch and on the scoreboard, I really fear the worst.

Now, as I check in, a late Portuguese rally is on the way as they look to cancel out those early goals from Jimmy Floyd Hasselbaink and Patrick Kluivert. Pauleta pulls one back with seven minutes to go, as I make my way through passport control. Then, in the dying seconds, Portugal are awarded a penalty. Figo hits it as I walk up the stairs to the departure gate. And he scores.

I shout, loud enough to be heard by the players and fans waiting to get on the plane. It's Portugal 2 Holland 2. You little beauty.

Our luck is changing at last. The Dutch have now dropped five points against the Portuguese and two against us. They are the team to beat now when they come to Lansdowne Road in September. They are the team we can push out of the qualification picture.

Thank you, Figo.

ANDORRA 0, REPUBLIC OF IRELAND 3

WEDNESDAY 25th APRIL, LANSDOWNE ROAD

World Cup Group Two Qualifier

Republic of Ireland v Andorra

Portugal's late equaliser against Holland last month has cleared a lot of the haze from the Group Two picture. Thanks to our draw in Amsterdam, and Portugal's subsequent four-point tally against the Dutch, we now have the ability to seal our own fate. The home games with both the Portuguese and Dutch were always going to be crucial. Now we must avoid defeat against Portugal at the start of June and ensure that the September clash with Holland holds the real key to our qualification hopes. Beat them then and we remove them from the equation. Then we can start to dream.

The trick now is to take more points from Portugal than the Dutch did. We already have that Lisbon draw in the bag so it is hard not to look at that June fixture as we await Andorra's arrival in Dublin, complete with another packed defence.

Two issues are already decided in my own head before the squad is named. Firstly, I will not risk the players on yellow cards in this game. Roy Keane, Jason McAteer, Kenny Cunningham and Robbie Keane are all one booking away from a ban that will keep them out of that Portugal match. For Roy it becomes less of an issue when Manchester United withdraw him with another hamstring injury.

More worrying in this instance is the absence of Niall Quinn, again with a back problem, along with Damien Duff, Lee Carsley, Dean Kiely and Rory Delap. Gareth Farrelly, Barry Quinn and Dominic Foley earn late call-ups.

Duffer's absence ensures the second decision is an easy one. Mark Kennedy is back in the squad for the first time since his Harcourt Street *faux pas* and he will start my fiftieth game as Irish manager. Mark is back on merit. I sent my scout Seamus McDonagh to watch him at Wolves recently and he was more than impressed. He looked like the senior pro on the Wolves team, and played like a Premiership player in a First Division team. The thing Seamus really liked about Mark on the day was his maturity. That is music to my ears about a player I have known and loved since I signed him for Millwall as a skinny sixteen-year-old from Dublin.

Mark has had to put up with the rough and the smooth in the days since he babysat for Fiona and me. That great goal he scored in the 94–95 FA Cup against Arsenal at Highbury made a real name for him and he was never going to turn down the big move to Liverpool when it came along. In hindsight, Mark might have been better staying at Millwall for another year or two because I know the lack of first-team opportunities at Anfield really affected him, but for financial reasons, Millwall had to sell him.

At Liverpool he fell between two stools really, not starting for the first team but too good to stay in the reserves. A player in that situation ends up playing with the reserves and not training with the first team or training with the first team and not playing with the reserves. I know from experience that it can do your head in. Mark was a big player at Millwall, everyone loved him there. Then all of a sudden he's behind John Barnes in the queue for a first-team shirt at Liverpool and his game – and career – suffered.

The one thing I drummed into Mark throughout that period was to have belief in his own ability. He is the most natural player I have come across in years, more skilled than he ever gets credit for. Mark is also the best crosser of a ball we have in the Irish squad. That's what I want him to do against Andorra. I want him to take defenders on, get his foot around the ball and send in those crosses.

The one thing we didn't do early on in Barcelona was throw the ball into their box and I am determined not to make the same mistake in the return match. I tell Mark and Kevin Kilbane that I want them to hit Gary Doherty and David Connolly with as many crosses as possible.

Two stories dominate the build-up to the game, aside from my selection as the Philips Sports Manager of the Month for March, thank you, very much. Bernard O'Byrne resigns as chief executive of the FAI on the day before the match and some eyebrows rise when I publicly announce my regret at his departure. There is a lot of opposition to Bernard over the Eircom Park issue but I am genuinely sorry to see him go. I didn't know Bernard before I got the Irish job but I did develop a very healthy and productive working relationship with him over the years. From my point of view he was professional and likeable and was good to me, both professionally and personally. Like Pat Quigley, Bernard was loyal to me and my future at a time when a lot of people wanted me out of the job and I will never forget the faith he put in me. I wish him well.

The other story to dominate the press conference on the day before the match concerns the drug allegations against Portugal's Fernando Couto and Holland's Edgar Davids. Quite what this has to do with me or the Irish team is beyond me but one journalist even asks me if I have any knowledge of such incidents among my own players. Now, they are making me laugh, they are winding me up. What can I say to a question like that? And have any of these journalists ever seen Ireland play so well, in their opinion, that the players must have been on drugs? Give me a break. If I ever discovered any of my players taking anything approaching a banned substance they would be out the door with a kick up the backside.

Next question please.

How many goals will you put past Andorra's flat back ten? Show some respect. I am sick of being asked how many we will win by on Wednesday night. Yes, Andorra will come here and defend in numbers. They are a small nation, learning how to compete at this level and if I were their manager I would pack my defence as well. There is nothing to be gained from coming to Dublin and getting absolutely hammered. And no, I don't think nations like Andorra should be asked to pre-qualify for the World Cup or the European Championships. When did we become so high and mighty in Ireland that we can look down our noses on countries like Andorra?

As it turns out, Andorra show those journalists – and the rest of us – a thing or two when they go and score a goal against Ireland and at Lansdowne Road. Yes, that's right, little Andorra take the lead in Dublin after thirty-two minutes of action.

I can barely believe my eyes. A word that rhymes with 'hit' crosses my lips as a Justo Ruiz free-kick is headed home by the unmarked Lima. Andorra cannot contain their joy. They have never scored away from home in a World Cup qualifier before and here they are, 1–0 up in Dublin.

Oh dear, this was not in the script. I knew we needed to be patient tonight but this is stretching it. How do we get out of this one? We score actually, precisely two minutes after their shock opener. A high ball into the box from Mattie is knocked on by Gary Doherty and Kevin Kilbane steers it between 'keeper Sanchez and his post. Whew.

Just two minutes later normal service is restored. Mark Kennedy does what he is in the team for and beats his man all ends up on the right wing. The cross is inch-perfect and Gary's header is denied only by the crossbar. As the ball crashes back into play, Mark Kinsella is on hand to smash the rebound home. That's more like it.

We are on the front foot now. David Connolly, victim of some heavy challenges all night, has a penalty appeal turned down and Sanchez saves from Gary off an Ian Harte cross. I am a happier man than I could have been in the dressing-room at the break, where I get the message across to hit the crosses from diagonals, not from the back.

We create chances after the break, lots of them, but the third goal takes its time. The crowd shout for Robbie but I ignore them. I cannot afford to see him booked before the Portugal game. That third goal eventually arrives in the seventy-sixth minute when Ian Harte's free-kick is parried by Sanchez and Breeny hits the rebound home.

Gary Doherty and Hartey both hit the woodwork before the Icelandic referee blows the final whistle. Big Gary had a good game. He is still not a classic centre-forward but he's got a great aerial threat and he is learning all the time. I feel for him having to chop and change positions but he was excellent out there and I hope he continues to develop at this rate.

It's another win, another step closer to the dream. We have played six games and are top of the group with fourteen points. Portugal have eleven from five games and Holland eleven from six matches. It is getting interesting now. Very interesting.

At the press conference after the match I am asked the inevitable questions, were we too cautious out there tonight? Will those three goals be enough if it comes down to goal difference?

You have to approach a team like Andorra with a degree of uncompromising respect. They rough players like David Connolly up, they stick big centre-backs on and tell them to get stuck in, they go down easily looking for free-kicks, they look to disrupt your rhythm. And good luck to them, I would do exactly the same thing if I were David Rodrigo, their coach. When Andorra scored, I did wonder where a goal was going to come from. I did think about putting Robbie in to try and liven it up. But the players responded straight away, they did what I had encouraged them to do all week and got a diagonal ball into the box. As a result of Gary's knock-down, Kevin scored. Simple. Once we got the second, two minutes later, we were in control of the match.

Of course, I would have liked more goals than the three we scored but they didn't come. And anyway, goal difference will only count if we don't beat Portugal and Holland at Lansdowne Road. My aim is to win those two matches and make goal difference irrelevant.

The first of those challenges comes in a little over a month when we take on Portugal. I don't even dare to look beyond that game.

Republic of Ireland 3, Andorra 1

WEDNESDAY 2nd JUNE, LANSDOWNE ROAD

World Cup Qualifier

Republic of Ireland v Portugal

Clinton Morrison, the young Crystal Palace striker, is finally an Irish player. We have been chasing his paperwork for some time now and he is to make his debut in the under twenty-one match on Friday, the day before the senior game, at Shelbourne's Tolka Park on Dublin's northside.

He is included in a Republic squad after a long and drawn out process, and to be honest, a lot of hoo-ha. When I first discovered that Clinton has an Irish grandmother, through one of those famous letters, I asked Ray Houghton, then on the staff at Palace, to enquire about it for me. He spoke to Clinton but there was never a definite answer for him. To be fair to Clinton, I think there was a lot of pressure from within the club for him to bide his time and wait for an England call-up. Eventually I went straight to SFX, the management company who look after Clinton, and arranged to meet him for lunch one day in an Italian restaurant in Bromley, southeast London, with his agent, Neil Fewings.

The meeting was designed to clear the air, find out exactly what was going on in Clinton's head and determine, once and for all, if he wanted to play for Ireland. Instead, it was almost a disaster. After waiting at the restaurant for an hour, and after a couple of frantic phone calls, I was just about to give up on them, and Clinton's international career, when they finally come through the door. Neil took the blame, saying he was running late, but as far as I was concerned, that was no excuse. I explained to Clinton there and then how important punctuality is to me. If a player is late for a bus, the bus goes without him, simple as that. This was the first time I had ever arranged to have a chat with a player about his prospective international career in these circumstances and I was not impressed. It's about respect. Would they have been late for Sven-Goran Eriksson?

Eventually, I accepted Neil's apology and discovered that Clinton did want to play for Ireland. I half knew that already, having met his great mentor Ian Wright at the BBC and asked him to have a word for me. Wrighty spoke to him, and that went some of the way to landing us one of the brightest young strikers in the English game.

Clinton is going to be a major asset to the Irish squad. I decide to play him with the under twenty-ones in Tolka and then again in Estonia four days later and see how he gets on. I have a feeling he will be in the senior squad soon enough.

Glen Crowe is another young striker making noises at the moment. Despite what some people think, I do know all about the Eircom League, the national league in Ireland, and am kept well up to date with which players are going well for their clubs. Glen, a striker I know all about from my days as Millwall manager when we looked at him before he went to Wolves, has been banging in the goals at Bohemians, with thirty-five to his credit for the season. Initially, I invited him along to train with the Irish squad in the build-up to the Portugal game, but since Gareth Farrelly is ruled out with injury, I have promoted Glen to the squad proper. He is in there on merit, looks good in training and, like any Eircom League player, he has a chance of playing for Ireland with just one provision – he must be good enough. That is the only criterion that matters.

The other news on the injury front before the biggest game we have played in a long time is mixed. Kenny Cunningham reports in with the squad but he is struggling with a serious stomach muscle problem. Richard Dunne has filled in more than admirably for Kenny earlier in the campaign but I want all hands on deck for this one.

Gary Kelly, Robbie and Breeny all have minor knocks when we meet up but should be fit for the match if they are needed. The biggest smile on my face is reserved for the moment Niall Quinn walks through the door. He is moving freely after his back problems and he assures me he will be able to play on Saturday if selected. We missed Niall for the last three games against Cyprus and Andorra, home and away, so it is a relief to know he will be okay.

The buzz about this game is phenomenal. We spend the early part of the week out at Citywest, a hotel near Rathcoole that we use before big games like this, and the hotel is alive with fans and great expectations. The players are as worked up about the game as the supporters.

We have always worked on the theory that Lansdowne is a fortress and that home results play a huge part in our qualification bids for European Championships and World Cups. The fact that we took a point in Lisbon last October is a bonus going into this game. Another three points on Saturday would be a major coup against one of the best teams in Europe.

Portugal arrive on Thursday and theirs is not a happy camp. They are not impressed by comments attributed to Hartey about how he is going to deal with the great Figo. Like any seasoned pro, Hartey says he will get a few hard tackles in early on. Translated into

Portuguese, it seems that means he is going to kill Figo, to judge by their over-the-top reaction.

They have other problems. Conceicao is out injured and a major question mark hangs over the availability of their captain Fernando Couto, charged with nandrolene offences at Lazio in Italy. He has been suspended by FIFA and only a last-minute appeal will clear him to play. Portuguese officials are going mad on the issue, even accusing the FAI of collusion with FIFA to get their captain banned. Considering FIFA have rarely done anything to help Irish football, I find that one hard to believe. The Portuguese FA president even has a go at the FAI for sending an Opel to collect him at the airport and not a BMW or a Merc. I kid you not.

The whole Couto affair throws an ugly smokescreen around the game and I stupidly get dragged into it. At my Lansdowne press conference on the day before the match, I am asked my opinion on the Couto case and the inference from Portugal that we had something to do with his ban being upheld by FIFA before such a big game. I treat the question as a joke, saying that I can't remember sitting in Couto's bedroom and injecting him with a banned substance, nor can anyone else involved with the Irish team. There's a big laugh and I think that's the end of the matter. Silly mistake, I should just have kept my mouth shut and said no comment. By Saturday, I am public enemy number one with the Portuguese party in Dublin.

Before the match, I go to shake hands with their manager, Antonio Oliveira, in the tunnel. He offers me the limpest bit of wet cod you have ever come across in your life and quickly turns his head to look the other way. I laugh and he replies that I won't be laughing after the game. I am livid now, my blood is boiling. Something else is said as I go down the tunnel and I pretend not to hear it. His behaviour is not what I would expect.

I go back into the dressing-room, as much annoyed with myself as I am with Oliveira. I shouldn't have answered the question at Friday's press conference and I should have just ignored him in the tunnel, but I wasn't brought up that way. Surely a handshake and a hello isn't too much to ask for from the manager of the team you are about to play against.

My final team talk is easy after that insult. Revenge, I think they call it.

It is probably the best-kept secret in the history of Irish football that Gary Breen is out of the Portugal game. He put his hernia injury to the test at Friday's training session at Lansdowne and it failed miserably. With Kenny Cunningham already out, the choices are limited. Richard Dunne was always going to replace Kenny so it's down to a straight fight between Steve Staunton and Andy O'Brien to play alongside the Manchester City star. Andy has youth and enthusiasm on his side but he is untested at this level, despite a good season in the Premiership since his move to Newcastle. Stan has all the experience you could want in a centre-half and his natural ability to play on the left offers a better partnership with Richard. I opt for Stan but nobody going to Lansdowne Road has a clue that my two first choice centre-backs are out, especially not the opposition.

With the selection Stan equals Tony Cascarino's record eighty-eight caps for Ireland, and there is every chance he will break it against Estonia on Wednesday. I have faith in him and, in the dressing room before the match, I tell him to talk Richard through the game and generally calm everyone down on the pitch.

The players are nervous, naturally so. Dublin is alive with World Cup talk. Everyone thinks we are one win away from the World Cup finals this afternoon but I know it is more important not to lose. I never play for a draw, however, certainly not at Lansdowne, so the message to the players is to be positive. Quinny is back, re-united with Robbie upfront and I go for Stephen Carr's pace at right-back with Gary Kelly's experience in front of him. Hartey has a big job on his hands marking Figo but I have every confidence he is up to the task with Kevin urged to help him out when necessary.

Portugal's team sheet surprises me. Oliveira has a new goalkeeper in Ricardo and has left Joao Pinto and Nuno Gomes on the bench for some reason best known to himself. Still there's always Figo and Rui Costa to worry about so there's no point jumping through hoops when their list comes into the dressing-room.

A huge wind is swirling around Lansdowne and the players are not impressed in the warm-up. It proves to be a massive factor early on as we struggle to control the ball and the tempo of the game. Stan and Richard look all at sea for the first twenty minutes or so but it is our passing all around the field that is truly desperate. We can't get the ball down, we can't keep it.

Portugal have the lion's share of the possession and the chances in a very nervy and very poor first-half from our point of view. We should be behind at the break. Captain Figo, a constant threat, plays a great one-two with Pauleta before flashing an early chance just wide of Shay's left-hand post in the fifth minute. Then Rui Costa, magnificent through the middle all day, drives his first shot off the post and the rebound at Shay. Roy Keane denies Pedro Barbosa before Pauleta inspires another great save from Shay just before half-time.

Then comes a stupid and needless booking for Roy. He is yellow-carded for insolence towards the referee over a decision and is out of Wednesday's game in Estonia, after his second booking of the series.

At the break, I am annoyed by the card and by the first-half performance. I think about making a change going into the dressing-room but where do I start? We created just one real chance when Roy headed at the 'keeper in the twenty-fourth minute. Something is clearly wrong on the pitch. I believe the wind is the big factor. It is so strong we can't get the ball out of our own half. I decide to leave well enough alone for the moment and see if the conditions switch in our favour in the second half.

Sure enough, the game is transformed after the break.

Roy spends the afternoon engaged in one of the great midfield battles with Rui Costa and begins to gain the upper hand in the second-half. Keano's determination and focus are quite something as we finally move forward. Mark Kinsella forces a great save out of Ricardo and Niall and substitute Damien Duff, on for Robbie, all go desperately close before the great breakthrough arrives in the sixty-sixth minute. A quick throw-in from Stevie Carr finds Roy in the box and his shot deflects off Litos and past Ricardo. Elation. Lansdowne erupts. I dance for joy.

We have taken the lead against Portugal. We are in the ascendancy. Duffer is running them ragged. We are close to the greatest

World Cup win of my managerial career. And then it all goes pear-shaped. Suddenly Portugal are running the game. I take Quinny off and try to batten down the hatches, take what we have and hope to catch them on the break.

Mattie Holland is sent on with instructions that the team is to go to a 4–3–3 with Gary Kelly and Kevin pushing up in support of Duffer. They have thrown on Luis Boa Morte and Capucho and are starting to take risks at the back now. There is every chance that Duffer's pace will expose them when they are at their most vulnerable but we need to support him, to have something to aim at.

Instead, we revert to a 4–5–1 for five minutes, we fall back to our eighteen-yard box and even Duffer gets pushed back. By the time I get to sort it out, Portugal have already made the most of our indecision.

Figo wins a great ball in the seventy-eighth minute, substitute Joao Pinto releases Nuno Frechaut down the right and Figo pops up at the far post, unmarked almost, to head home the equaliser.

We could have defended that goal better but now we have to get a message to Portugal that we are not going to give up. I get Gary Doherty on for Kinse and get a target back upfront. The plan to go to 4–3–3 was the right thing to do in my mind but it didn't work because we sat back after the goal. Gary's introduction gives more structure to our play but the game peters out and both teams settle for the draw in the end.

The point is hard-earned and well received. The dream lives on. We have played a great game of football, a magnificent, pulsating and flowing game that brought warmth to every heart present in a packed Lansdowne Road.

As I prepare to go down the tunnel I see Oliveira coming off the bench. I want to shake hands and congratulate him on his team's part in the spectacle. I put my hand out and he blanks me. I ask him if he is going to shake my hand and he just turns away.

I lose it. I call him a horrible, obnoxious little s**t. He mutters something in Portuguese and starts to get angry. I tell him to shut up and there is a confrontation. Thankfully, Eusebio, in Dublin as an ambassador for the Portuguese FA, drags me away. I had met him once before, at a charity dinner, and he was an absolute gentleman. He saves my bacon at Lansdowne, pulling me away and onto the pitch. I will always be grateful to him for that.

Figo is the same. He throws his arm around me and gives me a hug. I'd sooner have a hug off him than their coach any day. He is a true Portuguese gentleman, so much more representative of that lovely race of people. The other Portuguese players are great too. There is no animosity, no bitterness from anyone except Oliveira.

That's what the game should be about. I have been involved in some real ding-dong clashes with some of the best centre-forwards in the game in the past and I have always swapped handshakes with them. It is the mannerly thing to do.

I apologise for my part in the incident later, at the press conference. I should not have allowed Oliveira to drag me down to his level. His behaviour that day marred a great sporting occasion. The game was too good a contest to be spoilt by events at the end of it. We could have won it, they could have won it. We are both happy with the point that keeps the pressure on Holland.

As for Oliveira – who cares?

Republic of Ireland 1, Portugal 1

WEDNESDAY 6th JUNE, TALLINN

World Cup Group Two Qualifier

Estonia v Republic of Ireland

There were so many questions at the press conference after the Portugal game. Would you have done this if you had known that? Would you have tried that if you had known this? In the end, I produced a little prayer that Fiona gave me years ago when I got the Millwall job. She reminded me about it on the morning of the game. It read: 'God, grant me the serenity to accept the things I cannot change, the courage to change the things I can and the wisdom to know the difference.'

It is a lovely thought and a lovely prayer. There are things I cannot do anything about. That was the point I was making, and it is just as applicable in the build-up to the game in Tallinn.

Firstly, Portugal are now in the strongest position of all the three contenders in Group Two. Figo's late equaliser on Saturday ensures that their fate is in their own hands. They will win all their remaining games, barring an unforeseen disaster somewhere, and will finish the group with twenty-four points.

We have three games left, nine points to play for and fifteen in the bag. We can finish on twenty-four points and still lose out on top spot to goal difference. If that happens, it will still be a good day's work because we will have come through the group unbeaten and into the play-offs.

It is, of course, all conjecture as we fly to Estonia for the trickiest away tie we have faced since Lisbon last October. We have to win this game now and that is a difficult enough task in itself. It is made all the more so by Roy Keane's absence.

The game against Portugal on Saturday was Roy's best performance for me yet, mainly because he was up against a real world-class opponent in Rui Costa. The two of them would make some midfield partnership at club level. But as a result of that second yellow card, Roy is spared the trip to Tallinn and can start his summer holidays earlier than everyone else.

The rest of us are up early on Monday and off to Estonia with the under twenty-one team and a group of supporters on our Aer Lingus charter.

The fact that the game comes just four days after Portugal is a bonus. I have never made a secret of the fact that I miss life in the asylum that is club management and these back-to-back fixtures are the closest I get to that schedule. Working with the players for ten days at a time, as I am currently doing, is a godsend. It was definitely one of FIFA's better decisions and I really look forward to my time with the players on these trips. There is only so much you can do tactically on the training pitch when you meet up two or three days before the game. With a long stint like this, we get a chance to imprint how we want the game played on the players' brains and they are less likely to forget about it when they go back to club duty.

We have done well in these back-to-back fixtures into the bargain. Cyprus and Andorra were a success and I know that so much depends on Wednesday night as we leave Dublin.

Estonia were nothing if not rugged in Dublin and I have a couple of team decisions to make as we leave. Robbie Keane has been struggling with an ankle injury since a heavy challenge from Tony Adams at Highbury, late in the Premiership season. He did not look himself against Portugal on Saturday and I was happier with the impact Damien Duff made when I threw him on alongside Niall.

My inclination is to start with Duffer as Quinny's strike partner and leave Robbie on the bench. It's something I have been toying with for a while. Duffer has a quality that Irish football has been crying out for for some time now, genuine pace. His turn of speed can be blistering and when you consider that he can turn and dribble with the ball as well as any Premiership player, you can see why his talent excites me so much. He also holds the ball up well and that quality makes me suspect he can be a hit as an out-and-out striker. Would I want to mark him if I was a centre-back? Absolutely not. He was great when we played him through the middle against Portugal on Saturday so am going to leave him there for this game. If he can play off Quinny and run at those big centre-backs, then he can create real chances for us.

Duffer is just one of a host of youngsters coming through the ranks. The European Championship success at under-sixteen and under-eighteen level and the way Brian Kerr's teams have performed in the World Youth Cups augurs well for the future. We have more kids than ever playing the game now and I know there are a dozen more aspiring Duffers and Robbies waiting in the wings. The more the merrier as far as I am concerned.

I go to see some of those youngsters on the Tuesday night when Don Givens' under-twenty-one side play Estonia at the new Lillekula Stadium that will also host the senior game on Wednesday. The term 'new' is an understatement in this case. The ground is a building site and the pitch is a shambles. It is actually unplayable, full of ruts and divots and very uneven. How this was passed for Holland's 4–2 win here on Saturday night is beyond me. My worry is twofold, it is both dangerous for the players and a potential leveller in terms of our chances of winning the game.

I give the players who didn't go to the under-twenty-ones match the bad news when I get back to the hotel but I warn them not to say anything in public about the state of the pitch. The Estonians are a proud people and they will be deeply offended if we insult their new stadium. We cannot say anything that will wind them up ahead of the match. Shut up and put up.

The players half knew what to expect anyway as the training ground was just as bad. A massive crowd turned out to watch us every time we trained there and we struggled to find a decent part of the pitch to do some shooting practice on.

The under-twenty-ones win well, 3–0 thanks to two goals from Graham Barrett and one from Jim Goodwin. A number of the players, including Clinton Morrison, Steven Reid, Colin Healy, John O'Shea and Thomas Butler impress me. They are names to watch closely in the coming months. I have already taken Andy O'Brien off Don Givens for the senior squad ahead of tomorrow night's match, as cover for Gary Breen back in England for a hernia operation.

The players give Steve Staunton a standing ovation when he comes into the dressing-room for the senior game the following day. Stan will captain Ireland in Roy Keane's absence and he will make a record eighty-ninth appearance for his country. That is some achievement, all the more so because Steve was out of the first-team picture with Ireland in recent times and only got back in against Portugal last Saturday because of Breeny's late injury.

I never doubted Steve's ability to play at this level again but I did have words with him on the pitch in Lisbon, when we trained the night before the game at the Stadium of Light. I was concerned that Steve was drifting away from the squad and lacking a bit of motivation. It is hard for a senior player to see kids come in and take his place in the team. I have been there and I knew what he was going through. I just wanted Stan to realise that he has an awful lot left to offer this Irish team and the youngsters coming through. I told him then to be ready, that his chance could come at any stage. That happened on Saturday and now he is captain as he breaks the Irish appearances record.

The pitch, as we feared, is absolutely dreadful, the surface almost treacherous. We need the likes of Stan and Niall to lead by example, to show the youngsters that you just get on with it in circumstances like this. Roll your sleeves up and fight for the cause.

Estonia have a new coach in the Dutchman Arno Pijpers and he has improved them since Dublin but tonight they are without their well-known 'keeper Mart Poom, of Derby County. They do have a flying machine playing down the left by the name of Andres Oper, a 10.8 second man for the 100 metres. After watching the video of Oper against Reizeger in Holland's 4–2 win here at the weekend, I asked Stevie Carr how fast he could run.

I think he's fast enough to give Oper something to think about and the fact that Gary Kelly will add his experience in front of Stevie will help. The pair worked well as a unit down the right for twenty-three minutes against Andorra and I have no worries about their ability to gel tonight.

Matt Holland replaces Roy in midfield. I have said it before but the biggest compliment I can pay Mattie is that we don't miss Roy half as much as we used to before he came along.

Kells is in on the right because Duffer will partner Quinny. I have a major concern over Niall's back going into the game but he is confident he will last the ninety minutes. This is definitely a game when his cuteness will count for a lot and we need him to feed Duffer as often as possible.

Duffer wins a corner after just eight minutes. Stan swings it in, Quinny flicks it off at the near post and Hartey puts the ball back into the six-yard box. Richard Dunne has stayed up for the corner and smashes it home from close range. It's like his Lansdowne Road effort against the same opposition, they clearly have not learnt how to pick Dunney up at corner-kicks.

The goal settles nerves on the bumpy pitch and their replacement 'keeper Martin Kaalma has to react quickly to deny Duffer on the double with two quick saves in the fifteenth minute.

Quinny then lands awkwardly under a challenge from Andrei Stepanov and is in some discomfort with his back. He struggles on for fifteen minutes, during which time Estonia enjoy their best spell of the game. Dunney does well to intercept an Indrek Zelinksi effort before Shay pushes a Raio Piiroja shot out for a corner. Marko Novikov and Jevgeni Kristal go close but we regain our composure and Kevin reminds them we are still in the game when he flashes in one good effort but with no reward. Quinny's game is over when he concedes defeat in his battle with pain in the thirty-sixth minute and Gary Doherty again answers the call as an emergency striker.

He obviously has the touch. Within a couple of minutes of his arrival, we score, just like we did when he replaced David Connolly in Barcelona. Gary Kelly creates the chance again with another clever throw from the right wing, Stevie Carr sets up Hartey and when his shot is blocked, Mattie drives home his third World Cup goal.

The second goal is a killer blow as far as Estonia are concerned. Oper gets no change out of Stevie, Stan is man of the match in the middle of our defence and we have total control for the remaining fifty-two minutes. Kevin almost adds a third late in the game, after a fine set-up from Gary off a Kells cross, but the game ends with a two-goal win for the Irish. And three more World Cup points in that bag.

It is probably the most mature performance by an Irish team in my time in charge. If anything, it was better than the games in Holland and Portugal at the start of the group. We controlled the game from start to finish. We made the best of a bad lot with the pitch and even managed to pass the ball on it. We kept at Estonia, we picked holes in them and we dictated the tempo of the game. We were professional, quietly and efficiently. They were well organised and well coached and we had the measure of them from the first kick.

We had some outstanding individual performances. Stevie Carr never gave Oper a kick and linked superbly with Gary Kelly down the right. Stan was a leader at centre-back, Duffer a joy to watch at centre-forward. And I'll repeat myself, we don't miss Roy as much now as we once did, Mattie and Kinse dug it out time and time again against Estonia. They were excellent.

What more can a manager ask for? Very little really. This is more than I dreamed of a year ago. We have now put together an eleven-game unbeaten run away from home. We are top of the group with eighteen points from eight games and two more to play, at home to Holland and Cyprus. We can finish with twenty-four points, the tally I believe will be good enough to see us through.

We can even win the group, though I can't see Portugal slipping up against Andorra, Estonia or Cyprus. If anything they could wipe any goal difference advantage out in one game.

So let's be positive as we go off on our holidays. One win against Holland next September and we are guaranteed the play-offs at worst. We can do that. With everyone fit, we are well capable of beating the Dutch at Lansdowne Road.

Hands-up all those who predicted we'd make the play-offs when this group began last September. And be honest.

ESTONIA 0, REPUBLIC OF IRELAND 2

FOUR

August–December 2001

Ireland are two wins away from a play-off for the World Cup finals at worst as we await the arrival of Holland and Cyprus in Dublin. Beat the Dutch in September and we can start to think about packing our bags for Japan and Korea.

WEDNESDAY 15th AUGUST, LANSDOWNE ROAD

International Friendly

Republic of Ireland v Croatia

The biggest game of my life is less than a month away. It is time to get to work, time to get the players back to work.

The summer was good. No worries, no anxiety, a few weeks in the sun in Portugal and a big game at the back of my mind. A very big game. Croatia are in town this week but everything is geared to Holland. I want to get the players thinking about the game, looking forward to it, reminding themselves how we play and what we need to do to beat the Dutch and knock them out of the Group Two reckoning.

Croatia is a chance to bring people together and ease them into a new international season, the big season, World Cup season. It's also a chance to look at some new faces, including Clinton Morrison and Steven Reid, both in the squad after their impressive under-twenty-one performances, Stephen McPhail, Gary Doherty and John O'Shea.

There is a big clamour to promote John to the senior squad but first I want to see him establish himself in the team at Old Trafford. He is a great prospect, there is no doubt about that, and looks the part, a real silky footballer. His United boss Alex Ferguson rates him highly, but there is a big difference between playing for the United reserves and playing for a club's first team, whether it's Manchester United, Manchester City or Aston Villa. I try to explain that to people when we talk about some of the youngsters coming through but sometimes I feel like I am banging my head against a brick wall.

The Croatia friendly is a perfect game to blood John in at this level, but there is no way I can take a chance on an inexperienced international against the likes of Ruud van Nistelrooy next month. I have always been one for giving youth its fling but it has to be done in a measured and controlled way. I have no doubt that down the road, John is going to become a very good international footballer. Croatia will represent his first steps on that road but we will take it slowly, for his sake as much as anything.

John will feature as a sub against our visitors. I've struck a deal with Croatia boss Mirko Jozic that allows us both to use nine substitutes. He has a big World Cup game coming up as well, against Scotland at Hampden, and is just as interested in trying out players and systems as I am.

Steven Reid is another to make his debut in the match. A while back he mentioned to his Millwall team-mate Robbie Ryan that his grandfather was from Galway and Robbie passed the news on to Taff. Now Steven will play on the right side of midfield against the team that did us with a late goal in Zagreb a couple of years ago. I have seen a lot of Steven on the left at Millwall but he is naturally right-sided so the position won't be a problem for him.

Mark Kennedy is back in the team. I know Kevin Kilbane isn't best pleased at starting this one on the bench but he should know that he is first choice when it comes to Holland in a fortnight. Mark has had a succession of injuries recently and needs a game.

Niall Quinn has an ankle injury picked up in a pre-season friendly. Thankfully he has assured me his back is just fine after a good rest,

The Master and I. Just having Jack Charlton around the place gives me a big lift.

Robbie Keane celebrates the opening goal against Holland in the Amsterdam Arena, during the September 2000 qualifier.

Happiness is Matt Holland's equalizer in the October 2000 qualifier at the Stadium of Light. It is a goal of some beauty. Portugal are stunned.

The marksman. Mark Kinsella enjoys his first goal for Ireland against Estonia, October 2000.

Playing the waiting game against Cyprus in March 2001 – a match we have to win if we are serious about World Cup qualification.

The Duffer. He is a joy to watch as the Andorra players allow Damien Duff to run at them for fun in the Barcelona qualifier, March 2001.

Take it away. Matt Holland goes around the Andorran 'keeper, Sanchez, at the Lansdowne Road qualifier, April 2001.

Ireland v Portugal, June 2001. A quick throw in from Stevie Carr finds Roy Keane in the box and his shot deflects off Litos and past Ricardo. Elation. Lansdowne Road erupts.

Steve Staunton makes a record eighty-ninth appearance for his country, away to Estonia, June 2001. That is some achievement.

The haka. Elation once again as Holland are beaten at the Lansdowne Road qualifier, September 2001.

The Irish team line up to play Iran in Dublin, November 2001. If we win this play-off match and keep a clean sheet, I am confident we can go through. Quietly confident.

A hug from Iranian manager, Miroslav Blazevic. I love this guy. He is what I call a tulip, someone who is a real larger than life character.

Home supporters predict the score line at the November 2001 play-off in Tehran. Nothing can prepare players for the atmosphere in the Azadi Stadium.

We have done it! It's November 2001. We have seen off Holland, we have beaten Iran over the two legs and we are in a major final at last. I am walking on air.

We have qualified for the World Cup 2002 and all hell breaks loose. The players and staff are ecstatic.

The best of friends. Standing with Saudi Arabia's coach, Nasser Al Jawhar, at the World Cup draw in Busan, December 2001. We will need five points to guarantee our passage through to the second phase and it may all come down to the last game against the Saudi team.

Top man. To see a crowd of this size turn up to Niall Quinn's testimonial in May 2002, paying tribute to the player and raising so much money for children's charities in Dublin and Sunderland, is special.

Taoiseach Bertie Ahern takes time out from the general election to add his weight to the farewells at Dublin airport, as we leave for Japan.

which is music to my ears. Mattie is also out, with a knee problem picked up in a friendly in Ireland, as it happens, but the main thing is that both of them will be fit for Holland.

With Niall out, I go for a frontline partnership of Duffer and Robbie. Last season I saw Jaap Stam struggle when Manchester United played Fulham and he had to mark Louis Saha, the French striker with blistering pace. Jaap is a fantastic defender but the pace and movement of Saha caused him real problems and he had a nightmare that afternoon. I have a feeling he may not fancy the idea of Duffer and Robbie running at him when Holland come to town and this is the perfect opportunity to try them out.

We are still missing Gary Breen and Kenny Cunningham so Stan and Richard play together again at the heart of our defence, Stan winning his ninetieth cap. The way he's going, he could make the hundred. What an achievement that would be for an Irish footballer.

Stan leads by example in the opening twenty minutes of the game as we pass Croatia off the field. The dominance is rewarded when Damien Duff opens his international account with a brilliant goal in the twenty-first minute. Steven Reid, Robbie and Roy set it up for him and Duffer finishes into the top corner after dragging the ball back with a great piece of skill. Robbie and Duffer spend fifty-two minutes on the field together and they work really well as a unit. I might just play them upfront against Holland after this performance.

Andy O'Brien and Steven Reid also make impressions. Steven spends the first-half out wide on the right and, though clearly nervous, his touch and power are good. He is replaced by Steve Finnan at the break but he will be back, I have no doubts on that front. Not everyone takes to international football as easily as Robbie but Steven is definitely one for the future.

Richard Dunne reminds me of his Amsterdam performance before he makes way for Andy at half-time. The step up to the Premiership and the move to St James's Park are bringing out the best in Andy. He looks the part, accelerating, tackling and clearing the danger when a Croatian forward gets between our defence and the goal. Richard and Stan are still ahead of Andy in the queue for the

Holland match but he is making noises. Central defence has been an area in which we lacked strength in depth but my options at the back are improving.

Wimbledon's new signing David Connolly is another player with the bit between his teeth. Clinton, on for Robbie in the fifty-second minute, destroys Dario Simic with his first touch in international football and sends in a great cross for David but the Juve defender Igor Tudor denies him a goal.

David is busy around the field and plays a big part in the second goal with a clever pass for Jason in the seventy-second minute. His shot is blocked by 'keeper Stipe Pletikosa but Clinton is on hand to shoot into the empty net and score his first Ireland goal from very close range. They all count. Clinton is picking up the confidence and swagger of an international footballer.

Croatia bounce back when substitute Davor Vugrinec heads home an Igor Biscan cross in the eightieth minute.

We begin to lose our shape and it's my fault. I have already made eight changes by the time the Croatian goal arrives and make it nine when John O'Shea makes his debut as an eighty-second-minute substitute for Gary Kelly. John is unlucky, three minutes into injury time, when a Robert Prosinecki corner hits his hand and the Swiss referee points to the spot.

Two years ago Davor Suker broke our hearts with a ninety-third minute winner in a Euro qualifier in Zagreb. Tonight, he beats substitute 'keeper Alan Kelly from the spot and saves the game for the Croatians. Deja-vu all over again, as they say!

Still, that's thirteen games unbeaten and two more well-created goals. The old Millwall chairman Reg Burr used to tell me he'd sooner be superstitious with a good side than a bad side. Superstitious? Not me, touch wood. I have a good side now. We are making progress and we are buoyant a fortnight ahead of the biggest test we will face in this World Cup bid.

The result says Croatia took a draw from Lansdowne Road but I tell the players in the dressing-room not to beat themselves up over that equaliser. The performance was excellent, the raggedness was down to me and all the changes I made. There are far more positives than negatives to take from tonight's game, this glass is definitely half full.

The press conference is alive with talk of Holland's win over England at White Hart Lane tonight. Great, let them think they are world-beaters again. Suits me to face a cocky Dutch side in Dublin. The bigger they come, the harder they fall. Bring them on.

REPUBLIC OF IRELAND 2, CROATIA 2

SATURDAY 1st SEPTEMBER, LANSDOWNE ROAD

World Cup Group Two Qualifier

Republic of Ireland v Holland

Another big game, another injury crisis, another week in the life of the Irish manager. Mark Kinsella, Stevie Carr, Kenny Cunningham and Gary Breen are all ruled out when I name the squad to play Holland, not long after the Croatia game. Clinton Morrison and Steven Reid are in, rewards for fine debuts on both their parts.

I am down to bare bones now at the back. When Ian Harte's shin is cut open by Paulo Di Canio at West Ham on the Saturday before the game, I start to question my luck. That night I speak to the Leeds physio and he assures me that Hartey will be okay, given rest and treatment, but there is no guarantee that he has enough time on his side to play against Holland. Time to pray.

Stories have been circulating that Keano is out for three weeks with an ankle injury but he plays against Villa on the Sunday, aggravates an old hip injury and opts to stay in Manchester again for treatment and report later than the rest of the squad. I just hope he is fit.

Mark Kennedy arrives in Dublin with the rest of the lads ahead of our first training session on the Tuesday and is promptly sent back to Wolves. There is no way his groin injury is going to allow him to play on Saturday. More headaches but at least I am not the only one with problems ahead of the game. Edgar Davids is handed a five-month ban for drug offences by the Italian FA on the Tuesday and the Dutch are furious. Louis van Gaal has included him in his nineteen-man squad and he will travel to Ireland but it is virtually certain he won't be able to play.

Even without Davids, the Dutch squad is a lot stronger now than it was in Amsterdam a year ago. Marc Overmars, Boudewijn Zenden, Jaap Stam, Jimmy Floyd Hasselbaink, Ruud van Nistelrooy and Pierre van Hooijdonk are all back in contention. They are clearly hyped up for this game and they are talking up their chances, according to the Dutch media who have started attending my press conferences. Some Dutch players are even talking about retiring from international football after the World Cup finals. I wouldn't be quite so confident about getting there if I were them.

I have watched the video of their White Hart Lane win against England a few times and it's the best comedy I have seen for years. The game was so slow that I could have played centre-back for Holland, and I'm forty-two. Nobody tackled, nobody put a foot in, no-one chased back. If Louis van Gaal reads anything into that game he is badly mistaken. It took thirty-two minutes before a tackle was seen that night in London, I have a feeling we might not even have to wait thirty-two seconds for the first tackle on Saturday.

That is what I tell my players as we watch the video together. They have a good laugh when I say I could have played in the game myself, and watching the tape works wonders for us. I show the lads all the pretty little patterns that Holland use against England and tell them it will be different for the Dutch on Saturday.

It seems we are the only ones who can see that match for the charade it is, however. From what I can pick up, the Dutch are as fooled by that England result as everyone else. They were swanning around like world-beaters that night but one good tackle should bring them back down to earth with a bang.

I have a little surprise for the Dutch. I pull Quinny on the Tuesday out at Citywest and tell him he won't be playing. I explain that I am going to go with Duffer and Robbie upfront and he understands my logic perfectly. He is an intelligent guy, understands how I am using him and has no problem with it. He doesn't lose his head or storm out when things go against him. I ask him to go along with the notion that he is playing if the media ask about the game. Let the Dutch believe that Stam is going to have a battle royal with Quinny.

Roy arrives in after an early morning flight on Wednesday but he is too tired to play in a practice game against the under-twenty-ones at John Hyland Park in Baldonnel on the Naas Road. Duffer scores the only goal, playing as a centre-forward.

The Dutch are in town the next day and Louis van Gaal is starting to annoy me. He has been quoted on my employment prospects if Ireland lose on Saturday and he seems none too concerned at the prospect of Ireland sacking their manager and me losing my job if his team wins. That disappoints me. There is no need for Louis van Gaal to get involved in Irish football politics. Hopefully we can wipe the smile off his face.

Jaap Stam has just completed a move from Manchester United to Lazio and the press want to know if it will influence Saturday's game, somehow put him off before the Ireland match. Will it heck. If I was changing jobs and going from £50,000 a week to £75,000, I'd be doing cartwheels. He's old enough and wise enough to deal with all the controversy that has surrounded the move from United. It won't have any effect on his form in a Holland shirt. Duffer might be more of a worry for Stam.

When a Dutch journalist asks me what I make of the Edgar Davids ban, the alarm bells ring. I have made this mistake before, when my comments on Couto sparked World War Three back in June. This time I have no opinion on the matter, thank you. They can bring two Edgar Davidses to Dublin for all I care. I'd rather beat a Dutch team with Davids in it than one without him. I'm learning.

The week flies by at Citywest. There is a huge buzz about this game. The supporters are at the hotel, asking for autographs, hoping to meet the players. Someone suggests we should go out the back door to training but I refuse, point blank, to even consider the idea. I love that special bond we have with the fans. We owe them a big game on Saturday for their loyalty.

Friday is a quite bizarre day thanks to FIFA. For some incredible reason, they have decided to make the draw for the play-offs on the day before the penultimate game in our group. As we are driving to Lansdowne Road, the news breaks on the radio that the team which finishes second in Group Two will play one of the Asian teams in the November play-offs.

The radio presenter is almost wetting himself. He says it's great news for Mick McCarthy and his Ireland team. Great news for us? What about the Dutch. Don't for a second think this won't help them going into the game. They'll be sitting in their hotel thinking great, beat the Irish and we have a ready-made route to the World Cup finals with only a little Asian team to get past. It's only great news for us if we beat Holland. Lose and it won't matter at all.

I go with my instinct when I tell the players the team. Duffer and Robbie are upfront. Gary Kelly gets the nod to mark Overmars, ahead of Steve Finnan. Mattie is in for Mark in the middle and will sit in front of the centre-backs Richard Dunne and Steve Staunton. If Kluivert drops he's to pick him up. Jason has played his way back into the team but I need him to deliver. Kevin and Jase have to tuck in when the Dutch are on the attack. More importantly, I want them to supply and support Robbie and Duffer. We need to be positive at home. Ian Harte, I am glad to say, is fine. He's in a bit of pain but he will play through it. I hope people realise how much effort he has made to make this game.

Before the match the dressing-room is awash with adrenaline. Lansdowne is packed to the rafters, the Dutch have turned one half of the North Terrace orange, everywhere else is green to the gills and the fans are singing already. Like the players, they can sense how close we are to the big one now.

My final team talk is short and simple. It's the one about passionate hearts and calm heads. I ask the players to give me the opportunity to walk up to Louis van Gaal afterwards and say 'unlucky'. Just give me the chance to look him in the eye, shake his hand and say 'bad luck'.

The game begins at a hectic pace. Roy clatters Overmars inside the first sixty seconds. Welcome to Dublin Marc.

Holland mean business. They attack in droves in the first-half with Overmars ever dangerous down the left. Kluivert is sent through early on and puts the ball past Shay's post. When I see him go through, I think to myself that he scores these nine times out of ten. This is the tenth time, thankfully. Maybe the luck, for once, is with us.

The Dutch continue to force the pace. Mark van Bommel tests Shay with a decent effort from twenty yards. Robbie has our first real chance but gets little power behind the shot. Zenden responds but fails to lift the ball over Shay Given. We are digging deep in the middle of the field. Roy lifts those around him, Jason and Kevin cover every blade of grass. Mattie is doing the shadow job on Kluivert that I asked him to do.

Gary Kelly is booked for a foul on Overmars, borne out of frustration as he loses the ball, and Zenden's free-falls for van Nistelrooy at the far post. I can barely look. Somehow the Manchester United striker fails to connect and the ball drifts away, past the post.

We keep it scoreless until half-time. The Dutch have to make the running and they are struggling to contain Duffer when he gets on the ball, as I suspected they would. We have a lot of comfort to take from the opening half, a lot more hard work to do after the break. The full-backs are told to tuck in alongside Stan and Richard again, to keep it narrow and stop them playing in and around us.

The plan is working until Kells forgets the cool heads part of the passionate hearts speech and cuts Overmars down again in the fifty-seventh minute. The second yellow card from German referee Helmut Krug, and the red to follow, is inevitable but a little harsh. Now we need to do something. Robbie is sacrificed and Steve Finnan goes on at right-back. I will take the draw now. It's no use to the Dutch but should be enough to see us through to the play-offs so let's see if we can keep the ball and frustrate them.

Seconds later Stan's headed back pass goes past the advancing Shay Given. Van Nistelrooy is in like a flash but Shay manages to get his body across him and Hartey and Richard Dunne combine to get the ball off the line and behind for a corner.

My heart stops. At first, I thought Stan's header was going in. Then I thought a penalty would be given against Shay for impeding van Nistelrooy, now I can't believe how we have got away with it.

Should it have been a penalty? I've seen them given in similar circumstances. The Dutch are going mad on their bench but I think Shay has been quite clever. He stood up and it looked like van Nistelrooy was impeding him as much as anything. Play on, please.

Holland are getting desperate now. They have Hasselbaink on for Zenden and van Hooijdonk on for Numan. They are playing with four upfront and lumping the ball forward. Then we hit them with a killer blow.

Roy Keane is fouled as he breaks down the left but the referee is inspired and waves play on. Keano gets it inside to Duffer who switches the play to the right and finds Stevie Finnan on the overlap. Cocu stands up to Stevie but the full-back comes inside, switches onto his left foot and sends a great ball to the far post. Jason is in and around the box, loitering with intent, and plants the ball into the roof of the net with the sweetest half volley of his life.

Lansdowne Road erupts. Holland are a goal down to ten-man Ireland. We are twenty-three minutes away from the greatest result this team has managed yet.

What a twenty-three minutes it is. Louis van Gaal gets more desperate by the minute. For some bizarre reason he takes Overmars off and asks van Hooijdonk and Hasselbaink to play as wingers. We can't believe our luck. They lump high balls into the box and Stan and Richard lap them up.

The crowd become the eleventh man now. They can sense history in the making here. They lift the noise to a level Lansdowne has never heard before. It is us against them, Ireland against Holland. The East Stand is visibly rocking with the emotion.

Sure, we ride our luck but you make your own luck in this game as well. The final whistle goes and I walk up to Louis van Gaal. 'Unlucky, Louis,' I smile. And then I celebrate with some very, very happy Irishmen.

Lansdowne Road is still swaying, the East Stand shaking, as I depart for the dressing-room. My body aches with the exhaustion. I feel like I have just played the ninety minutes against Holland myself. This is Christmas and all my birthdays rolled into one. We have pulled off the greatest win of my time managing the Republic of Ireland thanks to the skill and dedication of a very committed group of players. We were short five regular internationals. We had a man sent-off early in the second-half. We were up against the Euro 2000 semi-finalists. And we have knocked them out of the World Cup.

Japan and Korea will be the poorer without Holland but I am not about to shed any tears for them. They went head-to-head with us and we won. We took four points from six off them and we might even win the group yet. There is hope. Portugal are red-hot favourites but we have one game to come, at home to Cyprus, and we will carry on until it is mathematically impossible to go through to the finals without the need for a play-off. That is all for the future though. For now, I can bask in the glory of the press conference.

This is my moment. I tell anyone prepared to listen that this is the sweetest win of them all. A famous victory, hard-earned by a very honest bunch of fellas.

How did I feel when Gary Kelly was sent-off? Oh great, actually. I knew we were on top and with ten men we could take the game to them! I am, of course, being sarcastic. I can't answer that question, it's too stupid. How did the guy think I felt when Gary was sent-off? Instead, I admit I'd have settled for a 0–0 draw when Kells was red-carded.

What did you think of the ref overall? I don't believe this one. We've just beaten a great Dutch team with ten men and someone wants to know what I thought about the ref. Help me, please.

Best win ever? The current win is always the best but yes, this is special. It was something else to go on from that red card and win it.

I'm delighted for Jason McAteer that he got the goal. I can never understand why Jase gets so much criticism. He does the job on the right-hand side of midfield so well for me. He understands the needs of the position as well as anyone, when to tuck in and defend and when to push forward and get crosses in. It amazes me that he can't get a game at Blackburn or a team to buy him. I know eyebrows were raised when his name appeared on the team sheet because of my preference for players involved in first-team football but I had no worries at all about his ability to go from the Blackburn reserves to the World Cup stage. Jason is too good a player to be rotting in the stiffs. He epitomises the spirit of this team and the gamble of playing him today paid off. I don't look for vindication but I am proud that my support for Jason has been rewarded.

Stan is the same. He can't get a game at Villa yet he can turn in four faultless international displays with Ireland. He deserves a change in fortune.

Do you feel personally vindicated tonight Mick? Of course, I do. When I took the two away fixtures at the start of this group, people were sending for the straightjackets. I bet half the country thought I was off my rocker, and the other half were certain. I knew it was a gamble but I also knew that was the right time to play them, straight after the Europeans. I also knew we needed to get results at home, that Lansdowne would make or break our bid to qualify for the World Cup. Today proved just that. We are unbeaten in the group, we are unbeaten now for fourteen games. And we are, at worst, through to the play-offs.

Is that vindication? You bet.

Republic of Ireland 1, Holland 0

SATURDAY 6th OCTOBER, LANSDOWNE ROAD

World Cup Group Two Qualifier

Republic of Ireland v Cyprus

We are still dealing with ifs and buts at the top of Group Two in the European section of the World Cup qualifiers but their importance is diminishing.

Portugal, as expected, won their penultimate match in Cyprus. I was in Dublin at the time and Taff was at the game. I did try to ignore it but people kept ringing to tell me the score. One guy even rang every time there was a half chance for Cyprus and a possibility that they might produce the first real upset of this group. They didn't, of course. Our demolition job on the Dutch has the monopoly on surprises and we are level on twenty-one points apiece with the Portuguese going into the final game.

Their manager, my old friend Antonio Oliveira, is still moaning, as is his way. This time he is upset that Cyprus have left a handful of their top stars out of the squad to travel to Dublin at the request of their clubs.

Does this man ever smile, I wonder? If I were him I would concentrate on Portugal's game with Estonia in Lisbon and forget about us. Is he seriously worried that an Estonian team with nothing but pride to play for is going to beat a side containing Figo, Rui Costa and Joao Pinto amongst others? I doubt it. I'd put the mortgage on Portugal winning that one and topping the group so I don't know what he is complaining about.

I have other problems to worry about. Thanks to FIFA's mistimed draw last month, we know that we will go to the Middle East for a play-off if we finish second in Group Two. My fear is that the current war in Afghanistan will throw the plans for the play-offs into chaos. I know there are some things in life that are more important than football. And we have been here before, particularly when we played Yugoslavia, Croatia and Macedonia during the Balkan crisis. But I would like some guidance from FIFA on the subject and, so far, very little is forthcoming.

My real fear is that they will decide to turn the two-legged play-off into a one-off game at a neutral venue. I would hate to think that all the hard work we have put in over the last eighteen months will come down to just ninety minutes of football. Play-offs, to my mind, only work when you have the chance to play home and away. I have no worries about going to Asia, provided FIFA guarantee our safety. That is more acceptable than a one-off game as far as I am concerned.

Don't get me wrong, I am no hero. If the third place play-off in Asia is anywhere near the war zone, I will stay at home and watch the video. But I do believe we should be given the opportunity to bring whoever the opposition is to Lansdowne then play them on their own turf. It is the fair way to do it and we know how keen FIFA are on fair play.

I have another worry concerning the play-offs. Four of my players are on yellow cards and we still don't know if they will carry over into the knock-out series. Robbie, Mark Kinsella, Kenny Cunningham and Jason McAteer are all in the squad for the game against Cyprus but I will not risk them if their cards are going to carry over. What happens if they get booked again, pick up a one-match ban and then the play-off is changed to a one-off game. I don't fancy seeing my team weakened in those circumstances, thank you.

FIFA eventually make their decision on the Thursday. The yellow cards will carry over. So that's the end of those four starting the game. I will leave them on the bench and consider using them only if we are stuck.

Training is low-key in the build-up to the game and that worries me as well. We cannot afford to start looking to the play-offs now. We have to prepare to win this game and attempt to win the group. I remind the players of that all week.

Team selection is straightforward once the yellow card issue is sorted. Richard Dunne is out with a back injury and Kenny is on a card so Gary Breen, himself carrying a knock, will partner Stan.

Stevie Carr's knee is now a major concern and he is joined on the sidelines for this game by Gary Kelly, suspended after the Dutch game. As a result Steve Finnan joins the back four on the right with Hartey out left. Curtis Fleming is in the squad to provide cover at right-back in case anything happens Steve.

Mark Kennedy comes in for Jason in midfield, alongside Roy, Mattie and Kevin from the Holland match. And Quinny is re-united with David Connolly upfront.

The potential upset is the key element of the team talk before the match. It may be a long shot but we can still win this group. I can't for the life of me see Portugal slipping up at home to Estonia, but hope springs eternal. The one thing we must do is win this game. That's all we can do. Take care of our own business and worry about what is going on in Lisbon when this match is over.

There is an air of anti-climax about the place as the game kicks off. Lansdowne is nowhere near as animated as it was a month ago for the Holland game but that is only to be expected. The old ground soon bursts into life, however. Niall Quinn, playing on his thirty-fifth birthday, is upended by Petros Konnafis after only two minutes. Free-kick to Ireland, twenty-two yards out and there's only one man for the job. Ian Harte steps up and buries the ball with that sweet left foot of his. The perfect start.

The Far East is calling just nine minutes later when Kevin Kilbane swings in a cross from the left and Quinny heads home the twenty-first international goal of his eighty-eight-game Ireland career. He has finally broken Frank Stapleton's record. Lansdowne celebrates and the entire ground sings 'Happy birthday'. I join in.

Niall's strike partner David Connolly is blooming since his move to Wimbledon and he almost celebrates his return to the team with a goal when he gets on the end of a Mark Kennedy cross in the twentieth minute but heads wide.

Cyprus field just six of the team that stood up to us in Nicosia last March, when the 4–0 scoreline in our favour failed to do them justice. They are nowhere near as dogged in their opposition tonight and if it wasn't for the heroics of goalkeeper and captain Nikos Panayiotou they would be well out of sight by half-time. He produces a series of fine saves, denying Quinny, Roy, David and Kevin.

David does put the ball in the back of the Cypriot net on the stroke of half-time but referee Juan Ansuategi Roca from Spain disallows it, claiming that Kevin had fouled the 'keeper as Ian Harte's corner swung in.

I have no idea what Portugal are up to in Lisbon as we head for the dressing-room and little interest. I stress again that we need to do our own job first and forget about them until after the final whistle. The group may yet come down to goal difference but I doubt it. The three points are the important thing here.

We guarantee them in the sixty-third minute when Hartey, Quinny and Kevin combine before David Connolly gets the goal he deserves with good control and a fine finish. It is David's first goal in thirteen internationals and it will do his confidence a world of good.

Shay has little or nothing to do all night. He joins the applause in the sixty-eighth minute when Mattie sets up Roy and my captain finishes clinically from just inside the box. That's that then. I finally enquire how Portugal are doing and discover they are 5–0 up in Lisbon. My mind drifts east, to the Middle East to begin with. And then the Far East, we hope.

Elation, pride, joy, relief and frustration – all those emotions and more flow through me in the minutes after the end of Ireland's participation in Group Two of the World Cup qualifiers. We have finished the group unbeaten. We have scored seven wins and three draws and amassed twenty-four points, enough to win all but one of the other eight European groups. Along the way we have drawn in Amsterdam and Lisbon, beaten the Dutch on our own soil and sent them crashing out of the World Cup for the first time since 1986. And still we are not through to the 2002 finals in Japan and South Korea. Not yet.

That is the one thought I want the players to take away with them in the aftermath of the four-goal win over Cyprus. We are not there – yet. This team is good enough to go to the World Cup finals now. This team is good enough to join Portugal in the Far East next summer and make an impression on the greatest football stage of them all. I am full of pride in these players, pride they have earned over the last fourteen months of blood, sweat and tears.

And I have no regrets. Someone asks me after the match if I regretted not winning in Holland or not beating Portugal in Dublin. No. If I were to regret events gone past, I'd make my life miserable. And right now, I am far from miserable. I am happy and I am optimistic.

Privately, I always reckoned we would end up in the play-offs. That's why I was not prepared to expose Robbie Keane, Jason McAteer, Kenny Cunningham or Mark Kinsella to the risk of another yellow card against Cyprus.

Some people have expressed the view that I should have played them and gone hell for leather for the goals that would have caught Portugal's superior goal difference, all nine of them as it would have transpired. That was one way of looking at it. Personally, I never thought for a second that Portugal would slip up at home to Estonia.

When we went four up, I did check to see how Portugal were doing. If they had been only one up, I might have been tempted to throw Robbie in for the last twenty minutes or so but there was no need. Our play-off fate was sealed at that stage. And I am not worried by it, despite disappointments in the past.

I thought we could beat Belgium in 1997, I thought we could beat Turkey in 1999 and, despite those previous setbacks, I firmly believe we have matured as a team and can beat whoever the play-offs pit us against this time. My team have given me that faith over this Group Two campaign. They have played like never before, they have competed like never before. And they have shown the world that they are ready to take the step up to the big stage, even if we have to do it through the play-offs now.

Along the way, there have been some great individual stories, none more deserved than Niall Quinn's new goal-scoring record. I want Niall with me in Japan and South Korea and I believe he will play a big part in getting us there through the two games next month, if we play two games.

Niall is not the only star of this campaign to date. Jason McAteer has scored some great goals, Roy Keane has set new standards for everyone to aspire to every time he has played for Ireland in this group. And then there's Steve Staunton. No one deserves to play in the Far East next year more than Steve. He has been the big bonus of the tournament so far. He waited patiently for his chance and when he got it against Portugal last June, he took some woeful stick. Steve was bigger than all of that though. He has settled in at centre-back, he has locked himself into the position and he has made it impossible for me to drop him now. Not that I want to, of course. When we look back at this group, he will be recognised as one of the real stars of this campaign.

They have done us proud these players, all of us.

Republic of Ireland 4, Cyprus 0

SATURDAY 11th NOVEMBER, LANSDOWNE ROAD

World Cup Play-off

Republic of Ireland v Iran

A week after the win over Cyprus and I head off to the Middle East. Saudi Arabia have qualified automatically for the finals after a shock defeat for Iran in Bahrain, a result that prompted some civil unrest in Tehran. Miroslav Blazevic, my old sparring partner from Croatia, must now guide the Iranians through a two-legged play-off against the United Arab Emirates with the winners to meet Ireland on a home and away basis, Lansdowne Road first in the order of play.

There is, of course, a crisis lurching in the background as I head east with Taff, our travel agent Ray Treacy and the team's logistical expert Eddie Corcoran. The ongoing conflict in the region has already caused a number of Chelsea players to stay away from a UEFA Cup game in Israel. As a result, speculation is rife that we will have a problem travelling to Iran or the UAE. Thankfully, any such fears are ill-founded. I spend two days in Iran and five days in Dubai without so much as a hint of trouble.

The people in Tehran could not be friendlier. There is no sign of poverty or deprivation, no hint of the war a few hundred miles away in Afghanistan. The standard of living appears to be fine, the food and the hotel are first-class and the locals cannot do enough for us. There are twelve million people living in this proud city and about five million Hillman Hunters from our observations. One of them is driven by a Des Lynam lookalike who becomes our guide for our stay. We promise to meet up again if we return.

After the first-leg of the Asian play-offs, I am convinced we will be going back to Tehran. Iran batter UAE but end up with only a one-goal advantage to take to Abu Dhabi for the second leg. Five days later class tells and Iran win comfortably away from home.

They look a decent side, have a good old-fashioned centre-forward in Ali Daei and a real livewire beside him in the shape of Karimi. The only aspect of his game that lets him down is his finishing. He has everything else, a good touch, pace to burn and an eye for an opening. He is Iran's dangerman by some distance.

Injury worries interrupt my spying mission. Damien Duff rings me in Abu Dhabi to say his hamstring injury has flared up again after five weeks on the sidelines. He is definitely out, Mark Kennedy joins him on the casualty list, Kevin Kilbane is rated as doubtful and there are serious doubts about Roy Keane's knee. Just a normal week.

The one lesson I take home from Tehran is the need to go about our business professionally at Lansdowne Road. Previous play-off experience will point to the need to take a win from the home leg and keep a clean sheet. We didn't manage that against Belgium or Turkey in a past life and it cost us dearly on both occasions. We really need a good result in Dublin. The Iranian support is fanatical. They build up to the game with an eerie prayer that floats from one side of the Azadi stadium to the other and sends shivers down your spine. The only way to take the sting out of the crowd is to kill the game in Dublin and render the second leg all but meaningless.

I have no worries with regard to security or hotel arrangements. I explain to the players that everything in Tehran was as good as we need it to be and I assure them that I would not expose them to any security risk. If I am prepared to travel there, that should be good enough for them.

It is, but first we welcome the Iranians to Dublin. Miroslav is up to his usual tricks, talking us up as the best team in Europe then claiming he will hang himself from the goalposts in Tehran if his side fail to qualify. I love this guy. He is what I call a tulip, someone who is a real larger than life character. I mean no insult when I use the phrase to describe him at a press conference a couple of days before the game but he is not amused. Maybe my meaning is lost in the translation but he uses the comment to wind up his players, claiming I have accused him of a lack of sincerity. I should have known better.

Miroslav repeats his suicide threat when he lands in Dublin and also asks the Gardai to arrest Roy Keane and give his side a chance. That, he claims, is the only way they will stop our captain. It makes for good headlines but I know that Miroslav is too cute to believe we will walk all over his team. He will defend in numbers here at Lansdowne and look to hit Karimi and Ali Daei on the break.

Roy arrives on Thursday, the same day as the Iranians. He has stayed in Manchester for treatment on the knee that has kept him out for three weeks, but says it is now no more than a niggle. He's had his rest and Alex Ferguson has no problem with him being here, he knows that Roy wants to play. He should be available for Saturday's game and if he plays in that, then we'll look at him again before the next one. So long as he doesn't get a bang, he should be fine for both matches against Iran.

Keano takes a full part in Thursday's training session in Baldonnel and it is good to be able to stop answering questions about him. In fact all twenty-four players train, which means I am now in the difficult position of having to decide between players who have come into the team against Cyprus, and those they originally replaced due to injury or threat of suspension. It is inevitable that in any successful team some players come in, do well and retain their position. Others miss out through injury or suspension and then find it hard to get back in. In this case, Mattie Holland, Gary Breen and Steve Finnan are the men in possession but Mark Kinsella, Richard Dunne, Kenny Cunningham and Gary Kelly are all available again. My head tells me that possession is nine-tenths of the law in this case.

I am in a good mood as the game approaches. We have been here before with play-offs and the players know what we need to do on Saturday. Their spirits are good as well. When Gary Kelly asks me how long the flight to Tehran will be on Monday, I tell him forty-five minutes, and he seems to accept that! He was on the Leeds plane that caught fire at Stansted airport some years ago and is a nervous flier now, so he would be quite happy to accept a forty-five-minute flight. It takes an effort for him to get on a plane but he is quite happy to do it for his country.

I get a laugh from the press when I tell them that Fiona and I have been discussing the security situation in Tehran and have decided that only one of us should go, so she's flying out on Monday and I'm staying at home!

The team is announced on Friday. Roy is fit and plays. Mattie

Holland, Gary Breen and Steve Finnan retain their places. It was hard telling the likes of Kells, Richard Dunne, Kenny and Kinse that they were on the bench but telling the others that they were dropped would have been even more difficult.

Iran are the best team in Asia, they have some very good players and they are talking a good game. But we have a team that has improved as a unit and as individuals over the last six years. We are ready for this like never before. If we win in Dublin and keep a clean sheet, I am confident we can go through. Quietly confident.

I meet Miroslav in the tunnel before the match and we exchange handshakes and hugs. Managers at war? I don't think so.

Iran set their stall out early. They are happy to sit back and let us do all the running. They swamp midfield and leave five across the back. Quinny comes in for some close attention and they are quick to close down our supply lines. The first-half is tetchy and tight. We start brightly but never quite get past their rearguard.

The first real chance falls for Robbie when Niall gets a flick to a Jason cross. Robbie's connection is scrappy and the ball flies outside the post. A minute before half-time the breakthrough finally comes. Jason is flying inside the box when Rezaei hacks him down. The referee points to the spot and Hartey hits his customary penalty high into the left corner. Lansdowne goes mad.

We need a second, need a cushion. That arrives on fifty-one minutes when Quinny causes havoc as he contests a Jason free-kick. The ball falls to Robbie just inside the box and his left-footed volley has goal written all over it.

At 2–0 down, Iran have to come out and play. They do and almost with disastrous consequences. Ali Daei puts Karimi clear with a great through ball. He has only the 'keeper to beat but Shay dives bravely at his feet and saves the day. Seconds later Karimi is in again but he can find no way past Shay. We break quickly and Jason almost scrambles a third before Karim Bagheri lets fly with a late effort that sails wide.

The final whistle sounds and we are halfway there, halfway to Japan and Korea. We can't get carried away, the return leg on Thursday will be a very different affair, but we have given ourselves a chance. The 2–0 win, and the nil is the important bit, means we are in the driving seat going to Tehran.

We are not safe yet, far from it, but those goals from Ian Harte and Robbie Keane are enough to give me the result I want. The two goals will alter the shape of the game on Thursday as far as Iran are concerned, they will dictate the way Miroslav Blazevic prepares for the match. He has to go for it now, he has to throw caution to the wind. And that, I believe, will play into our hands. The team knew they had to dictate the pace of the match in the first leg and they didn't let me down.

Shay wins man of the match for his world-class saves but there are a few players who must have run him close. Roy Keane is one of them. Mick Byrne and I speak to Roy after the game and he says his knee is fine and he will be travelling with us to Iran on Monday. We will need him out there. The 120,000 Iranian fans at the stadium will present a unique atmosphere but my players are professional and have been through play-offs and away games in front of threatening crowds before. They know what they have to do now and they are ready to do it.

The only prediction I will make is this. If we qualify, I will have a hangover on Friday morning.

I suspect I won't be alone.

REPUBLIC OF IRELAND 2, IRAN 0

THURSDAY 15th NOVEMBER, TEHRAN

World Cup Play-Off

Iran v Republic of Ireland

Sunday morning brings a bombshell. Roy Keane is flying home to Manchester. He is out of the second leg of the World Cup play-off. I am stunned when he tells me the news. In the Lansdowne Road dressing-room after the match he assured me and Mick Byrne that he would be there when the World Cup goes to the line in Tehran. He busted a gut in the first leg, he came through with flying colours after three weeks out and he was one of the best players on the pitch, as you would expect. He felt fine afterwards and told me to count him in. I went public at the press conference and assured the nation that Roy would make the second leg. And now he is gone. He says his knee has reacted badly to the game and he is going home. He is out the door and off to the airport without as much as a goodbye to the other players before I get to tell them the news. I am perplexed.

I want him in Iran. We need Roy's leadership and his experience and his drive. Now he is on the way back to Manchester ahead of the biggest game we have ever played as a squad. A 2–0 lead is a good scoreline to take to the Middle East for the second leg but it is not enough to guarantee qualification for the World Cup finals and that is what we are working towards here.

Aware that he has important fixtures for his club as well as his country to think about, I spoke to Alex Ferguson about his concerns for Roy last week and the possibility of him only playing in the first leg if the result was cut and dry. Roy knew about my discussion with his boss, yet despite that he was happy to commit himself to going to Iran on Saturday night. I was delighted when he then said he was coming to Iran. I knew how much his presence would help to safeguard our 2–0 lead. I do not believe 2–0 is cut and dried.

Now he is not coming, despite that Saturday night promise. I have to put a brave face on it for the press, insisting that Roy's knee stiffened up overnight and he is not up to two games in five days. We will miss him but we have to get on without him. The door is opening for Mark Kinsella.

Roy Keane is not my only worry the morning after the night before. Niall Quinn's back is in bits. He was tormented all through the first leg and he can barely walk the next morning. Niall is going to travel, though. If there's the slightest chance that he can play in the match, he will be there for Ireland.

Steve Staunton is another man in trouble. His hamstring forced him off late in the second-half last night but he reckons it's more of a back problem this morning. We will take it one day at a time with Stan in the build-up to the match.

Crisis aside, the camp is positive. We train in Dublin on Sunday then fly out first thing on Monday morning, premier class for the players and staff, you'll be glad to know.

The reception in Tehran's international airport is good-humoured if partisan. The Iranian fans all want to know where Roy Keane is. They also taunt us with 3–0 placards but they are delighted to see us here. Despite all the stories we have been hearing, it seems that Westerners are more than welcome in this part of the world.

The players realise all my comforting words about this city were true when we check into the hotel. It is as comfortable as we have seen anywhere in the world. The biggest problem for the players over the next four days is boredom. They have their creature comforts with them, their CDs, mini-discs and DVDs, but time drags. The fact that they get on so well together makes a big difference. Some play cards, corridor football matches or putting competitions and Kenny regularly organises football quizzes and even 'Who Wants To Be A Millionaire' style games on away trips, though modern football has a few millionaires in its ranks already!

Tehran presents a problem that is more serious than boredom. The altitude means a lot of the players have problems sleeping due to a combination of the light air and the six-hour time difference and Martin Walsh, the team doctor, is inundated with requests for help. I have no problem in that department. This is the biggest week of my life but I am as relaxed as I have ever been.

Quinny is brilliant around the hotel. He knows he has no chance of playing because of his bad back but he is here nonetheless and constantly geeing the lads up, reminding them how close they are to a World Cup finals and what that means to the people back home. Just to have him here is reassuring for the other players.

The week moves along at a curious pace. We train well, eat well and eventually sort out the sleep problems. The press conferences are quite bizarre. I am continually asked about Roy Keane and eventually tell the locals that they can call our team the Republic of Roy Keane for all I care if we win a place in Japan and Korea. He is not here and we have to get on with it. One journalist questions my Irishness and my Barnsley birthplace. Get this game on quick, please.

On the afternoon of the game I go up to my room for an hour or two before our scheduled visit to the stadium. I have a great book with me, the aptly named *McCarthy's Bar*, and I fancy a bit of peace and solitude before we resume action. I lie on the bed, open the book and find my mind drifting from Belgium to Macedonia and on to this game. It suddenly dawns on me how important the next twenty-four hours are for me. My life is hanging on the edge here. Win and I am a national hero, off to the World Cup and up there with Jack Charlton. Lose and I am out of here. I will quit. I cannot face the thought of a European qualifying campaign on the back of a World Cup failure.

And then I fall asleep. For a good hour and a half I sleep the sleep of the innocent. We are ninety minutes away from determining our World Cup future and I am relaxed. I know I have done my best to get us to this point. Now we will find out if my best is good enough.

Nothing can prepare the players for the atmosphere inside the Azadi Stadium. The place is swarming. The Iranians have been in here for hours, chanting back and forth from one side of the stadium to the other. They let us know what sort of a ride we are in for as soon as we arrive. We are hissed at on our way to the dressing-room. Down in the bowels of the stadium, the lads can hear the din above. Taff asks them if they want to stand up to these guys, to go out there, stare them in the eye and see what they're made of. The lads are out the door.

Now they know what we were talking about. There are bottles of iced water raining down on the pitch. Firecrackers go off. Welcome to Tehran.

Back in the comfort of the dressing-room it is time for the passionate hearts and calm heads talk again. By match-time the atmosphere is almost frightening. The Irish anthem is first. Then over a 100,000 Iranian fans sing their prayer. The lads think it is the national anthem. Our players go to shake hands with the opposition then realise what is happening. Their nerves have to be rattling now. If they can come through this, they can come through anything.

The game kicks-off and some sense of reality returns. Iran force the early pace, they have to. Ali Daei sets up Karimi for a header but he puts the ball wide of Shay's left-hand post.

I am so proud of my players as they chase every ball and every shadow, hassle and harry. Iran are huffing and puffing but with no penetration. Mattie Holland and Kinse are stifling them in the middle. Any time they do get through, they run into the brick wall of Shay, Stan and Gary Breen. Shay is a contender for man of the match again with Steve Staunton right up there alongside him.

It stays scoreless until half-time and the pressure is really on Iran. We almost steal a goal early in the second-half when Robbie plays a great through ball for David Connolly but his shot hits the side-netting. That proves to be our best chance of the night.

Shay makes an incredible double save, first from Bagheri and then from Ali Daei. He follows that with another stop from Karimi. He is blessed tonight.

As the clock counts down, Iran grow more desperate. They eventually score through Yahya Golmohammadi but it is in the ninety-first minute and too late to make a difference. They need another goal to equal us and take the game to extra time. We take the kick-off too quickly and give possession back to the Iranians but I am prepared to forgive and forget this time. Seconds later the Costa Rican ref William Vega blows his whistle and we are through to the World Cup finals.

It is all a blur when that final whistle goes. We have qualified at last and all hell breaks loose. Taff, Packie, Mick Byrne, Johnny Fallon, Ciaran Murray, Martin Walsh, Eddie Corcoran, Tony Hickey and Joe Walsh surround me. The players are ecstatic and mob me. The BBC tell me later that their soundtrack is unusable because the language is so bad. It was all 'you effing beauty' and words to that effect, so the Beeb just showed the pictures.

We have done it. We have seen off Holland, we have beaten Iran over the two legs and we are in a major finals at last. I am walking on air.

I get dragged to a big ballroom under the main stand for a press conference which is bizarre in the extreme, with pushing and jostling and a lot of stuff I can do without from over-zealous locals. I want to get to the dressing-room, I want to share this moment with my players but first I must talk to the media.

There are so many emotions buzzing around my head. I am delighted for the Irish nation, for Fiona and my family back home, for the FAI and everyone who supported me over six very tough years. I am thrilled for the staff and for the players, for the ones who put the effort in tonight against all the odds and got us through. And I am, of course, so glad for myself. I have done it now, I have followed Big Jack into the big time. I am entitled to my vindication now as much as anyone.

Eventually I get back to the dressing-room and the players, who have waited patiently for my arrival, give me a standing ovation. That was the proudest moment of all, to share it with them and to receive their applause.

A few hours later we are off to the airport through streets paved with broken glass. The Eircom champagne has to wait until our Aer Lingus plane is out of Iranian air space but the party is worth waiting for. I have waited six years for this and I am not going to waste a drop now.

Nobody sits down for most of the flight. We sing and walk our way back to Dublin where 500 loyal and great fans are waiting to share our joy. I look at their faces and I just know it has all been worthwhile. We are going to Japan and Korea now and we are going to try and win the World Cup for those fans. I am not saying we will win it, I would never be that presumptuous, but I can promise you one thing, we will try.

IRAN 1, REPUBLIC OF IRELAND 0
(*Ireland win 2–1 on aggregate*)

SATURDAY 3rd DECEMBER, BUSAN

World Cup Draw

Qualification guaranteed at last, I am off to the Far East with FAI travel agent Ray Treacy and our liaison officer Eddie Corcoran. Our final destination is the World Cup finals draw in Busan, South

Korea, but before that we are men on a mission. Acclimatisation camps, training grounds and our base for the World Cup itself are on the agenda, the sort of things we can only really plan for until qualification becomes a reality.

We have had our eye on the ball since the win over Holland back in September, to be honest. We knew then there was a good chance we could make it to the finals and we began to plan our strategy. My wish list is simple. Firstly, I want somewhere hot that is quiet and relaxing, a hideaway I can bring the squad to for some R'n'R for about a week at the end of the Premiership season. Right now the favourite for that job is the Pacific island of Saipan, some three hours beyond Tokyo, which has been recommended to us by John White, an Irishman who has been resident there for some years now. John contacted Ray after the Dutch result and suggested we have a look at Saipan and all it has to offer as soon as possible.

After the rest period, and some acclimatisation sessions in the heat and humidity, we will move to a training camp in Japan ahead of the World Cup finals. A base in Izumo, an agricultural city whose mayor has been in contact with the FAI for some time now, has been recommended and we will have a look at that on this trip as well. I need the training camp to have the best facilities possible available to us. I will not leave anything to chance in this World Cup preparation.

The third element of the package is more complicated and concerns our base for the World Cup itself. Obviously that depends on the draw and will have to wait until after Saturday. Fortunately they are queuing up for the chance to host the Irish team and our wonderful fans.

Saipan is our first port of call and, I have to say, I am impressed with this beautiful Pacific retreat. The Hyatt Regency hotel on the beachfront in Garapan, Saipan's main town, is five-star and luxurious. Saipan is a haven of peace and tranquillity. One of the Northern Mariana islands, it sits in the deepest ocean in the world, and has stunning sandy beaches and coral reefs. It is 8,000 miles from home and nine hours ahead, 1,000 miles away from the World Cup and ideal for our first week of preparation. Football is an unknown quantity here. Nobody we meet on this island paradise knows who I am let alone that my team has just qualified for the World Cup finals. They won't have a clue who Roy Keane is or who we are when we come here in May and that will suit us all just fine. He deserves some anonymity before the goldfish bowl that is a World Cup finals and this retreat will offer Keano just that.

The island is steeped in history with Spain, Germany, Japan and the US all fighting for control of its strategic location over the years. The Americans were based here when they bombed Hiroshima and Nagasaki, and there are haunting tales of Banzai Cliffs and Suicide Hills, where Japanese parents threw their children to their deaths for fear of US repression at the end of World War II, stark reminders of the tragedy and suffering in Saipan's past. Today the island, just twelve miles by six, is American controlled and home to just 25,000 people. Tourism is its main business but it also boasts a clothing industry that supplies all the top labels from Levis to Polo.

The heat and humidity here in May is exactly what we will need for acclimatisation purposes ahead of the World Cup. The only thing missing is a proper training pitch. The locals promise to provide all the facilities we need at Ada's Gym, some five minutes from our proposed hotel in Garapan. They have a pitch already and promise to bring it up to the standard of the fairway at Coral Ocean Point Resort, one of several world-class championship golf courses on the island. Considering I shoot a very low round on Coral Ocean Point and take the money off Ray Treacy, I will be more than happy if the pitch is up to that standard.

I emphasise the need for quality when it comes to the training surface and they promise to meet my demands. Everything else is first-class. We will be able to let our hair down in Saipan in May and do some work – nothing too strenuous – when we come here for a week before the serious business gets underway.

Izumo is next on the list and it is just as suitable as Saipan for our purposes. It is here that we will do all our work on tactics and formations, free-kicks and corners, during the second week of our World Cup trip, and the facilities have to be top class. Everything about the place comes up to standard. The training pitch beside the city's Dome sports complex is like a billiard table and the mayor promises to leave nothing to chance in fulfilling our requirements. I decide to base the squad here for at least a week, regardless of whether the draw puts us into Japan or Korea for the World Cup itself. We can work in comfort in Izumo and move on for the tournament. Deal done.

As we leave Izumo for a night's stopover in Tokyo, I begin to realise how long it takes to acclimatise. I am suffering from jetlag, managing only four or so hours of sleep a night, and I know we will have to get the players out here early to allow plenty of time for their sleep patterns to adjust. The beer isn't cheap either, by the way, but it's not as expensive as I was led to believe.

Arriving in Busan, I begin to really appreciate what we have achieved, what this team representing Ireland has managed to do in the World Cup qualifiers. Everywhere I go people want to talk about the Irish team, about the players, about our potential match winners.

In the run-up to the draw I am asked frequently who I want to avoid in the finals on Saturday's exposure to pot luck, FIFA style. My answer is definite – no one. I am not bothered who we play come the summer. I have every faith in the players and their ability to do the country proud in June. There is not a team in this World Cup that scares me. My only hope is to get a glamour draw against Argentina, France or Brazil. I would love that for the fans, they deserve a bit of romance this summer and, personally speaking, I would love to pit my wits against the greats of world football. All I want from this draw is a just reward for the team and the supporters for all the effort it took to get us here.

When I enter that convention hall in Busan and the World Cup anthem starts up, goosebumps appear on my neck as I realise what it all means, what we have done by getting here. The draw itself takes an eternity as FIFA president Sepp Blater goes through the very complicated procedure.

I get the big guns I was hoping for when Ireland are drawn as second team to Germany, three times world champions and a side with obvious European style, something we are well used to. They played England in the qualifiers and that will be a big benefit to us when it comes to playing against them because I know Sven will help us and the tapes of the two games will be beneficial as well. I know all about England's famous result in Munich, the 5–1 win in October, but that will count for nothing come June. History and tradition are with the Germans but I don't think we have anything to fear from them. This side does not look like a World Cup winning team and if we can get results against Holland and Portugal, we can get a result against the Germans.

Cameroon, the defending champions going into next month's African Nations Cup, are next. Like us, they are capable of upsetting the big guns as they have proven so often in their impressive World Cup past. The fact that they will play competitive football in January means we can send Taff to watch them and be totally up to date with their team and tactics by the time we play them in the opening game of the group on 1st June, the first game on Japanese soil.

The final team in our group, and the one we will play last, is Saudi Arabia. I have already seen a couple of tapes of the Saudi team, who were one of our potential opponents for the play-offs. They do not look as good a side as Iran so we are well capable of beating them. At first glance, the game with the Saudis looks like it will hold the key. We will need five points to guarantee our passage through to the second phase and it may all come down to that last game.

The draw is favourable, as good as I could have hoped for. I know exactly what we need to do now and I am sure Sven-Goran Eriksson was only half joking when he suggested we swap. I'd certainly rather have Germany, Cameroon and Saudi Arabia than Argentina, Sweden and Nigeria.

My one disappointment in Busan is the non-existent Irish press corps. Only Peter Byrne, now writing for the *News of the World*, has come this far, everyone else wants my comments by phone. Surely the presence of an Irish team in the draw for the World Cup finals deserved better.

FIVE

February–April 2002

There are no easy games in World Cup year. I hate the term 'friendly', in fact I may ask the FAI to brand these games as 'non-qualifiers' in future. 'Friendly' suggests, to my mind, a measure of slackness in our approach. And if we say the games are 'non-competitive', then that suggests that we are only along for the ride. Nothing is further from the truth. The 'friendly' games at the start of this year, against Russia, Denmark and the United States, are the start of the World Cup campaign as far as I am concerned, the last stepping stones to the 2002 finals.

WEDNESDAY 13th FEBRUARY, LANSDOWNE ROAD

International Friendly

Republic of Ireland v Russia

Jack Charlton is in town for our friendly against Russia. I am delighted to see him, happy to have a pint or two with my old boss and a man I regard as a close friend. He's here for the Eircom FAI awards at the Citywest Hotel where he is to be honoured for his services to Irish football, and rightly so. Just having him around the place gives me a big lift.

I invite him to mix freely with the squad for the week we are here in the build-up to the match, but Jack is a very reticent man. He doesn't want to be seen to be interfering with the squad and my way of doing things. I know he deliberately stayed away from Ireland games early on in my reign because he didn't want to cramp my style. Now we have qualified for the World Cup, he believes the urge for people to compare our teams and our styles is gone. I enjoy his company at Citywest and can't wait to hear what he thinks of the team when he watches them play again on Wednesday night.

I also spend some time with the FAI in the build-up to the game. We have finally agreed a new deal to keep me in the job until the 2004 European Championships. The negotiations turned into a long, drawn-out and very public saga in the media, which was never my intention at all. I left all the talking to Liam Gaskin, the man who looks after these matters for me, and thankfully it is sorted now. I haven't actually signed the contract yet but the deal has been agreed by Liam and FAI general secretary Brendan Menton and that is good enough for me. I want to concentrate on the build-up to the World Cup.

Not surprisingly, with the World Cup squad selection just three months away, I have almost a full crew on board for this game with Alan Kelly, Stephen Carr and Mark Kinsella the notable absentees through injury. Stephen is the major concern for me at the moment. He is the best right-back in the Premiership but he hasn't kicked a ball all season following knee surgery, and time is running out. I want him on the plane to Japan. He contributed as much as anyone to the qualification process and it would be a shame now if he misses out. I won't set Stephen any deadlines. I just hope he is fit by the end of the season and able to play his way into the team ahead of the flight to the Far East. If he comes back with five or six games left to play in the Premiership, that will be good enough for me.

This being World Cup year everyone wants to play. I am even getting offers from wannabe Irishmen all over England, players anxious to jump onto the World Cup bandwagon. I have bad news for them. As I have said many times before, we don't do easy caps with Ireland.

We are back to work now. I enjoyed my break over the Christmas and New Year period but I am keen to get down to business on the training ground. I want to take a close look at a couple of youngsters who are starting to push for regular recognition at senior level.

Colin Healy is probably the most surprising candidate for a senior cap in the twenty-three-man-squad assembled ahead of this friendly. I have known about Colin for some time now, thanks to his appearances in the under-twenty-one squad and some good displays in training games against us but, up until Christmas, he was going nowhere fast in the Celtic reserves. Now he has moved to Coventry, in the Nationwide First Division, on a three-month loan and his life is about to change forever.

I caught sight of Colin at Crystal Palace last month, just after I got back from holiday. Mark Demuth, a friend of mine, does some television work there and asked me if was I going to the Coventry game. I was just back from a Caribbean break and unaware of the fixtures so I jumped at the chance to see a game with so many Irish players on view. Little did I know that the cameras would beam pictures of me sitting in the stand onto the giant screen behind one of the goals before the game kicked off. I am not sure what that did for Colin's nerves but he was excellent that night. He was busy and commanding in the centre at Selhurst Park and I knew straightaway that he would come into the squad for the Russia game.

Colin is disciplined and intelligent, he knows what to do and the right time to do it. You can't teach a player that, you either have it or you don't. With Mark Kinsella out injured, I decide this is the perfect opportunity to throw Colin in at the deep end. He will partner Roy Keane in an all-Cork midfield, a prospect I am looking forward to.

Newcastle's Andy O'Brien is another who will start the game, alongside Wimbledon's Kenny Cunningham. Andy's club form with Newcastle has been superb all season and I am anxious to start him in a senior international for the first time.

Steven Reid gets another chance on the right-wing, the position he filled on his debut against Croatia last August while his Millwall team-mate Richard Sadlier is guaranteed a first cap from the bench. Like Steven and Colin, Sads is one for the future. We set up the deal to sign him when we were at Millwall, so Taff and I know how good a prospect Richard is at centre-forward. People always compare him to Niall Quinn because of his size but I feel that is unfair on both players. Like Niall, Richard has a better touch than he gets credit for and he has a real eye for goal. He looks the part in training this week. Surrounded by quality players, he fits in with no problems at all. That's a good sign in my book. He looks ready for international football.

I make it clear to Richard and all the youngsters in the build-up to the game that the World Cup door is open to them. I admit that first and foremost, I will be loyal to the players who got us there. But circumstances can change between now and May when we fly to the Far East. Our history with injuries would have to suggest that someone will be forced out of the finals. And there is always the chance for Colin or Steven or any of the youngsters to play out of their boots now and force me to take them to the World Cup. That is the incentive for them against Russia.

The Russians are not happy with the state of the Lansdowne Road pitch. You can see that in their expressions when they go out for the warm-up before the start of the match. Great. If it gives us an advantage, I'll take it. We have a proud record at this ground. We may be tenants here but I will hold our Lansdowne record up for comparison against the home statistics of any nation in the world. I want to maintain that home form tonight.

A year ago this month the weather did me a favour when snow forced a postponement of a friendly against Denmark. We had a weakened squad for that game and I feared we would lose. My real worry was that a defeat then would severely dampen our prospects in Cyprus the following month. That's why a little part of me was quite happy when the conditions were deemed unsuitable for football and we all went back home. Tonight is different. I want to start the World Cup year with a bang. And revenge against the Russians, winners here in my first game in charge, would be nice as well.

The game is just three minutes old when an Ian Harte free-kick is only half cleared and a Steven Reid shot from the edge of the area deludes 'keeper Ruslan Nigmatullin and almost breaks the back of the net. The goal is the catalyst for a supreme first-half showing. Colin Healy looks a natural beside Keano in the middle of the field, Andy O'Brien is solid at the back and Duffer is just good old Duffer upfront.

Steven Reid is the real bonus. He plays a superb ball down the right in the twentieth minute and Steve Finnan's cross is worthy of the pass before Robbie steers a header home to prove he's on the way back.

Russia have little to offer to counter our bright start. Shay saves from Yegor Titov on twenty-six minutes and Vladimir Beschastnykh puts a header just over the bar but that's as good as it gets for the visitors.

Before we reach the interval, Roy and Hartey both go close to a third. And then the changes come. Before the game, I agreed with the Russian coach that we could make as many changes as we wanted. I take advantage at half-time with Gary Kelly, Mark Kennedy, Gary Breen, Lee Carsley, Richard Dunne, Dean Kiely and Clinton Morrison on for Reid, Kilbane, Cunningham, Healy, O'Brien, Given and Duff.

The make-up of the team is changed dramatically but the momentum is still with us. We dominate the rest of the game with both Ian Harte and Clinton, set-up brilliantly by Richard Sadlier, hitting the woodwork. By the time the second-half is over, I have used all twenty-three players in the squad with Niall Quinn even replacing Jason in the last minute.

Jason is none too pleased. He asks me if it is within the rules of the game to substitute a substitute. I tell him it is but the switch backfires on me. The clock on the East Stand had actually stopped when I dragged Jason off and put Quinny on. I thought there was six or seven minutes left, enough time for him to make an impact. Instead he got about sixty seconds and I am not even sure if he touched the ball!

Colin Healy won the man of the match award in forty-five minutes and it was totally deserved. He ran the midfield in the first-half, just as Lee Carsley did in the second. I am glad that I went to see Coventry that night in London but I am also glad that Martin O'Neill at Celtic allowed Colin to go out on loan. I have made it clear in the past that I do not see the reserves as the place to watch a potential new cap in action. The fact that Colin is now playing for Coventry in the First Division got him this chance tonight and he took it. Too many players go out on loan and go through the motions, but not Colin. He has impressed with Coventry and now he has repeated that with Ireland. It must be a record to win a man of the match award so quickly into an international career. If it is, it's a deserved record.

Steven Reid is another player with a great future. Taff is claiming all the credit for his goal. He reckons he taught him how to shoot like that when he used to train Steven as a kid at a Millwall School of Excellence over at Sheen in London!

I wanted a selection headache from this game and I got it. I deliberately mixed youth with experience and the young players have given me plenty to think about. The likes of Sadlier, Reid, Morrison, O'Brien and Healy are ready for international football but it is important to take this one stage at a time. As I have said, the players who got us to Japan are the front-runners to fly there in the summer, I will be loyal to them when it comes to picking the World Cup squad, but these youngsters have given me plenty of food for thought and plenty of hope for the future. I know that they are ready now, if not for the World Cup then for the European Championship campaign that will follow it.

There is a big difference between playing in the World Cup finals in Japan and playing against Russia in a friendly but they did show that they can compete on this stage and they have proven, once again, that we have the strongest squad of my reign now. It has taken time to get to this point. The players who came in when I took over from Jack are mature now and understand what international football is all about. We have improved individually and collectively, as players, management and as a team. I am a better manager now than I was when I got this job. I have learnt along the way and I am excited now about the future, not just for the World Cup finals but also for the European Championships that follow.

Republic of Ireland 2, Russia 0

WEDNESDAY 27th MARCH, LANSDOWNE ROAD

International Friendly

Republic of Ireland v Denmark

We are three months away from the World Cup and the momentum is building. At the start of March, I fly to Tokyo for a conference attended by the managers of all thirty-two finalists. For me, new to big tournaments as a boss, it is a fascinating exercise. And I am clearly not the only one who can't wait for the tournament to begin judging by the behaviour at the seminar.

As with any group of people, some are active and some are passive. France's coach Roger Lemerre is the most colourful. He walks with the swagger of a man who has won the World Cup and the European Championship. Roger is heavily involved in the workshop, in which FIFA invite us to air our views on everything from referees to the humidity the players will face in the Far East. The French coach has a bee in his bonnet over the passive offside rule. He wants FIFA to enforce it strictly come June.

Personally I am more concerned with FIFA's instructions to referees ahead of the opening games. Will they, as I fear, tell refs to hit players hard in the first few games and dish out cards willy-nilly? We have seen that in World Cups before and it has ruined previous tournaments.

Germany's Rudi Voeller and Denmark's Morten Olsen raise their concerns about the humidity levels in Japan. FIFA assure us that they will have water carriers up and down every pitch and they will be instructed to encourage players to take water as often as possible. There will, they promise, be no repeat of the dehydration problems experienced by the players involved in World Cup '94 in Orlando.

We discuss everything from kick-off times – Denmark are annoyed that their game with Senegal will kick-off at 3.30 in the afternoon, when the temperature is at its highest, to suit television schedules – to team strips. And then, after a couple of hours, we have a coffee, shake hands and wish each other well. It is convivial, informative and very laid back. The next time we meet, in June, the battle lines will be drawn.

As part of my trip, I spend time in Izumo City, the venue of our training camp, and Chiba, our host location for the majority of the first phase. The facilities we asked for when we were last out in Japan are now up and running and the training pitches are, I have to say, world-class. So is the reception that awaits us. The Irish fans have looked for more tickets than anyone else going to Japan for the World Cup and the locals I meet can't wait for their arrival.

I travel again the week before the Denmark match. This time I go to New York. The World Cup is fairly irrelevant in America at this moment in time – New York is rebuilding in the wake of the 11th September tragedy and the Irish and the Irish-Americans are focusing their thoughts on the future. I spend time with some of them during my stay in New York, visit Ground Zero with Captain Paul McCormack, an Irish policeman stationed at the Bronx, and pray for those lost at the World Trade Centre. The courage and the hope on open display in the city in the wake of such sorrow is quite inspirational. I know from talking to them that the Irish in America will be rooting for us when the World Cup kicks-off in June. I promise to give them something to cheer about.

As I fly home from New York, Stephen Carr is on his way to see Richard Steadman, the Colorado specialist who operated on his injured knee last summer. He has suffered a reaction and the knee has flared up again in training. The club want his surgeon to have another look at it. I speak to Stephen before he goes and assure him that he has enough time to regain fitness and make that World Cup plane.

My first thoughts are for Stevie. I know how much he wants to play in the tournament, like all the players, and I know that if he can't, his loss will be bigger than the team's. We will still go to Japan, even if Stevie doesn't make it. He is the one with everything to lose now. I know the pain he is going through, mentally and physically, and I want him to know that the World Cup is still alive for him.

Mark Kinsella is another with Japan on his mind. He is back in the squad for the Denmark game, his first appearance since he replaced Roy for the second leg of the play-off in Iran. Mark is over his knee injury and his return is perfectly timed with injury making Roy absent. Lee Carsley, Kevin Kilbane, Mark Kennedy and Andy O'Brien also miss out through injury.

David Connolly is back too, in a straight swap for the unfortunate Richard Sadlier who has a long-term hip injury that may bring a premature end to his season with club and country.

As the squad trains together in the days before the friendly the emphasis is on preparing for the World Cup. I tell the players that the squad that goes to Sunderland for Niall Quinn's testimonial in May will be the squad for Japan. They have two games now to make my mind up for me.

One player seems determined to secure his place in that line-up, judging by his performance against Denmark. Welcome to the Damien Duff show.

With Robbie paired alongside Clinton Morrison, Damien plays down the left wing and he is sensational. A packed Lansdowne Road enjoys every minute of it as Duffer turns Danish full-back Thomas Rytter inside out. He is at the heart of everything that is good about a great Irish performance in which we attack from the word go.

Ian Harte is denied by Sunderland's Thomas Sorensen after only five minutes and the Dane then has to react smartly twice to deny a lively Clinton. A goal is on the cards and it arrives in the nineteenth minute. When an Irish corner is only half cleared, Duffer is fed the ball close to the touchline by Jason, beats two defenders and supplies a sublime cross. Hartey has to score as he rises to meet it and he does. It's a sign of things to come.

One Dennis Rommedahl shot aside, saved by Dean Kiely, Ireland control the game but we have to wait until the second-half before we add to the tally. After a foul on Mattie Holland, Steve Staunton stands over a free-kick just midway inside the Danish half, rolls the ball quickly to the unmarked Robbie who proceeds to beat the 'keeper all ends up from outside the box. A great goal.

Clinton has done everything but score but that is put right when he takes advantage of a clever David Connolly flick and hammers the ball past substitute 'keeper Peter Kjaer as the referee prepares to blow his final whistle.

There is a real feel-good factor about the place after this game, most of it inspired by Duffer. I have said all along that he is going to be a star at the World Cup finals but the more he plays like this, the less chance we have of keeping him a secret. Teams are beginning to know what to expect of him but the great thing is that he takes it all in his stride and still beats defenders for fun. The Danes tried everything they could to stop him but to no avail. The playing surface wasn't great but Duffer paid no attention to that. He destroyed the full-back and will destroy a few other World Cup reputations as well on that showing.

Damien's man of the match award was guaranteed from very early on. In fact Niall Quinn turned around on the bench after only three minutes and said Damien would win it. We had a forty-five minute man of the match winner with Colin Healy against Russia but that must be the first three-minute award!

Robbie is another one who can be pleased with his night's work. At the press conference after the Russia game, I suggested he needed to work on his sharpness and some saw that as a criticism. It wasn't meant to be. Robbie was coming back from injury at the time and I knew there was a lot more to come from him. Against the Danes he was closer to the player I know he can be. He has been getting a bit of stick for not scoring enough but his goal was a real rocket. It was breathtaking.

Clinton will take great encouragement from his goal as well. He kept looking for it and he got it right at the death but his best bit of skill came earlier in the second-half when he nutmegged the defender out on the touchline. He pulled that trick right in front of the dug-out and I swear four or five of us on the bench pulled ligaments just looking at him twist and turn the guy.

The best story of the night concerns the way the crowd booed the wrong player. Peter Madsen was introduced as Peter Lovenkrands, the Glasgow Rangers man, when he replaced Allan Nielsen at half-time. The crowd booed Madsen every time he touched the ball, thinking he was from the 'other team' in Glasgow. When the mistake was rectified, they booed the Irish team and cheered the Danes before finally getting the chance to boo Lovenkrands when he did come on.

It was a classic Irish joke gone wrong.

REPUBLIC OF IRELAND 3, DENMARK 0

WEDNESDAY 17th APRIL, LANSDOWNE ROAD

International Friendly

Republic of Ireland v United States

April begins with bad news all around. Stephen Carr is ruled out of the World Cup finals at the beginning of the month and I am heartbroken for him. He rang me as soon as the verdict was delivered by the Tottenham medical staff and his deep disappointment was clearly audible. Stevie has worked so hard over the last eighteen months to get us to Japan. He was a contender for man of the match in Amsterdam, he was magnificent in Estonia. We will miss him. The biggest compliment I can pay him right now is that he is one of the few full-backs in the world that I would fancy to do a marking job on Damien Duff.

I try to offer him some consolation as we chat and tell him a story from my own playing days that allows me some insight into his current suffering. I sat in the stands in Malta, back in November 1999, when John Aldridge's first international goals sent Jack's team through to the World Cup finals for the first time in the country's history. I was the captain of that team but a knee injury kept me in the seats, beside the supporters who experienced such difficulty getting to the island for that game. I was there but I wasn't, if you know what I mean. I was there in body and spirit, as excited about the game and the result as any of the fans sitting around me. But I wasn't part of the team that day and that hurt. I felt isolated from the celebrations in front of me. My worries about the injury didn't help. It cost me my first-team spot at Lyons and ultimately pushed me into a move to Millwall because I needed first-team football before Italia '90.

The same feeling came back to me when I went to the 1998 World Cup finals and watched our Euro 2000 opponents Croatia in action against the Reggae Boyz from Jamaica. There was a great buzz, great colour about that game but my head was full of what ifs after our play-off defeat in Belgium. It hurt to see others enjoy the World Cup back then, just as it will hurt Stevie when we kick off against Cameroon on 1st June. He is welcome to come to the games in the Far East but I doubt he will take up my offer.

Roy Keane is in the injury wars again, as well. I am in Sarajevo, on a UNICEF trip to raise awareness of the plight of the children who have lost limbs in landmine explosions, when my phone rings repeatedly. Half the world wants to tell me that Roy has been stretchered off playing for Manchester United in a Champions League clash with Deportivo La Coruna. The pessimism is clear, even so far from home. The first two callers reckon his knee is gone again and one even suggests I may as well rule him out of the World Cup.

I decide to wait until I hear from Roy or his club. The United doctor rings three days after the injury, to say there is no damage to anything other than Roy's hamstring. His knee is fine and he should be okay within a month at the latest. It is a relief. We need a fit Roy Keane in Japan. I do not want to go to the World Cup finals without my best player. He deserves to be there for the way he performed in the qualifiers and I am confident, after speaking to the doctor, that he will make it.

The visit to Sarajevo, by the way, is a harrowing experience. It is now seven years since the conflict in Bosnia ended but the children are still living through the horrors of war. These kids have to watch out for landmines like we watch out for cars crossing the road. There are still sixty-five million unexploded mines in sixty-four countries across the world. They cost $3 to make and $1,000 to disarm. Sometimes football can seem trivial.

Events before kick-off of the friendly against the US prove, at least, that the game does have a heart, when the FAI present a very large cheque for $275,000 in aid of the September 11 funds to a group of American fire-fighters. The money has been raised by the Irish fans and the players and the total figure from those sources has been matched by the Association. As you can imagine, the gesture is warmly received by our visitors.

It is an important night on the pitch. I will name the squad for Japan a couple of weeks after this game and time is running out for those on the fringe.

Gary Doherty is back for this game, after recovering from a broken leg, as a late replacement for the injured Niall Quinn while Rory Delap features for the first time since he made the squad that went to Iran. Rory gets to start the game when Jason McAteer pulls out with a groin injury. Richard Dunne is also forced out so Andy O'Brien will start a game for only the second time, clear in his own head that this is his World Cup opportunity. I may take five centre-backs to Japan so it is down to him now.

Colin Healy benefits from Roy's absence again and I have also promised to go easy on Damien Duff in this game. His club boss Graeme Souness, fighting relegation at Blackburn, was none too pleased that Damien played for eighty-seven minutes against Denmark last month. I promise to treat him gently this time. I might just play him for the first forty-five minutes as a striker and as a winger for the second forty-five. Do you think I'd get away with that?

The conditions are dreadful. It has been raining non-stop all day in Dublin and Lansdowne Road is flooded, there is no other way to describe it. There are pools of water down both wings and floods coming off the surface and I am seriously worried that the Swiss referee Philippe Lueba is going to call the match off when he examines the pitch. There is no sign of any improvement as kick-off time looms but the ref decides to go ahead and we have to make the best of a bad lot.

Somehow the players cope. Duffer is back in the middle tonight to accommodate Kevin Kilbane's return but he is just as effective there as he was against Denmark a month ago, and teaches another defence a lesson.

The Americans try every means, fair and foul, to stop him. If this were a qualifier, at least one of their players would have been sent-off. They offer stubborn opposition but we find a way through in only the sixth minute. Good work down the right from Rory Delap and Steve Finnan creates the opening and Mark Kinsella provides the finish to a move he started as he flashes the ball into the net.

The US, ranked thirteenth in the world and five places ahead of us, prove to be as awkward as the weather. They are nothing if not persistent and they earn their reward when Eddie Pope, one of Duffer's chief tormentors, heads home a John O'Brien corner on thirty-four minutes.

Half-time sees me make six substitutions and the game, naturally, loses some of its shape until Gary Doherty makes the most of his introduction as a replacement for captain Gary Breen in the seventieth minute. He gets on the score sheet when he rises majestically to head a Steve Staunton cross past Spurs team-mate Kasey Keller in the eighty-third minute. It's a good striker's goal but I still prefer Gary as a centre-back.

Robbie Keane is coming good at just the right time for the World Cup finals. He doesn't score against the US but he doesn't have to, to prove his worth to me. He is fit, sharp and hungry as his man of the match award confirms. He is playing football with the cheek and brashness of his youth and he is enjoying it. A month before we go to the World Cup, it is good to have him back in that sort of form.

Robbie is not the only one to come good against the States. Andy O'Brien's half-time substitution may have surprised some people but I see enough of Andy to be impressed with him in those opening forty-five minutes. Colin Healy, Rory Delap and Steven Reid also do well in my estimation.

People keep asking if Colin and Steven will go to the World Cup. I can't tell you at this moment in time because even I don't know. I know the twenty-three players I want to bring to Japan, but some of them are injured so at this stage everyone involved in the US match has a chance of making the flight to Saipan. That obviously includes Colin Healy and Reidy, but there are no guarantees for them. I say as much to both of them in the hotel after the match. And I reassure them that, no matter what happens for Japan, they have long careers ahead of them with Ireland.

Games like the American one are important for these players. Which is one of the reasons why I cannot agree with Sven-Goran Eriksson's suggestion this week that we should abandon friendly internationals and just have training get-togethers in between competitive dates. I cannot see us ever going down that road. There are a number of reasons why it will just not work for us, no matter what the English decide to do.

For a start, we do not have the financial resources that would allow us to abandon friendlies. We had 39,000 people at Lansdowne for the USA match and the revenue that sort of game brings in is crucial for the FAI. More importantly, on a personal level, these friendlies are vital to me in the development of young players. I need to blood them in these so-called meaningless games and I need these fixtures to give the youngsters caps and experience.

And I would struggle to get players to Dublin for training camps rather than internationals. I know I would not have been that interested in two days' training in Dublin when I was a player. I don't think many players would come here to train when they could do it with their clubs and stay at home with their families.

It is a different story when you are playing games and players are getting caps. That means something. The fact that we are World Cup finalists meant I had players falling over themselves to get to Dublin this week. If we had not qualified for the finals, I am sure some players would have been under pressure to stay with their clubs in England.

REPUBLIC OF IRELAND 2, UNITED STATES 1

TUESDAY 7th MAY, DUBLIN AIRPORT HOTEL

World Cup Squad Announcement

This is the day I have waited over six years for, the day I finally get to announce a Republic of Ireland football squad for a major finals. I have dreamed of this day ever since I was appointed Irish manager back in 1996. It is an historic moment for Ireland and for me personally. We are just ten days away from our departure to the Far East and I cannot wait.

I am showing my hand over a fortnight ahead of the FIFA deadline for World Cup squads and that is deliberate. It is all down to the situation that developed around Gary Waddock, the former QPR and Charleroi midfielder, when we qualified for the 1990 finals in Italy. Gary was named in the squad that left Dublin for the World Cup finals, via an away friendly against Turkey, but he never made it to Italy. Big Jack had serious concerns over the fitness of Liverpool's Ronnie Whelan, struggling to regain his strength after a long-standing thigh muscle injury. After a scoreless draw in Turkey, Jack decided to bring Swindon's Alan McLoughlin into the squad as a potential replacement for Ronnie, at the expense of Gary.

He made the decision as Alan was starring for Swindon in their promotion play-off win at Wembley. And he announced it to Gary by the luggage carousel in Malta's airport as we arrived for our World Cup training camp after a marathon journey via Istanbul and Rome. Gary, gentleman that he is, has never made an issue of the timing of that decision but it had a profound effect on me.

I can remember Gary having to hang around the hotel in Malta for a couple of days, waiting for a flight back to London. He was distraught, naturally, and though he did his best to keep his disappointment from the rest of us preparing for Ireland's first World Cup finals, we were all hurt by it. Saying goodbye to him was one of the saddest things I have ever had to do. It stayed with me for many days, almost to the time we left Malta for Italy.

As a result, I always said that if I ever got to name a World Cup squad, I would do it well enough in advance so as to avoid any similar situations. That is why the twenty-three players who go to Sunderland for the Niall Quinn testimonial on 14th May will be the players who go to the World Cup finals, injury permitting.

I make that clear now, as I sit down in a conference room at the Holiday Inn here in Dublin Airport and announce the names of the twenty-three players who will carry Irish hopes onto the World Cup stage.

The goalkeepers are Shay Given, Dean Kiely and Alan Kelly. The defenders are Steve Finnan, Gary Kelly, Gary Breen, Steve Staunton, Andy O'Brien, Richard Dunne, Kenny Cunningham and Ian Harte.

In midfield I will look to Jason McAteer, Mark Kennedy, Roy Keane, Mark Kinsella, Mattie Holland, Kevin Kilbane and Lee Carsley and upfront I have gone for Niall Quinn, Damien Duff, Clinton Morrison, David Connolly and Robbie Keane.

These players already know they are coming. But I also spoke to the lads who have lost out, to the players whose dreams were shattered when they received my call yesterday. I would have liked to speak to them face to face, but that was simply not possible.

Some of them are very unlucky. Colin Healy has been brilliant in the two and a half friendly internationals he has played to date but, as I've said in the past, there is a big difference between friendlies and World Cup games. Likewise, Steven Reid was very close to this squad. He has never put a foot wrong in an Irish shirt and he must wonder why his name is not on this twenty-three-man list. I explained to both Colin and Steven last month that their day will come in the future. They have youth on their side and just because the World Cup has passed them by, it is not the end of their international careers, not by a long shot. Before we know where we are, we will be playing Finland in an August friendly and then Russia in the opening European Championship qualifier. The future is theirs.

Rory Delap did well against the United States in April but that was his first start for us in a long time. Likewise Gary Doherty has been out for most of the season with a broken leg and I just feel he ran out of time. I know he scored for me as a centre-forward against the USA and he played in that position in a couple of the qualifiers but I regard Gary as a central defender and I have plenty of options in that department. I have assured him that next season will offer new opportunities, once he is fully fit.

Nicky Colgan loses out to Alan Kelly in the goalkeeping stakes. Nicky has understood all along that Alan will travel if fit and that is the case now.

Loyalty is the key word with this squad. I said all along that I would be loyal to the players who rolled up their sleeves in the qualifiers. The players who got us to the World Cup are the players on their way to the finals. Of the squad selected, only Clinton Morrison and Andy O'Brien were uncapped when the qualifying series began in Holland and they now have six and five caps respectively. You cannot match experience when it comes to a World Cup finals. As far as I'm concerned, it is not the place for experimentation.

Not everyone at the press conference agrees with me. The questions today centre on the choice of Mark Kennedy, still to recover fully from his groin injury, and Lee Carsley, just over a knee problem, to the detriment of Steven Reid and Colin Healy.

Mark's fitness is a key issue. He has been to see a specialist in London and is confident that he has enough time on his side to recover fully before the World Cup finals. I am a big admirer of Mark's, have been ever since I signed him for Millwall, but I will only take him to Japan if he is a hundred per cent fit. I have made that clear in all my recent conversations with him. If he does not look fully fit when we play in Niall's testimonial in Sunderland, then he will not travel.

Lee Carsley's fitness, on the other hand, is not a concern at all. He got back into the Everton team at the tail end of the Premiership season and assures me he is fine. Lee's selection does appear to ruffle some feathers. I am always surprised at the media reaction to Lee in Ireland. They seem to blame him for the Turkish penalty that led to the equaliser in the last European Championship play-off and that is wrong. The ball hit Lee on the arm, he did not try to concede a penalty. I have every faith in Lee's ability to fill a central midfield role for me. If I didn't, he wouldn't be in the squad.

Lee was in Tehran when this team had to roll up its sleeves and fight for their World Cup lives. The experience those players gained at the Azadi Stadium last November will stand them in good stead in the Far East next month.

I am asked what I expect from the World Cup finals, what we will aim to achieve in Japan and, hopefully, Korea and I let the world in on a little secret. We are going to do everything we can to win the World Cup. I am not saying we will, but we will give it our best shot.

We have nothing to fear and everything to be excited about going East. I have a squad that knows how to win, a squad that wants to win. We have so much going for us ahead of the group games with Cameroon, Germany and Saudi Arabia. We have experience, we have youth and we have that fighting Irish spirit.

Bring it on. Let's get on that plane now. Let's get ready to face the world.

PART II

The World Cup Finals

SIX

13–17 May, Sunderland and Dublin

MONDAY 13th MAY

The tent is open for business and the World Cup starts here. Registration is about to begin for the twenty-three players and ten staff who will journey to the 2002 finals in the name of Ireland. I am excited and expectant. We have dragged ourselves halfway around the world for the last two years to get to this point. We have fought our way through the Group of Death undefeated, seen off the Dutch and come through the play-offs against Iran. We have worked our backsides off and we have qualified for the World Cup finals on merit.

At the end of the week, we will fly from Dublin to base camp in Saipan but first come a couple of games, one for Niall Quinn tomorrow night and the other against Nigeria at Lansdowne Road on Thursday.

Today we travel north, from all corners of England and Ireland, to Sunderland for Niall's much-publicised testimonial. I fly to Newcastle from Gatwick, happy to play my part in a game to honour one of the few great guys left in football. Niall has been everything a manager could want from a player, everything any father could want from a prospective son-in-law. He deserves to be recognised in his adopted English home and I am delighted that my Irish team will provide the opposition tomorrow night.

A secret travels north with me. Roy Keane, my captain and Ireland's best player, won't be with us until Wednesday. I have known this for twenty-four hours now and have managed to keep it mostly to myself. The Manchester United doctor rang to inform me that Roy is going to France for treatment at a French FA clinic.

Roy is going there, on the recommendation of United team-mates Fabien Barthez and Laurent Blanc, to get some treatment on long-standing hip and knee problems. The French staff will also do some stretching with Roy, prepare him for the World Cup and ensure that he is one hundred per cent right when he finally reports to Dublin for World Cup duty on Wednesday.

Roy has not called me to confirm all this personally but I have no problem with his method of communication via the club. He is their player until he departs for the World Cup and I know he will call me to explain what is happening when the time is right. I am just happy that he will make it to Dublin on Wednesday, in time for the game against the Nigerians and the Friday departure to the Far East.

My immediate concern is to keep his absence private and within the group. I know the ferocity of the storm that will kick up if I announce that Roy is out of the game at Sunderland so I keep quiet on the subject. If I release the news, Roy's absence will become a bigger story than the testimonial. Niall is still trying to sell tickets in his efforts to make a million pounds for charity and I am not going to do anything to jeopardise that. I know I am a football manager and not a PR guru, but I am not going to make any statement that will affect ticket sales or damage my relationship with Roy or United. The last thing Niall needs right now is a story breaking that the best midfielder in the world is out of his testimonial.

Roy does not need a media scrum surrounding his World Cup fitness. That subject has already been on the agenda ever since he damaged a hamstring in the Champions League game with Deportivo La Coruna back in April and I don't want to resurrect it. Anyway, the United doctor said they'd appreciate it if I keep quiet on the nature of the injury so I am happy to shut up, full stop. I have no desire to let this news out, no wish to prompt a barrage of telephone calls, press conferences and intrusions before we have even settled into World Cup mode. We have anything up to six weeks ahead of us in the media spotlight so there is nothing to be gained from igniting the stampede any earlier than necessary. The questions will come thick and fast as soon as he fails to appear tomorrow night but there is no need to pre-empt them.

Instead, I look forward to meeting the rest of the squad as they check in to the new Marriott hotel on Sunderland's seafront. The deal is that the players must arrive in time to sleep in the hotel tonight and then train in the morning. It is too early in our World Cup trip to begin laying down the law.

Two players in particular have my attention as I travel to Sunderland. Mark Kennedy and Lee Carsley have both had their injury problems in recent weeks. Some eyebrows were raised when I included them both in the twenty-three-man squad for the World Cup finals but they are both in there on merit. My only concern is if their fitness is everything they are telling me it is.

Lee got back into the Everton team towards the end of the Premiership season and reported no reaction to his knee injury. He says he will be fine and I have no reason to doubt him.

Mark is more of a worry. He has had a long-term groin problem and managed just forty-five minutes of action in the play-offs as Wolves missed out on promotion to the Premiership. His club boss, Dave Jones, reckons Mark should be okay, given time, but I will reserve judgement until I see him in action in the next seventy-two hours.

I desperately want to bring Sparky to the World Cup but I am not afraid to make the hard decision, no matter how much it will break my heart if I have to leave him behind. Mark must prove on the training ground, and in the games against Sunderland and Nigeria, that he is ready to play in Japan, that his injury will stand up to the demands of the World Cup finals.

TUESDAY 14th MAY

The training ground is no test for an injury that threatens your World Cup participation. I know that as I look at Mark Kennedy in training this morning and worry for his immediate international future. Players can always get through training sessions and handle situations that would quickly expose an injury under match conditions. Most things on the training ground can be anticipated, the element of surprise is missing and an injury can be protected.

That said, Mark still does not look comfortable as we go through a very light work-out. His movement is not right. Tonight, I will make my mind up on his World Cup, but only after he has pushed himself to the limit against Sunderland. I doubt it is going to work but we will give him the chance.

The build-up to the game is everything we want it to be, the atmosphere very special as Sunderland and the Republic pay tribute to Quinny. Thousands of fans have travelled from Ireland and Glasgow to add a touch of green to the red and white on show in a 35,000-strong crowd.

I decide to give most players just forty-five minutes, with one exception. Mark Kennedy is now on World Cup trial. He must prove himself tonight.

The first half does offer Mark some hope, at first glance anyway. He scores one goal and sets up another for David Connolly as we build up a 2–0 interval lead, but I know he is not right. Physically he is not contributing in a manner that would suggest he is up to the demands of a World Cup finals. He is getting crosses in and running up the wing but he is not closing down, not chasing back. At half-time I speak to Mark in the dressing-room and tell him that he is not contributing to the game as a team player. He needs to up the tempo to convince me he is fit enough for the trip to Japan. It doesn't work out. By the end of the game we have added another goal from Kevin Kilbane and substituted Sparky. We have some serious talking to do when we get back to the hotel.

Quinny plays briefly for both sides. He is tired and emotional after a game that highlighted a side of football I thought had gone forever. To see a crowd of this size turn up to pay tribute to Niall and raise so much money for children's charities in Dublin and Sunderland was special. Niall looks drained afterwards but he has every right to be. This whole testimonial has demanded so much of his time and he has thrown himself into it at full tilt. He can relax now, happy in the knowledge that he has a World Cup to look forward to and happier still that his efforts have raised one hell of a lot of money for two very good causes.

Once the festivities are over, I am thrown back into the cauldron of modern-day football.

Just one player dominates my press conference at the Stadium of Light, and it is not Niall Quinn. Surprise, surprise, Roy Keane's non-appearance sparks a deluge of questions and accusations from the media, as I suspected it would. There are even suggestions of a snub, for me as much as for Quinny, as I face the media from home and England.

Such talk has been the norm in all debate about my relationship with Roy ever since I got the Irish job six years ago. How can I change people's perceptions?

I explain, almost till I am blue in the face, that I have known about Roy's non-show since Sunday and have no problem with him at all. I add that he is having treatment for a long-term injury, that he will arrive in Dublin on Wednesday, that Niall and I both knew he would be missing tonight's game. I turn the table. How can it be a snub when I knew about it?

And yes, maybe he should have called himself but that has never been the way between us. We don't have that sort of relationship. He rings me when he thinks it is necessary and that is fine by me. I have had my fair share of phone calls over the six years and I am not such a weak character that I need Roy to ring me every day and assure me that everything is okay between us. I have accepted things as they are over the years and got on with it because it has been for the better of the team as far as I am concerned.

This is no different. Roy is coming in on Wednesday and I am happy with that. He is going to the World Cup and we will all get on with it. That is all that matters, that he is sitting on the plane for Saipan come Friday morning.

Mark Kennedy won't be on the plane. He comes up to me in the hotel a couple of hours after the match and asks for a chat. Sparky knows he is not fit enough for the World Cup finals and he is brave enough to say it.

Mark could have cheated me. He could have cheated Ireland and himself and boarded that plane. Other Irish players have travelled to World Cup finals in the past knowing they were not fit enough to take any part in the competition, but Mark is bigger than that. He has had his problems over the years, but Mark is as honest as the day is long. We have known each other since he was fifteen, I love him like a son and he knows how much I want him to be fit for the World Cup. He also knows how much it would break my heart to tell him he is not going. Mark takes that decision out of my hands. He stands up to be counted and tells me to rule him out.

There are tears as we accept the finality of it all. I just hope this honesty redeems Mark Kennedy in the eyes of the Irish public. He deserves nothing but credit for the way he has handled himself tonight.

WEDNESDAY 15th MAY

I am up early and off to Dublin ahead of the squad. Mark Kennedy has already left for his home in Manchester. He is heartbroken but realistic as he leaves.

Sparky will bounce back from this disappointment, he will play for Ireland again, just as we will see fellow injury victims Stephen Carr and Gary Doherty in the green next season. First, though, Mark must come to terms with his loss. The World Cup will carry on without him, Ireland will travel east without him and the next few weeks are going to be difficult to stomach when he switches his television on. I wish Sparky well, tell him to keep the head up and to ring me if he fancies a trip out to any of the games in Japan. I don't expect him to take me up on the offer but it's there anyway.

Next up is the scramble to get hold of Millwall midfielder Steven Reid. He is the logical replacement for Mark, more of a wide player than Colin Healy who would have come in if Lee Carsley had failed to make it. Although he's still only twenty, Steven has played on both sides of midfield for club and country and was very close to making the squad in the first place.

I had told Steven to stay around until the Friday in case Mark had a problem so I am not best pleased to discover that he got my message on his mobile as he sat in his brother's car en route to Gatwick airport. It turns out that once the squad had assembled in Sunderland on Monday, Steven booked a holiday in Barbados with his girlfriend and was on his way when I rang. I'm not too sure what she has to say on the subject but he promises to get back to his London home, pick up his stuff and grab the first available plane to Dublin.

It's a good job we got him before he had left for Barbados. I am not sure how a trip halfway around the other side of the world would have mixed with an eighteen-hour journey to Saipan days later.

Anyhow, there's no harm done, which is more than can be said for the latest Roy Keane story. I arrive in Dublin to discover that the snub angle has hit the front pages. There are even suggestions in some of the papers, and on a couple of radio shows, that we were wrong to expect Roy to turn up for any of the work before the second World Cup camp in Izumo, that he should be treated differently from the rest. It is all nonsense. I have no problem with the fact that Roy didn't make it to Sunderland because I know he will arrive later today, in time for the World Cup. He will play against Nigeria and he will be there when it matters, when we face Cameroon in sixteen days' time. It seems some people just won't believe that.

The squad have a light work-out back in Sunderland before they follow me to Dublin on an afternoon flight. On their arrival at the Holiday Inn, kit man Joe Walsh and Umbro's Johnny Fallon hand out the squad numbers for Thursday night's match against Nigeria, the numbers we will use for the World Cup campaign. The players, as they are bound to, try to read something into it.

I attempt to explain that the numbers allocated do not correspond to the eleven players who will start the opening World Cup match against Cameroon on Saturday fortnight but I know some of them don't believe me, and with good reason. I wouldn't have been happy in 1990 if Jack Charlton had given me nineteen instead of five, so I know exactly where they are coming from.

There is no easy way to do this. I had looked at every possibility, from numbering them alphabetically to throwing all the names into a hat and allocating the numbers on a first-out-of-the-hat basis. Nothing worked, so I am back to square one. The first eleven numbers are the players who will start the match against Nigeria tomorrow night, simple as that.

Shay Given will be in goal with Steve Finnan and Ian Harte at full-back, no surprise there.

I want to see how Kenny Cunningham plays alongside Steve Staunton at the heart of the defence. Stan, who is guaranteed a starting role in Niigata, gets number five, so Kenny gets four.

Gary Breen, a more regular partner for Steve in recent games, is worried that his number fourteen means that he will be left out in the cold when the real action begins. He asks if that is the World Cup team, cut and dried. I assure Gary that he has two games, against Nigeria in Dublin and the Japanese club side Hiroshima in Izumo City, and over a fortnight on the training ground to convince me otherwise before we play Cameroon. And Breeny knows as well as I do that he won't care what number is on his back if he gets to play in Japan.

Some players, however, just know that they will play in the World Cup. And they deserve their regular numbers.

Jason will play wide right and wear seven. Kevin Kilbane will start in his regular slot on the left and with his regular number eleven shirt.

Roy Keane will get the number six when he joins up tonight and that is an easy one to work out. He has worn that shirt for as long as I can remember and I know Roy wouldn't be comfortable with any other number on his international jersey.

Robbie Keane has played in the number ten shirt since he broke into the side and it would be wrong to ask him to wear anything else.

Damien Duff knows he is going to play upfront alongside Robbie so the number nine jersey comes as no surprise.

Mark Kinsella will feel hard done by. I know that he will read everything into the fact that Mattie Holland will wear eight on his back and partner Roy against the Nigerians tomorrow night. As I had done with Breeny, I assure Mark that everything is still up in the air. Who knows what will happen between now and the first of June? All he has to do is convince me that he should start that game.

One man with no convincing to do arrives in Dublin a few hours after the squad. Roy Keane saw some of the papers on his journey here and is livid that anyone would suggest he snubbed Niall Quinn's game. The good news is that he is fighting fit for the World Cup and looking forward to it. I am delighted to hear it from the horse's mouth. Inside, I am doing cartwheels. After all the injury scares and all the worries of the past two months, it is great to know that our best player is heading to the World Cup finals on Friday.

Roy and Steven Reid are safely in harness by the time the President Mary McAleese comes to wish us a *bon voyage* at the team's traditional base at the Dublin airport Holiday Inn hotel. Mrs McAleese is a wonderful woman, someone I have come to admire greatly in the time I have known her, and it says a lot that she is prepared to come and meet us tonight rather than summons us to Áras an Uachtaráin, the presidential residence in the Phoenix Park.

The President offers us her full support ahead of the trip to Japan and assures us that the nation is behind us. She also tells us she will expect us at the Áras if we fulfil her expectations at the finals. We promise to see her again but not too soon. Some time towards the end of June will do quite nicely, thank you.

THURSDAY 16th MAY

Republic of Ireland v Nigeria

Strange as it sounds, I am not that bothered about the result tonight. It is the Irish players' performance, individually and collectively, that is important to me.

As I explained to the players yesterday, there are a number of things I want to look at closely against the second-best side in Africa. The make-up of our opponents is important for a start. When the draw was made for the World Cup finals, I asked the FAI to find us some quality African opposition before our departure and they have obliged. Nigeria will present a stiff challenge as they look to fine tune their own World Cup preparations.

They are missing former captain Sunday Oliseh, who has fallen out with the coach, and Ipswich winger Finidi George, but they still have some fine players like Taribo West, Jay Jay Okocha, Nwanko Kanu and the young striker Julius Aghahowa, who scored against Scotland last month. But it is more their shape and their movement that I am really interested in. The qualities served up by Nigeria tonight will be very close to those we should expect from Cameroon next month and they are going to offer my players a valuable insight into African football. How we react to the opposition in this game will tell me a lot about our chances against the Cameroons in the opening Group E fixture.

I also need to look at a couple of our own players very closely tonight, none more so than Wimbledon defender Kenny Cunningham. Kenny is one of the unluckiest players in the Irish squad right now. He was practically an ever-present in the team for the first four years of my reign as manager but has had a torrid time with injuries since this World Cup campaign began and he has paid the price. A long-term knee problem meant Kenny wasn't available to me when we played Holland, Portugal and Estonia in the opening three games. That worried me at the time but we coped without Kenny and he has struggled to re-establish himself since then. He did get back into the side, at Richard Dunne's expense, for the victory in Nicosia in March last year before injury again stopped him in his tracks when Portugal and Holland came to Lansdowne. Kenny needs to start games at this level now and I need to see how he plays alongside Steve Staunton.

I also plan to use Gary Kelly at left-back sometime tonight. Ian Harte will start there against Nigeria and in the World Cup, there is no doubt about that, but I have no real cover if anything happens to him or we need to push Ian forward into midfield. Steve Finnan could play on the left if Stephen Carr is available to me at right-back but that option will not be possible until next season at the earliest. Stan is the only other player with experience in the left-back position within the squad but I regard him as an out-and-out centre-half now. Gary has played there for Leeds. He has the pace and the experience to cope with the position if need be and his ability to mark a winger is, I believe, good enough to get him through, no problem.

Nigeria look a decent side all night. We enjoy a lively start but the visitors take the lead with their first attack when young Julius Aghahowa scores after only fourteen minutes. Ireland, driven on by Roy, rally well and we have plenty of possession. Duffer again shines on the friendly stage and Jason, Hartey and Robbie all have chances to level it before the break.

At half-time I master the art of bilocation. As I hold court in the dressing-room, organising a handful of changes and telling the lads to carry on as they are in terms of possession and dominance, a video appears on a giant screen behind the south terrace. I have taken this opportunity to thank the fans for their support, not just over the World Cup campaign but over the last six years, and to promise them that we will do our best to do them proud in the coming weeks.

Those supporters have been patient with me and with the team over the years. They have acknowledged the changes we have had to make since Jack's time and they have warmed to me and my team as those improvements have paid dividends. They have been supportive for as long as it has taken us to build a team capable of competing on the world stage again. I believe they could always see where we were aiming and now that we have arrived, I am delighted to thank them for that support.

Back on the pitch, Kells gets his chance at left-back when Ian pushes up into midfield and does quite well there. Hartey will never offer us the style and width of a winger like Kevin Kilbane or Damien Duff on the left but he does enough in the position to give me some food for thought, as does Gary Kelly behind him. Gary has impressed me whenever and wherever he has played in recent games and I know from looking at him close-up this week that he is determined to give this World Cup a real shot. His timing is good in a game where, as I suspected, the result proves to be less important than the performance. This is the perfect game to play well in and push for a place in my team, so close to the finals.

We concede another goal very early in the second-half to Efetobore Sodje before Reidy, the man who should be in Barbados now, produces his second international goal with an absolute piledriver. Try as we might, the equaliser never materialises but I am not that bothered. The stats show that we created twenty-one attempts on goal tonight, won thirteen corners and scored just once. Nigeria, in contrast, had two chances and one corner and scored twice. So the Irish performance was a lot better than the scoreline suggests. There were many positives and only one real negative in the result.

And losing at this stage is no bad thing, it might just lower the level of expectation that was floating around the place beforehand. After knocking Holland out and winning the earlier friendlies against Russia, Denmark and the USA so convincingly, it would be easy to get carried away with this Irish team. So often we turn up at Lansdowne Road for friendlies, win them and convince ourselves that everything is rosy, that we are great fellas. We even have Jason dreaming of a World Cup winner in that great TV advert for a well-known beer shown on Irish television and Sky, probably. This result might just place reality back on the menu. It's like the showjumper letting his horse catch its hooves on the way over the first fence. The horse picks them up after that and we will do likewise over the next fortnight in Saipan and Izumo. Certainly, we need to work on our finishing and we need to be aware that Cameroon will present a much tougher challenge in the heat of World Cup battle.

German coach Rudi Voeller, in the Dublin crowd tonight, knows that as well. He will have learnt little he didn't already know about Ireland in this final international fixture ahead of our World Cup confrontation. You can bet your bottom dollar that he has a good idea which eleven Irish players he will face in Ibaraki in three weeks' time. Tonight he will have studied our movement on and off the ball, looked for patterns from corners and free-kicks and generally familiarised himself with the shape of my side.

I am sure that Damien Duff and Robbie Keane will have impressed him with their movement in the first half. Those two were my great surprise packets a year ago but now the world knows all about them. They have the ability to become household names in this World Cup. I am constantly telling them that and tonight the fans let them know exactly what they expect from all of us with a rousing Lansdowne send-off. Paddy Reilly comes on to the pitch to sing the 'Fields of Athenry' and both sides engage in a lap of honour, the reception as warm for our Nigerian visitors as it is for the home side.

We are almost on our way now. Ireland expects us to do the country proud and we expect to deliver.

REPUBLIC OF IRELAND 1, NIGERIA 2

FRIDAY 17th MAY

A few weeks ago, the England coach Sven-Goran Eriksson said in an interview that he couldn't wait to get away to the World Cup, to get into the zone and concentrate solely on football. This morning, I know exactly what he means. It will be a relief to get on the Aer Lingus flight to Amsterdam and finally escape to the finals. Once we take off, we have the World Cup and only the World Cup to worry about. Everything else goes on hold and we can, at last, live for the moment. That has been the light at the end of the tunnel for some very hectic weeks now.

There are so many sideshows when you qualify, so many people looking for a piece of the action. We have all been pulled from pillar to post these past few months, players and management alike. On the back of our World Cup success we have all made money from commercial endorsements, we have all been happy to do our fair share of charity work pre-Japan, we have signed countless autographs, we have made records and videos and filled sticker albums.

And we cannot complain about one minute of it. The public love us because we have qualified for the World Cup, not because we are great guys or good-looking or make interesting conversation over dinner. They want a piece of us because we have qualified to play Cameroon, Germany and Saudi Arabia in Japan next month. And they are entitled to their pound of flesh.

This is the Irish team we are talking about and we cannot have it both ways. We cannot lay claim to the best supporters in the world then tell them they can't come near their team. That has never been the way for as long as I have been involved with Ireland, as a player and as manager, and it will never change as long as I am in charge. There is an humility about the Republic team that we should never lose. We are not Premiership prima donnas, we are not Italian-style models, eyes wrapped in the latest designer sunglasses. We are the Irish team, your team. We are humble and we are accessible and we are proud to be as Irish as the supporters.

That is why we are always happy to throw the doors of our hotel open to the fans wherever we are in the world, why the players are happy to stop and sign autographs on their way to breakfast, lunch and dinner. It explains why fans can watch us train, why they can travel with us and end up having a pint with their heroes a couple of hours after the game, no matter where we are, home or away. That's the way we are and it is the only way to be, in my opinion.

I have never gone to a World Cup as a manager before but I don't ever want to see the day that the Irish team is whisked through the airport in a coach with blacked-out windows and brought straight to the plane without as much as a wave for the fans left behind. Once that happens, we will lose the support of the ordinary people, and rightly so.

Okay, so the airport is bedlam this morning. There are hundreds of fans waiting to say goodbye to the team, crowding around the check-in area as the players put their luggage onto the conveyor belts. Those fans want autographs, they want photographs, they want to touch the players they will next see on a television screen lining up for the national anthem against Cameroon. Some players are a little hassled by the volume of the crowd awaiting them when we step off the coach at departures. What did they expect? This is the World Cup and this is the Irish team. This is the biggest tournament in world sport and those fans are proud that we are about to fly off to represent them in Japan and South Korea. Of course they want to send us on our way with a thousand slaps on the back. They want to see us, to touch us, to say goodbye.

And they will. We are Irish. We don't do back doors, we don't hide from the fans we are proud to call the best in the world.

A few months ago, in the week before the Holland game at Lansdowne Road, it was suggested to me that we leave our Citywest hotel through the side entrance because the fans were milling around the reception. I wouldn't even consider the idea then and I am not going to change now. Yes, we might well send the bags ahead of us if we qualify for Euro 2004 but I will not send the fans away. An hour of our time is not much to ask for before we fly to a World Cup finals. All we have to do today is give the supporters a fraction of our time, sign a few autographs, pose for a few photos and then head into the VIP area for a reception hosted by the team's sponsors, Eircom.

There we meet the press and the Taoiseach. The media, naturally, want to know what we all think about the World Cup before we leave. We will be in transit for the next eighteen hours and that, effectively, amounts to a news blackout.

I sit through countless interviews in the VIP room upstairs, cup of tea in hand. Roy Keane's absence from the Quinn testimonial dominates the conversation once again and I repeat there was no rift.

Are we tired after two games in three days? Sure, the lads are exhausted after a long hard season but they have a week's worth of R'n'R on a Pacific island hideaway ahead of them and that will recharge their batteries. Besides, there wasn't a lot I could do about having the two games so close together. We were never going to let Quinny down when he looked for the Sunderland match and playing it on the Tuesday meant the lads could spend the weekend with their families, which was important so close to World Cup departure. Nigeria were originally due to play in Dublin on the Friday but we wouldn't have been able to get a flight to Saipan until the Sunday then and that was too close to the World Cup finals to make it worthwhile. I want six days in Saipan to acclimatise and let the players relax. That's why we played last night and why we are flying today. Anyway, most of the lads only played forty-five minutes in each game and they will be fine by the time we play Cameroon.

How does it compare with the 1990 send-off? I actually remember very little about our departure for Turkey en route to Italia '90. I think we had a photograph taken at the hotel and a small reception up in the airport but that was about the height of it. The way the team performed in Italy changed everything, of course, even the way we looked on ourselves as a nation. That's why the fans are here today and why we are more than happy to see them.

Taoiseach Bertie Ahern takes time out from the general election to add his weight to the farewells. I am always flattered by the attention we receive from politicians and leaders of state. We don't have prime ministers knocking on our doors where I come from. He is very knowledgeable when it comes to football and he is a big Manchester United fan. We chat briefly about the Nigeria game and how we will do in Japan. I ask about the election and he offers me just one piece of advice – I already knew to stay well out of politics.

Two hours later we are sitting in an executive lounge at Schipol Airport in Amsterdam and the players are taking the Mick out of Roy Keane. Shay Given has the song 'Mick McCarthy's Baby' and excerpts of the 'Radio Roy' sketches from the Today FM radio show playing on his CD player and the lads are breaking their nuts laughing at the Keano impersonator. Even Roy can see the funny side but he is not smiling minutes later as we make our way to board the KLM jumbo bound for Tokyo.

At the departure gate, he finds the journalists responsible for the snub stories that had upset his flight from Manchester to Dublin on Wednesday. Roy snarls at them and I have no problem with that. They were wrong and he feels fully justified in having a go back. Fair play to him. He is quite entitled to his say and nothing he does in Amsterdam airport is going to impinge on his World Cup.

I leave Roy to it and head through passport control. I am dying for the guy checking my passport to ask me why we are flying to the World Cup with a Dutch airline. My vindictive streak wants to have the chance to reply ''Cos you're not' but he never asks the question.

Once on board, I change out of my World Cup suit, don my track-suit and settle back. I am blissfully happy as we begin our twelve-hour jaunt to Japan. We are on our way to the World Cup at last and everyone is happy. By the time we are flying over Siberia, I am ready for the sleep of the dead, which is just as well – Siberia goes on for hours and I miss it all!

SEVEN

18–23 May, Saipan

SATURDAY 18th MAY

There is little or no sign of the World Cup as we land at Tokyo's Narita Airport, ahead of our transfer to Saipan. Only a few posters here and there suggest that this is World Cup land, a fortnight ahead of kick-off in the world's greatest sporting event. We pass through fairly quickly, an hour or so spent in the transit lounge listening to Radio Roy and sipping coffee and orange juice before NorthWest Flight 0076 is ready to welcome us on board.

The players settle into their business-class seats, most of them, that is. Dean Kiely is left at the gate while Japanese passport control sort out that he is indeed Dean Kiely and not Dean Kelly. Some of the lads wind up Alan Kelly that he is behind this in a bid to boost his World Cup chances but the ruse doesn't work and eventually Dean makes it on board.

Three hours out of Tokyo we land in Saipan, base camp for the next six nights. The welcome is as warm as any cead mile failte. We are draped in Mwar Mwar garlands, the traditional headdress in this part of the Pacific. They make a pretty picture on my head. I'm making life easy for photographers Dave Maher and Andy Payton as they snap away in the arrivals hall.

The first thing that hits us when we make our way out through arrivals is the heat and the humidity. The temperature is hot, an average of thirty degrees Celsius at this time of year. The humidity is high, eighty-four per cent and rising, perfect for the work we will put in ahead of our time in the eye of a Japanese summer.

Saipan is not the fulcrum of our World Cup preparations, merely the foundation. I am not bringing the players here to run their nuts off, we will not do any tactical work until we head for Izumo City on mainland Japan, six days from now. Until then we will enjoy Saipan like any holidaymaker but we will also work up a sweat as we acclimatise to the heat and humidity. All I want from Saipan is acclimatisation and relaxation. The players will have a few days off to get used to the time difference, they will do some light training, get some rest in, let their hair down if they want to and then we will step it up as the week progresses. They need to recharge their batteries, just as I do. And Saipan, a million years from home, is the perfect place to plug in.

No one knows anything about football here and no one cares. We might as well be the Irish bobsleigh team as a World Cup-bound side. The players wander through the airport without as much as one request for an autograph. They are anonymous, just as I wanted.

Life is pretty good as we check in to the Hyatt Regency Hotel, right on the beach in the neighbourhood of Garapan. The players are more than happy with the facilities on offer in this five-star resort and all seems to be running smoothly. Until the first bombshell drops.

The skips that were sent from Dublin ahead of the squad have yet to arrive due to a customs problem. They contain everything from training gear to Nivea sun lotion, Lucozade and the official World Cup ball. I am not going to start a witch-hunt and look to blame someone for this fiasco. The kit should have been waiting for us in Saipan, it doesn't matter who sent it or how. It should be sitting waiting for us, not stuck in some airport or other.

It is not a good start but we will cope. We have the gear and medical supplies which we kept with us for the games against Sunderland and Nigeria. That will be enough to get us through the planned light workout on Sunday and everything should be here by the time we get down to a real sweat on Monday. I am not exasperated but I am annoyed. It makes me look bad in front of the players. Ultimately, the buck stops with me in terms of preparation and the gear should be here. Someone in the FAI will have questions to answer over this.

Worse follows. After check-in, I head up to the training pitch at the Ada Gym, some ten minutes from the hotel. Our local contacts have promised me a surface as good as the fairway at Coral Ocean Point, one of the championship golf courses on the island. That was the brief I gave them when I first visited the island last December. What we get is more like a bone-hard fairway on your local pay and play. I am annoyed and more than a bit upset at the state of it, there are bare patches that are just unacceptable. They promise to water it and I narrow down the piece of pitch that I know will be adequate for our needs, but I am disappointed. I had been promised better by our hosts and they have not delivered.

It's not the sort of news I want to bring back to dinner at the team hotel. After we eat, I sit the lads down for a team meeting. I hold up my hands and tell them about the training gear and the pitch. I admit that it is not good enough, that I have been let down and they, as a consequence, have been let down as well. I point out that we have to accept Saipan for what it is, a six-day break, with a little bit of work thrown in, on the way to the World Cup finals. We have enough training gear and strapping to get us through Sunday when all I want to do is some physical work, and we will send out for whatever sun creams and isotonic drinks we need for that first session.

I explain that we are not here to do full patterns of play, that will come when we move to Izumo on Friday and a pitch that is better than most carpets. The surface here is not ideal but is adequate. We can do enough running, closing down and five-a-sides on it as we build up the training schedule. This is merely the foundation for our World Cup, there are no walls going up here, no structures. All that will follow when we move to Japan.

I know from looking at Roy that he is far from happy. He demands the best, just as I do, and he has every right to have a sulk on.

I throw the debate open, tell the players they are quite justified if they want to whinge but nobody offers any contribution to the discussion. Roy keeps his thoughts to himself. As the meeting breaks up, the players joke about it all, as players do.

A couple of hours later, Roy comes to my room. He admits he should have spoken up at the meeting and then he lets fire. He knows this is not the way to start the World Cup and he says so. It is not good enough to travel around the world for two years to get to this stage and then see the training pitch fail to live up to expectations and the gear fail to arrive. He knows that if I am saying the pitch isn't great, it must be a problem.

I have no argument with him. I tell him he is right to have a go, that the fact I have been let down means we have all been let down. At the same time I re-iterate why we are on the island of Saipan, how it will be more than adequate for our needs this week. I repeat that the real work will be done in Izumo once we arrive there on Friday. I end the discussion by assuring him that he will have no complaints once he gets to Japan.

SUNDAY 19th MAY

Half the lads are up by sunrise. Some of them visited the Hard Rock Café last night but even that hard day's night has failed to adjust their body clock. They know now why we are here – even at this unearthly hour of the morning, the humidity hits you with the ferocity of an Ian Harte free-kick.

David Connolly is first to get up and go for a walk along the shore. By the time he returns to the hotel, most of the travelling party are walking on the beach. It is a heavenly way to start the day in a quite magnificent location.

After breakfast we head for the Ada Gym complex for a short session that can be best described as a loosener. The players get their first look at the infamous playing surface and they are not impressed. They know what I meant now when I apologised for its condition last night. It will do though and we will get on with it, as always. We have trained on worse surfaces in Turkey and Lithuania and we played on worse in Estonia in this World Cup campaign.

The session itself is easy enough. Taff takes charge for the hour and leads us through a bit of running and sprinting, enough to get rid of the jet lag. After that, it's free time for the players before tonight's barbecue with the media and some of the local dignitaries.

I've booked a mountain bike for the week and head out for a quick spin before my first official press conference of the World Cup finals. It is a casual affair with the fifteen or so journalists who have come out for the full duration of our Far East adventure. Amazingly another fifty will join them when we move to Izumo on Friday.

The inaugural conference is about as interesting as the training session that preceded it. Jason McAteer's ankle is the only injury concern of any note at this stage. Nothing to hold the back page for there. Instead, we talk about the pitch and the weather and the Fevernova ball, which they don't know hasn't arrived yet. I keep quiet on that one, instead becoming animated only on the subject of a football pitch.

No, not the one we are expected to train on here but the proposed national stadium back home now that Bertie Ahern has been returned as Taoiseach for another spell in office. After congratulating Bertie on his election success via the media, I express my hope that he delivers the promised stadium now that he is back in power. I have long advocated the need for a new home for Irish football, something I first supported when I played in the green shirt all those years ago.

I did back the Eircom Park project, I still believe that Croke Park will one day make a marvellous venue for an Irish soccer international and I just hope that Bertie builds his bowl in Abbotstown now. We have been very successful as a team at Lansdowne Road, thanks to the generosity of our IRFU landlords, but the time is now right to have a stadium that matches the ability and the stature of this current Irish team. Bertie, to be fair, didn't tell me how to play football when we spoke at Dublin Airport on Friday and I didn't tell him how to win elections. But now that he is back in power, I do hope An Taoiseach keeps that pre-election promise to build a new home for the Irish football team, amongst others, at the proposed national stadium out in Abbotstown.

The national stadium is about the most interesting thing we discuss at the press conference. We have at least four weeks of such gatherings ahead of us and no one is too interested in upsetting the apple-cart just yet, from either side of the top table. Realistically, I think the media are looking forward to a rest in Saipan as much as we are. They know how hectic things will become once we hit Japan and right now, they are as happy as I am to keep things low key.

Together, we establish a schedule for the week. I will arrive at their hotel, just down the beach from ours, every day for a four o'clock press conference. Then, every second day, they will be presented with four players for a pooled interview under the watchful eye of John Givens and Trevor O'Rourke, the PR men acting on behalf of the players' pool. The media can then decide when to release the news and the players' quotes back to the nation. It is all amicable, controlled and designed to make life more comfortable for all of us.

This spirit of co-operation is something I am keen to harness on this leg of the World Cup trip. I do not want an 'us and them' relationship between the squad and the press, not this early anyway. We are about to be away for anything between four and six weeks with these people so it is better, in my judgement, to start on a good footing and see where we go from there.

Tonight, I have invited all the media to a barbecue on the beach at the Hyatt. I remind them before I leave the press conference that the barbecue is strictly social. There will be no quotes, no cameras and nobody telling tales out of school afterwards. Those are the ground rules and anyone unwilling to oblige is not welcome. There are no dissenters. They agree to leave their notebooks and their cameras behind, even those who would love the chance to pick holes in my World Cup preparations. Some even seem visibly surprised that I am prepared to extend the hand of friendship to all of them in such a relaxed and informal atmosphere. Why?

More than anyone else in the travelling party, I have been pilloried by the media over the last six years. I have been humiliated, hammered and vilified in the past, even by some of the media here in Saipan with us now. My family have suffered as much as I have, more so on occasions. Some of the most critical attacks have come from men I am now inviting to sit down and dine with us. Yet, I am more than happy to socialise with all of them, even my most ardent critics, tonight.

My reasoning is simple. It is the right way to start this tour of duty. What is the alternative? Let wounds stagnate for years, isolate myself from the media and feed their hatred? Should I ban them from my conferences, speak only to those who toe the party line, if I can find any? I don't think so.

It was even suggested to me when we were planning this trip that the press be banned from Saipan. Why? What benefit would it serve to impose a blanket ban on them attending the week-long activities here, as England did in Dubai? All that does is encourage them to break ranks, dig behind the scenes, infiltrate the camp and look for something to write about. I do not want that mindset to creep into Irish football. Thankfully, we have managed to escape the worst excesses of the tabloid mentality over the years. My fear in this instance is that any threat to lock them out will create more problems than it will solve. I am not prepared to take that chance.

I'll tell you what I don't do – I don't read anything they write and I don't listen to what they broadcast. Of course, people back home in Ireland are always ringing me to tell me what this guy or that guy had to say but I don't pay any attention to any of it anymore. I get on with my life and my job now and anything they decide to say or write about me goes straight over my head. I did get involved early on in my time as manager, I did take it personally as a player, but I soon learnt the value of ignorance when I replaced Big Jack. What I don't know can't harm me, so I just ignore it all now.

I know certain players have problems with the press ahead of this social night together. Some have a better relationship than others with the media, some run a mile from the suggestion of an interview. The press, no doubt, feel the same way. They resent the fact that I no longer allow them to stay in the team hotel, something I stopped a few years back, but they certainly have their favourites when it comes to interview requests and off-the-record conversations. That is the way of the world in football and it always has been in my time as a player and a manager. The media are not all bad. We all do columns and interviews and press conferences with them, so we can't hate them all.

My message to the players before the night's entertainment is a simple one. Talk only to the journalists you like and ignore the ones you have a problem with. If you want to, ignore them all, that is your prerogative. This is our night out as well as theirs and you are all old enough and bold enough to make up your own minds about what company you keep in the course of the evening.

As it happens, the night is a great success. The staff meet in room 702 for pre-match cocktails and Taff presents us all with the Hawaiian shirts he picked up down the markets this afternoon. He paid ten dollars for each shirt, and he was done. At least the gaudy and very loud shirts raise a smile when we go downstairs. The press have a good laugh at our expense and damn the fact that their cameras are forbidden. Just as well.

There are no problems as the night develops and the drink flows. The two sides mingle without any incident, the island's governor graces us with his presence and the hotel chefs do us proud with the spread. Mario, the chief entertainer on site, provides a night's worth of South Pacific style variety and even persuades Robbie Keane to partake in what can best be described as a hula-hula dance. I won't name the press guy who danced alongside him but I will admit to a fleeting regret that I had banned cameras and couldn't get a snap of his ample beer belly.

Sometime around midnight, as proceedings wind down, I retire to the lobby for a night-cap with Taff, Ray Treacy and liaison officer Eddie Corcoran. The players go their separate ways. Some end up in the Beefeater, the media's established local for their sojourn in Saipan, and chew the fat with those they are supposed to hate. I have no idea what happened there and no desire to ever find out. The players are free to let their hair down for one more night. Tomorrow the real sweat begins. Others go to bed straight from the beach.

No one has a bad word to say about anyone else. Not yet, anyway.

MONDAY 20th MAY

The skips arrive overnight and the world is a better place. They are safely deposited in the hotel before the players get up and I breathe a sigh of relief. That's one headache out of the way. We now have all the clothing, all the Nivea sun lotion, all the Lucozade and all the balls we will need for at least the next month.

The Umbro training gear is state of the art, designed to cope with the heat and humidity we will face in Japan and, hopefully, South Korea. The spec is exactly the same as that used by England so there can be no complaints on that front.

The players have the morning off. Some will need it after their final night out before competitive duty last night, a night that apparently ended quite late in the press bar. Surprise, surprise. Others are up early, walking the beach, shopping, relaxing and generally taking it easy before the first strenuous training session of the trip this afternoon.

At lunch-time, I bump into Roy, quite by accident, on my return to the team hotel. I make a run for the lift and shout at whoever is inside to hold it. Roy is grinning like the Cheshire cat as I squeeze through the door. I say thanks and he claims he was trying to shut it before I made it. I say that he would and all.

He laughs, then says he hopes he wasn't too hard on me about the training kit and the pitch when we spoke on Saturday night. He is worried that he went over the top with his criticism. I tell him to forget it. He was entitled to have a whinge and he was right in everything he said. The training gear should have been here before us, the pitch should be better.

Anyway, he looks good in his Umbro gear and I tell him so. He agrees. As I leave the lift, I tell him that I hope he stands in my shoes one day and gets the chance to manage a team. If he does, I hope he gets Manchester United or Arsenal so that he can do it properly. He admits he is spoilt at United, where they have the money to go first-class on everything, on and off the pitch.

At training this afternoon, the lads really go for it, fighting it out in full-blooded five-a-sides. Later, some of the journalists express surprise at the ferocity of the exchanges on the training pitch, the way our defenders are prepared to get stuck in to Robbie Keane and Damien Duff in the heat of five-a-sides. I explain that it's fine by me. They can be competitive so long as they don't kick lumps out of each other. That may seem strange so close to the World Cup finals but I am not one for holding back in training, never have been.

I like it to be competitive and I do not believe that players who train without contact can then be expected to play at full tilt. It wasn't my way as a player and it is not my way as a coach. The only thing I don't allow are stupid tackles from behind. Otherwise, I trust the players enough to have faith that they will not go steaming in and do anything dangerous. Self-control isn't always easy for a centre-back on the training ground when a tricky so-and-so like Duffer or Robbie is coming at you full tilt, as I well know.

When I played at Manchester City, the manager Billy McNeill banned all contact in the practice match before one big game. I didn't like it but I put up with it until a little centre-forward by the name of Jimmy Tolmey nutmegged me and took the mick. He totally humiliated me in front of my team-mates. Just the once. The next time the ball came our way, I clattered him, upended him and left him in a heap, looking like the fool. Billy was none too pleased, especially as we had a game the next day, but Jimmy got the message.

It is the same with these players. Breeny, for example, is not going to take kindly to Duffer performing all his little tricks at his expense. So I have to allow them to make tackles and compete, so long as they are sensible. You cannot switch it on and off at this level and I have enough faith in the players to believe I will have a fully fit squad by the time we play Cameroon.

The subject dominates a twenty-minute dialogue at the conference that also features the new Adidas World Cup ball in our discussions. This is a topic that will rear its head on an almost daily basis as we move forward. The ball is lively. It moves differently in the air, the bounce is unique and its unusual colour scheme deceives the eye as it comes up off the turf. The 'keepers are already aware that it is going to cause them problems in match situations. It is the lightest World Cup ball yet and the technology appears to be weighted, excuse the pun, totally in favour of strikers.

That comes as no surprise to the goalkeepers. They are the last ones taken into consideration by FIFA in such circumstances. I know one goalkeeper who blames Craig Johnston, the former player who invented the Adidas Predator ball, for a famous World Cup goal when the flight of the ball caught him out quite badly. I am not sure who we should blame this time but I reckon the 'keepers will find out who invented this particular ball, just in case.

There is little else to report to the media. Jason McAteer is over his ankle problem and moving quite freely in training. The temperature and the humidity are both as high as we want them to be and I have abandoned plans to train twice on the Tuesday.

The press remark how unaffected the island is by the World Cup finals. I explain, again, that such total disregard for football is one of the main factors we are here and offer Roy Keane as an example. One of the reasons we stayed away from potential training grounds in the Far East is the popularity of Manchester United in that part of the world. He would be tormented in Thailand, Malaysia and even Japan. Here, Roy is able to walk freely around the hotel and the town without as much as one request for an autograph. It will be a lot different when he gets to Japan on Friday so he should enjoy the anonymity while it lasts.

TUESDAY 21st MAY

Another day in paradise. I breakfast with Roy. The sun is shining and life is sweet as we chat amicably for an hour or so. He's in good form and Saturday seems well and truly behind us now.

Training is late today. Packie arranges to take the 'keepers out early for a strenuous shooting session with the Fevernova World Cup ball and leaves a good hour ahead of us with Shay, Dean Kiely and Alan Kelly in tow. They have to know intimately how this new ball works before the end of the week. They want to work away from the group before training and I have no problem with that at all.

I have my own injury worries this morning. My back is acting up, a legacy from my playing days. It has been nagging at me for some time now and the best thing I can do for it is get out on the mountain bike and continue my tour of the island. With that in mind, I plan to spend a good hour on the road after the press conference this afternoon when my day's work is completed.

Taff takes training and I observe. After the warm-up, he pulls the 'keepers in for a full-blooded shooting session. They have already put some hard work in as the temperature hits thirty-two degrees and the humidity approaches eighty-four per cent. Taff then batters them with shots from all the outfield players. This is tough on the 'keepers. It is hard enough taking shots in this heat, harder again to throw a fifteen-stone frame around as shots come in from every angle. The outfield players get, maybe, one shot in every six. The 'keepers are working non-stop.

They are wrecked at the end of it, I have rarely seen them as tired, and Taff declines to throw the 'keepers in for the practice game that will end the session. They play by Taff's rules and that is fine by me. If Taff says they are too tired to play this game with the rest of the group, then they are too tired. They have done their work. This happens from time to time and Taff gets on with it, playing nine-a-side with the last man acting as the goalkeeper. We see some great defending and last-ditch goal-line clearances as the lads adapt.

One man is not happy with the decision. Roy is starting to moan at Taff over the 'keepers. He wants them in goal, Taff tells him to forget about it and play on, without them. Keano comes over and has a moan at me. I tell him bluntly that this is Taff's game and Taff's rules, so get on with it. He is not best pleased. He has a face like thunder as he goes back to the game.

He is the only dissenter. The lads are really up for this one, they are competitive and combative and even the outfield players attempting to keep goal are going at full tilt. As the match comes to an end, I am happy that the intensity I demand in training has been achieved. Three days in and the lads are chomping at the bit.

As I go back to the pitch to do some coaching with some kids from the island, Roy has words with Packie and the 'keepers, now well sheltered from the sun under an awning. I don't witness the row, but I am told all about it afterwards. He gets stuck in to Packie and then goes head-to-head with Alan Kelly. He suggests that the 'keepers may be 'too tired' to play now, but won't be too tired to play golf tomorrow.

I am not bothered by the outburst. It is a silly argument, the sort that occurs on training pitches the length and breadth of Britain every day of the football season. It's good to talk and there are times, like this, when it is good for footballers to shout at each other and let off steam as well. I'd have done it myself when I was Irish captain if something annoyed me.

Jack Charlton and Maurice Setters will confirm that many's the time I did. You give it, you take it and you get on with it. I even had a blazing row with Jack on one of the training pitches in Italy. I wanted to do some stretches and Jack wanted to start the session. We got stuck into each other big-time and he verbally slapped me around the place for acting like a prima donna. So I have been there, I have the tee-shirt.

Packie discusses the tiff on the coach afterwards but assures me he has had bigger rows with his kids over their homework. Considering I have had some belters on the pitch with Packie in my time, the subject is nowhere near the agenda as I head to the ritual press briefing in the media hotel.

The journalists don't raise the subject either. Some of them saw it, witnessed Roy swap verbal blows with Alan and Packie, saw him storm onto the bus with a red mist hanging over him, yet they never mention it once in the half-hour or so I spend in their company. Clearly, one or two believe they have a scoop and I can expect a telephone call or two later on.

Instead, we talk again about heat and acclimatisation and the way the 'keepers are adapting to the new ball. I elaborate on why Damien Duff will be one of the stars of the World Cup and talk a little about Group E opponents Germany and Cameroon. I am in and out in no time and ready for my own training session on the mountain bike as I make my way up the beach and back into the Hyatt.

A one-man welcoming committee awaits my return. Roy Keane clearly has something on his mind as he asks me to sit down on the balcony behind the lobby coffee shop.

I ask him what his problem is. He comes straight to the point. He wants to go home. He wants out of the World Cup. He is about to quit the Irish squad and international football. He tells me I still have time to call another player in before tomorrow's FIFA deadline for World Cup squads. He wants to retire here and now while I have time to call in a replacement and says as much.

I am staggered. I did not see this one coming, not at all. Not when we spoke on Saturday, not when he complained to me about the training match this afternoon. I manage to get some questions out, despite the state of shock I am in. Is it because of the pitch? The training gear? Have you got a problem with me? With the FAI? Is this all a result of your row with the 'keepers this afternoon? Is your mind made up? Can I change it?

Roy repeatedly answers no. It is all down to him. 'It's me,' he says again and again. 'It is personal.' He needs to go home. He could sit here talking all night but it will not change his decision. He won't. He can't tell me what it is. He has to be selfish and stop thinking of others. He has to think of himself for a change.

I am hit for six. I am gobsmacked. I had no inkling that Roy was about to land this bombshell on my doorstep.

I thought I had sorted things out amicably with him in my room on Saturday. We spoke in the lift on Monday when he said we'd all just have to get on with it. I had breakfast with him this morning, told him all about Izumo and how good the training facilities will be once we hit Japan.

Okay, so he had a row with my goalkeeping coach this afternoon but Taff and Packie were well within their rights to exclude the 'keepers from the training game. Coaches run the training sessions, not the players. And, yes, I did tell Roy to get on with it and play by Taff's rules. But that's football. He has to take it as well as give it when he plays a team game.

We go over the same ground as the reality of his wish sinks in. He repeats that this afternoon's events have nothing to do with the decision. He wants to go and he wants to do it while I have time to call in a replacement. Roy has no desire to see the squad cut down to twenty-two. I ask if this has anything to do with his family, does he need time to go home and see them, but he says no. It is not the pitch, it is not the 'keepers, it is not his relationship with me. He wants to go for personal reasons that he cannot expand on and I am never going to change his mind.

I take his word at face value. I have to believe that his reasons for quitting are all personal, that I cannot prompt any change in the decision. He has to go home, he has to retire from international football.

Eddie Corcoran, who looks after all the hotel and travel arrangements on behalf of the squad, comes into view. I call him over and break the news as gently as the shock allows me to. Roy is out of the World Cup and we need to sort out his flight back to Manchester. I also need to get hold of Colin Healy and get him out here as quickly as possible. We need Chris Ryan, FAI Administration Officer, to get hold of FIFA and let them know what's happening but I ask her to delay telling them or anyone else, even the FAI, until I say so. The need for swift action is overtaking the shock, but it is still so hard to stomach.

Roy heads back to his room. Eddie looks like he could do with a good, stiff brandy. So could I. I tell Taff and he is as gobsmacked as I am as the reality of it all sinks in. My best player wants to go home. My best player wants to quit the last World Cup of his career. Ireland and the Irish fans are about to be deprived of the one truly world-class player in our squad. Why?

I know Roy is single-minded. I know he is not one for changing his mind once a decision has been made inside that head of this. That thought fills my own head as I make my way up to the seventh floor and seek sanctuary in my room.

I phone Fiona and tell her the news. I don't want her to hear it from anyone else and once we start to fax FIFA and book airline tickets, it is going to leak out. She can hear the shock in my voice as we talk down a very crackled phone line.

Next on the list is Colin Healy. I ring him at 6.30 in the evening in Saipan, 9.30 in the morning back at home. He is on holiday from Celtic, in his native Ballincollig, just outside Cork City. I reach him on his mobile and the line is terrible. It breaks down about three times and I struggle to get through to him again. Colin, I reckon, can just about make out every second word. He gets the drift, something has happened and he should be ready to come out to Japan and join the World Cup squad.

I have to be honest, I do not know what to do for the best here. I understand the enormity of the issue at hand but I am not trained to deal with it. I have never been through this sort of crisis before, no Irish manager has. How could any football coach prepare for the day the best midfielder in the world tells you he wants to quit the Irish team on the eve of the World Cup finals?

I get hold of Mick Byrne, Roy's closest confidante within the group. I tell him what has happened and he is off to see Keano in his room. He spends quite a bit of time with Roy. On his return, Mick tells me that Roy is very upset, that he has had a good think about it and wants to stay now.

Mick and I go and see Keane in his room. Roy confirms he will stay but he never once says he wants to play in the World Cup. I ignore that, happy that he has come around, and ask him will it happen again. I am anxious because he has changed his mind on such a huge decision in the space of an hour or so. Will he change it again? Will we all have to walk on eggshells until the World Cup is over for the Republic of Ireland? He is not happy with that suggestion. His mood swings visibly even as he dismisses my fears.

Then I tell him that I have spoken to Colin Healy. The debate becomes quite heated now. He wants out again, based on the assumption that if I have indeed rung Colin Healy then I should leave Colin in the squad and count Roy out. He repeats two or three times that I should count him out in the midst of a very long and very fraught conversation.

I try to assure Roy that I want him in the squad. I tell him how much damage it will do to the squad if he goes home now. I repeat that I will gladly ring Colin Healy back and pull him out of the squad if Roy really wants to stay.

He won't. Again, he says he is going to quit, not just the World Cup but international football. I seek justification, anything to hang this decision on. He insists yet again that it is all personal, that he must think only of Roy Keane in this instance. It is not about me, Taff, the 'keepers, Packie, the training ground, the kit. He has his own private reasons, none he can share with me. I ask him to think about it again. He says he is not going to stew on this decision for anyone. He's going home and that's final.

I ask Roy to have one more think about it as I prepare to go back to my own room to take a shower. I tell him to make his mind up and let me know when he has reached a final decision. As I walk out the door, he tells me not to ring Colin Healy and cancel his trip, to leave Colin in the squad. He is going home, it is cut and dried. He is shouting at me now, he is quite agitated but I ignore it. I leave his room and Mick comes with me.

I finally get that shower. It clears my head somewhat, offers some sort of definition to my train of thought.

My doorbell rings. I am in the shower, so Mick answers. It is Roy. He says he is going home and, asks Mick to tell me to get his flight. It's over.

WEDNESDAY 22nd MAY

The morning after the night before.

I am awoken at 7.45 a.m. by a knock on my bedroom door from one of the hotel staff. They have spent the night shielding calls on my behalf and they would be grateful if I could place the phone back on the hook now. The porter explains that the switchboard has been hopping all night, even though I kept Roy's decision to quit within a very tight group. So much for confidentiality.

My phone goes into overdrive as soon as the handset is functional again. I ignore the calls. I know what they are about and I want some time to myself to think the day through. The one certainty is that we are going to have an eventful few hours ahead of us.

I know this is a big story, the biggest story of the World Cup ever from an Irish perspective. The news will certainly damage our preparations, damage the nation's faith in the squad's ability to get beyond the first phase. No doubt I will be thrown into the mire again. Despite all this, I feel refreshed. My conscience is as clear as my head after the best night's sleep of the trip thus far. It was phone off, earplugs in and the sleep of the exhausted as soon as I hit the pillow last night.

Now I am wide awake in a little corner of America with no regrets. I have nothing to hide from here. We are in Saipan because I chose to be here. I said it was the best place to come to for a training camp all along and my mind is still a hundred per cent strong on that decision. Nothing that has happened over the last twenty-four hours has shaken my self-belief. My preparations will still get the best out of the twenty-two players who want to be here. They are happy with the island and they are happy to stay.

Roy Keane is only going home because he wants to go home, because 'personal reasons' have forced his hand. I still don't know what those personal reasons are and I probably never will. He assured me countless times last night that it has nothing to do with me, Packie, Taff, the pitch, the gear or Saipan. All I can do is believe him, accept that he is out of the World Cup now and get on with the business of trying to get Colin Healy all the way from Cork to the South Pacific.

Could I have handled last night differently? Hindsight, as they say, is a wonderful thing. Perhaps I should have told Roy to sleep on it. Maybe I should have told him to talk to his wife, his parents, Alex Ferguson, whoever it is has his ear at this moment in time. I don't know – and I don't have the time to worry about it too much to be honest. The completed Irish squad has to be with FIFA in an hour and a quarter's time, as my captain reminded me in the course of his bombshell last night. I do not have time to play games with Roy Keane. If he wants out, I need to get someone else in who wants to play for Ireland. I must ensure that FIFA know that Colin Healy is our designated replacement for Roy Keane. I don't want to go to the World Cup with just twenty-two players.

Mick Byrne is in the room now. He is concerned for me and the team in the wake of Roy's decision to go home. He is taking calls for me and as soon as the first journalist gets through, we know the proverbial has hit the fan.

FAI president Milo Corcoran pops his head around the door and asks if he can do anything. The FAI have been on the case all night with a succession of phone conversations involving their general secretary, Brendan Menton, treasurer John Delaney and Roy's solicitor Michael Kennedy. They all want a bit of this and Milo's information is that Roy now wants to stay.

It's news to me. Roy has not been down to tell me, nor has he sent any message through to my room. Why has he left it so late? I can count the minutes to the FIFA deadline on two hands and I have still heard nothing from my captain about this alleged change of mind.

I send Mick Byrne up to Roy's room for one last check. Is he in or is he out?

The fax has already gone to FIFA with Colin Healy's name on it by the time Mick comes back and confirms the Roy Keane U-turn. If it wasn't for Mick going to his room, I would never have known that Roy wants to stay.

Panic stations. A new fax is sent to FIFA but there is no guarantee it will make Switzerland in time to confirm the latest twist in this game of musical chairs. We have no choice but to wait on that score.

Then I discover that a fax had been sent by the FAI half an hour earlier with Roy back in the squad, before I even knew he was staying. I am livid when I hear this news.

The players have already heard this morning that Roy is out of the World Cup. Now they discover he is back in again. Their captain has yet to speak to them on the subject either. Then he breezes into the room where they are eating breakfast like nothing has happened. Roy looks like a man without a care in the world. He even asks kitman Joe Walsh why there was no training gear outside his door this morning. It's almost as if the whole thing was a bad dream.

Roy eventually comes to see me before we go training. There is no explanation of his decision to stay, no mention of wanting to play for Ireland or for me in the World Cup. Instead, he is more interested in the practicalities now that he is staying.

I explain that I have already told Colin Healy to cancel his World Cup dream. Then I ask how we will handle the media circus already gathering in the lobby. Keano has no interest in talking to any of the press until his scheduled appearance on the players' pool interview rota next Sunday. Instead, we agree that I will say he wanted to go home for personal reasons and also because his old knee injury was acting up. He is happy to go along with that and leaves me to face the music.

The journalists are up early on the back of this one. Some of them have yet to go to bed. Thanks to the time difference their papers have not yet gone to print and their editors await the latest developments before their final deadlines. At least half a dozen microphones are stuck under my nose as I explain that Roy had quit but is now back in the fold. I confirm, as agreed, that his knee is acting up, he has personal problems he felt were impinging on the World Cup but he is ready now to devote himself to the cause.

I am asked my reaction to Roy's change of mind. I express my delight, explain how I did cartwheels when he arrived in Dublin last Wednesday, how I am delighted and relieved again now that he is staying. We need Roy Keane at the World Cup finals. I need him there if I am to put out the best Irish team in Japan. I say that we did not spend two years trying to get here to go into action without the man who is both our captain and our best player.

Peace is the buzz word by the time we train. It is all good-natured and well-mannered as the lads go through a rigorous morning session. There's not a peep from Roy. He is just one of the lads today and everyone is happy to see him back in the fold and apparently as committed as ever. By lunch-time he is back on top form. Roy even shares his meal with Alan Kelly and I laugh at the fact that they are bosom buddies again, twenty-four hours after they were screaming at each other.

Most of the lads go off to golf for the afternoon as Taff has organised a 'Texas Scramble' at Coral Ocean Point. As the lads tee off, a huge Airbus flies over the first tee. Resident joker Gary Kelly has the golfers in stitches as he shouts: 'Look lads, they're flying Colin Healy in to join us.' Trust Gary.

I am not with them as Robbie Keane's team shoots the winning score. I managed one of the lowest rounds of my life the last time I was out this way but my back is not up to a game of golf so I go out on the bike instead. Having spoken to the press already today, I am free as a bird until another barbecue with some local dignitaries tonight.

As I leave the hotel, Roy Keane is sitting down for the first of two newspaper interviews. It does strike me as strange that he is talking to two individual journalists so soon after telling me that he had no desire to talk to anyone until Sunday. I wonder just what he will say about his decision to quit the World Cup, and the subsequent U-turn, as I head out the gate of the hotel and disappear into my own little world.

THURSDAY 23rd MAY

The grapevine is buzzing with rumour. People can't wait to tell me what it is alleged is about to appear in print. Apparently, Roy has slagged off everything about Saipan, the World Cup, the FAI and all my arrangements in both his newspaper interviews. The first is due to be published in the *Irish Times* on Saturday, the second in the Irish *Sunday Independent* the next day. Already the content is up for discussion but I don't deal in rumour. I try to ignore the subject. We are twenty-four hours away from Japan now and I have other things on my mind. The real work starts in Izumo tomorrow and it is almost time to shut out all outside influences.

Before training, the staff and the players, Roy included, embark on a bus tour of the island. We visit Banzai Cliffs, Suicide Hills and look out over shark-infested Tiger Bay. Footballers can be blasé on such occasions, I am sure you have heard the old story about the West Brom player who opted out of the obligatory Great Wall visit in China because he reckoned 'seen one wall, seen them all'. Not my lot. They were happy to learn why this dot in the Pacific had such a part to play in history, and were genuinely taken with the impact such a small island could have on world events.

After a good workout in our final training session in paradise, lunch is fairly run of the mill, enjoyable and uneventful. Then I leave for a brief social engagement at a local primary school. The kids have absolutely no idea who I am or why I am on their island. They want to know my name, where I am from and what I do. It is refreshing to be so unknown this far from home. As I talk to the children, I am reminded how the anonymity of Saipan is in total contrast to the media blitz awaiting us in Japan. We should enjoy this while it lasts.

Normality arrives with my daily press conference. Today, we are getting closer to the bone. I have to defend myself against comments that Roy may be making with regard to the suitability of our World Cup training camp. So much for that nice quiet week in Saipan. We are definitely bordering on the absurd when I find myself defending the choice of venue against remarks that may be included in an interview scheduled to appear in forty-eight hours' time.

Gary Kelly follows me into the press conference and delivers a very informative insight into the players' relationship with their captain. He points out that Roy Keane is a great player but not the only player with Ireland. There are twenty-two other players here, Kells adds, and they are just as important to the Irish cause in his estimation. No one player is first amongst equals.

Gary says they are all happy in the South Pacific. In fact he says that he is so delighted with Saipan that he would love to stay here for the World Cup and just fly in and out of Japan twenty-four hours before each game. That's not possible under FIFA guidelines but it is heartening to hear such support from one of the senior players in my squad.

By the time I get back to the team hotel after the conference, journalists are waiting by the handful to tell me what Roy has to say in his *Irish Times* interview, now about to hit the streets ahead of schedule, in Thursday's edition instead of Saturday's as originally planned, back in Dublin. It will appear simultaneously on the internet across the world. Nowhere, it seems, is the article more eagerly awaited than in Saipan where the press are waiting with baited breath to confirm its content and get my reaction.

They have digested it all by the time they ask me to respond to the allegations made by my captain in the course of a very long piece that cuts practically the entire Irish World Cup preparation to shreds. Everything, or so it seems, is wrong with my best-laid plans. Roy is quitting international football after Japan, as he revealed to me on Tuesday night, but not before he publicly assassinates everything to do with the tournament, just hours after we had mended our fences.

I decline the invitations to discuss these allegations there and then. I am not going to spend another minute replying to something that an Irish player may have said in a newspaper and not to my face. I am not prepared to answer criticism of me, the Association, the team or my World Cup plans through the press. If somebody within the group has a problem, we will discuss it privately as a squad, not through the media.

I am surprised at this turn of events. After Roy's U-turn on Wednesday, I thought all this was behind us. I really did. I thought we were back on an even keel and working together towards the World Cup finals. Yet here he is, the man with a distaste for journalists, apparently using them to have a pop at everyone connected with the Irish team. To make it worse, the newspaper interviews were conducted on the very day that he said he was staying to lead us into the World Cup.

It is not good enough and I need to get to the bottom of it. I get hold of the *Irish Times* article, from *Irish Independent* journalist, Philip Quinn, someone I regularly take money off on the golf course. My blood begins to boil as I scrawl down the fax. Not only are my decisions with regard to our World Cup preparation taken to the cleaners, the entire squad is affected by this criticism, both of the arrangements and of individuals. Roy is putting his marker down with regard to his own team-mates a fortnight before we go into World Cup battle together. He is even questioning their ability, the level they play at, suggesting they are prepared to put up with any old rubbish when they play for Ireland. He claims that we all put up with sub-standard facilities and even results on the pitch just because we are Irish. Keano's remarks clearly undermine everything I have done since we qualified for the finals, he is casting a shadow over the entire World Cup for the team he captains.

I am disappointed and very annoyed as the severity of his words sink in. I am not alone. Players and staff are beginning to pick up the gist of the article and shock is spreading through the group like a cancer. As the man in charge, I have to address this situation. At 6.30, as the players start to arrive for dinner, I inform them that we will meet in an hour. I do not set an agenda.

I repair to my room with Taff and Packie. We have to tackle this as a group. One player cannot make such comments publicly without doing damage to team morale. Do the other players feel the same way? And how do they feel about their captain's attitude towards them now he has made these remarks? I cannot allow this to become an issue between us in the coming weeks, not with a World Cup about to begin. We must discuss it together, clear the air and attempt, once again, to move forward.

Packie and Taff both urge caution, advise me not to upset the apple-cart. I assure them I will not go screaming in. But I want this sorted and I want to move on. I want twenty-three happy players on that charter flight from Saipan to Izumo tomorrow morning.

Niall Quinn arrives at the meeting just ahead of me. He has been working on his newspaper column with a journalist and has no idea why we are all sitting down after dinner.

I enter the team's private dining-room and the sight in front of me is almost enough to bring tears to my eyes. There, twenty-three players are singing along with the resident band. The room is hopping as the band leads my players through a medley of South Pacific sing-alongs. I stand back for a second and watch my Saipan dream come to life in front of me. The lads are relaxed, they are having a good time, they have embraced what Saipan is all about. And here I am, about to get all serious. There is no sign of an end to the jollity so I leave them at it, for another few songs, before they launch into 'Stand By Me'. I have to ask the band to leave. My vision for this leg of the trip has finally been realised and I have to end it. Typical.

None of the players have been told the subject of the meeting in advance, nor have I discussed the article with any of them ahead of this private gathering with the people it concerns.

I go through the schedule for Friday, what time we will leave for the airport, when we will train in Izumo, normal run-of-the-mill stuff. Then I explain to the group, again, exactly why we have been in Saipan for the past six days. I talk about the need for stamina work, the climactic conditions, the opportunity to rest and have a good time, the anonymity it offers before the real World Cup work. I add that Izumo will knock them out with the quality of the facilities and reiterate that the problems over the training gear and the state of the pitch should not have happened.

I ask Roy, as captain, to air any grievances he has on behalf of the players. I have had my say on the subject of conditions here in Saipan and offer Roy his. I ask for his input and offer him the chance to air any grievances he may have so that I can address them personally, in front of the other players in our private meeting and not through the media. I want any issues in the camp cleared up before we fly tomorrow.

Roy is fuming. He throws the anonymity line back in my face, confusing the fact that we are anonymous on this soccer-free island with the fact that we are now talking as a group. He demands to know what right I have to call a public meeting about him. How dare I discuss something with him in a group situation? How dare I have a meeting about Roy Keane and criticise him in front of everyone else? He is heated, animated, almost out of control.

In response I point out that I have a 5,000-word article in front of me that publicly criticises me, the players, the arrangements, the FAI, everything to do with the World Cup. Why the hell should I respond to his criticism on a one-to-one basis, or worse still, through the media, when it affects all the squad? To emphasise the point, I pick the article up and begin to read out the comments he has made about his team-mates and the level they play at, the things they are prepared to put up with when they play for Ireland.

Roy Keane explodes. He shouts at me that he has a 'f***ing brain' and then he's off on a wild rant about our preparations, my management, his dislike of playing for me as a manager.

Roy says he missed friendlies because he didn't want to play for me. He admits he used to join the squad late for games to avoid me for an extra day or two. Saipan, in his opinion, has been a cock-up from start to finish. My training sessions are useless. He has a go at me for talking to journalists, for befriending them. He wants to play for Ireland but he doesn't want to play for me.

I struggle to get a word in edgeways. When I do get a chance to reply, I feel I have to ask him if he picks and chooses his games, does he deliberately miss friendlies? Are they below his dignity? He says yes, that friendlies are not for him.

I ask him why he missed the biggest game of all our international careers with Ireland to date, why he pulled out of the trip to Iran on the Sunday morning, just hours after telling me that he was going. That is the final straw. He shouts at me about 'your deal with the gaffer', Alex Ferguson. I ask him did he tell me on the Saturday night that he was going to Iran. He ignores the question and goes on about 'the deal with the gaffer' again.

He is fuming now and the room is stunned. No one can get a word in as he rants on. For about eight minutes I am every expletive imaginable from c to w. I was a crap player. I am a crap manager. I am a crap coach. I can't organise training. I can't make a decision. I can't get inside players' heads. I can't manage people, even though I have been managing him with kid gloves for six years now. I am an effing c*** and an effing w***er. He has no respect for me at all, as a manager or as a player. He only has respect for Alex Ferguson. He bizarrely claims I don't want him in the squad.

I have never seen any human being act like this before, never mind a footballer. He is delirious. He continues the abuse, dragging up an argument we had in Boston back in 1992. It goes on and on and on.

Eventually Roy starts to repeat one question. 'You want me to piss off, don't you? You want me to piss off.'

He has a point. I have had enough. He has crossed the line. I finally agree with him. I tell him to go. He tells me to stick the World Cup up my f***ing arse. With that, he is up and gone, out the door and out of the World Cup. As he leaves, I tell the lads I need their support now more than ever. One of the players says: 'Mick McCarthy well done.' The room erupts with a round of applause. Goalkeeper Dean Kiely then offers to do a job for me in midfield. Typical footballers, they see the funny side of anything.

As reality sinks in, I am as shocked as everyone else present. My best player, my captain, has just savaged me in front of his team-mates. He has just signed his own World Cup exit warrant and was quite happy to do so. The room looks to me for guidance. I tell the other players that it is over now. There is no way back for Roy Keane after that performance. I cannot allow him to play for me again after that assault on my character and my team. They are silent, rocked by it all. I tell them that Roy is history. If we are to move on then I need their support.

Packie and Taff speak. I have no idea what they say, it's all a blur. I wanted closure tonight. I expected to leave this meeting with everything sorted, with Roy back on an even keel and the squad united again ahead of our trip to Izumo. I did not call this meeting to lose my best player. Nor did I call it to listen to a bellyful of foul-mouthed abuse from a man most of Ireland looks up to as a role model. I was not brought up to behave like that or to accept behaviour of that nature. As a manager, I cannot allow any player to act in such a manner, no matter who he is. Had I accepted his behaviour, I could never have managed this team again, I would have had to go. It was him or me and maybe that's what he wanted. He had to go. As a result, we are a man down and my life will never be the same again.

My conscience is clear even as I leave the room and start the search for the FAI president Milo Corcoran and the press officer Brendan McKenna. I have to call a press conference ASAP and deliver this news myself, before the grapevine creeps in again. I have to get this out in the open and explain publicly why I was left with no choice but to send my captain home.

I go back to my room, talk to Fiona and to Liam Gaskin and tell them first-hand exactly what has gone off tonight. They don't seem as surprised as I am that Roy is gone. Perhaps I should have seen it coming when he quit three times on Tuesday night only to come back on Wednesday after a series of phone calls.

We locate Brendan and round the press up an hour or so later. They have no idea why they are being dragged away from all over town, from their diners, to sit in the hotel's Chinese restaurant, the only room available at short notice, and listen to me for the second time that day.

As I prepare to go into the press conference, the senior players in the squad approach me. Niall, Stan and Alan Kelly want to flank me in front of the media. They heard what Keane said in the meeting and they are as disgusted as I am. They offer their support and I am grateful. Unity is everything now.

The press corps look as stunned as the rest of us as the penny drops. They throw questions at me, none of them as severe as the criticisms that were thrown at me earlier by the man I made captain of Ireland. I get through the conference on autopilot. I am starting to realise how big this story is, the biggest story of the World Cup so far. I know it is only going to get bigger.

As the three players and Milo Corcoran begin to defend my actions, a series of thoughts race through my head. Was he right? Can I manage? Can I coach? Can I handle players? Hang on a second, we are sitting thousands of miles from home right now for one reason and one reason alone, because we have qualified for the World Cup finals. We are here because, yes, I can manage and coach and get the best out of the players who will wear the green shirt in Japan next month.

The press conference ends with a one-on-one interview with Gabriel Egan for RTE radio. Then I try to ring Alex Ferguson and get his answering machine. I leave a message. As a matter of courtesy, I want to let him know what has happened.

There are so many things that don't make sense in all of this. If Roy had decided to stay on Wednesday, why did he sit down and do those interviews just a few hours after telling me we could count him in for the World Cup finals? If he wanted out, why not go on the Tuesday night as he had planned? Why put us all through this hell when he could have ended it forty-eight hours earlier and walked away?

And why explode now? If he really wanted to play in the World Cup, Roy could surely stomach me and my ways for another few weeks and then let rip. Have a go at me out on the pitch after the last game of the World Cup, take me to task and call me every name under the sun in his biography for all I care. Just don't do it the day before we move to Japan for the tournament proper. It is all nonsense. I brought my players here to get them relaxed ahead of the World Cup. Instead, my captain has created the biggest fuss of all time and nothing will be the same again. Why?

I did not want to lose my captain, not when he quit on Tuesday and not when he lost his temper and the plot this evening. I am not stupid, I know he is the most valuable player in our squad, I have always had the height of respect for his abilities as a player and I still do.

I just cannot understand why he would do this to Ireland, never mind me. There are times as an international player when you have to bite the bullet, you have to get on with it for the good of the country, not that we are suffering in Saipan by any stretch of the imagination. Far from it in fact. We have thousands of fans on their way to Japan next week. They have spent a small fortune to get there and now they will be deprived of Ireland's best player. I feel guilty on that score. Could I have done any more to keep him here, to give those fans their hero on the World Cup stage? I don't think so. I have always done what I believed to be best for Ireland.

And from now on, I will always be known as the manager who sent Roy Keane home from the World Cup finals. The events of this evening will follow me to the grave.

EIGHT

24–30 May, Izumo

FRIDAY 24th MAY

One thing is still puzzling me as I awake, relaxed after a solid eight hours of sleep. Why is Roy Keane so obsessed with events in Boston ten years ago? Why was something that happened on an end of season tour to America in the summer of 1992 such a crucial factor in his outburst at last night's meeting? How could he allow something like that to fester in his head for a solid ten years? And, if he can put up with it for a decade, what difference is another four or five weeks putting up with me going to make?

Let me explain what happened back then, other than an embarrassing defeat to the home nation.

That June, I was one of the senior players of the Republic team, Millwall manager and Irish captain on one of my last tours of duty as an international footballer. My body was acting up and I knew my playing career was coming to the end. Keane was the new kid on the block, the up-and-coming star of the Irish team after a meteoric rise to fame at Nottingham Forest. The US Cup in 1992, a fairly nondescript tournament, was Keane's first serious tour with the senior Republic side.

On the final day, Jack left us to our own devices. The deal was simple, so long as the players were back at the hotel in time to pack their bags for the airport, we were free to do anything we wanted. Of course, footballers being footballers, some went on the beer big time, Keane included. And a group of them were late for the bus. So late that their bags were packed and sitting on the coach by the time they finally decided to join us.

Jack was not best pleased. Nor were the rest of us. A long season was over and as soon as we got home we were on our holidays. To get home, we needed to make that Aer Lingus flight out of Logan Airport. This delay was not helping. So Jack got stuck into those players when they did arrive and Keane, clearly under the influence, decided to give as good as he got.

I had a go back at him. As the captain and the senior player in the squad, I pointed out that he should know better than to turn up late for the bus on his first real trip with Ireland and then have a pop. He fired right back at me, had a go at me with one of those sarky comments of his, taking the water out of the shorts I was wearing and generally acting up. I wasn't having it. I asked him who he thought he was, keeping everyone waiting on his first tour away with the Irish team. It got pretty heated. I lost my head and if it hadn't been for Packie Bonner standing in between us, blows may well have been thrown from both sides.

I have since heard the claims made by Roy that I told him I'd get him back one day, even that I pinned him up against the window of the bus, but both claims are rubbish.

Boston clearly affected my relationship with Keane from his perspective but I am at a loss to know why. Yes, we had our differences in the summer of 1996, when he decided not to travel back to the US for my first tour as manager, but I subsequently met him in London before the Charity Shield that August and we sorted that one out, with Alex Ferguson's help. I have even been up to Keane's house in Manchester since in a bid to cement our relationship. In all those meetings and all our time together on international duty, he never once mentioned events in Boston. That's why his reference to it last night stung me. I cannot understand how he allowed it to stew for ten years.

If it was such a big problem all he had to do was sit down with me when I became manager and tell me that I was out of order when I spoke with him back in 1992. He could have sorted it out in one conversation, told me I was in the wrong, heard my take on the story and forgotten about it. It should never have dragged on like this.

Personally, I have had no problem with Keane based on anything that happened in Boston. I am not generally one for holding grudges, I prefer to get things out in the open and move on. I certainly never resented him in the years since that incident, nor did I treat him any differently to the other players because of it. If anything, I have bent the rules for Keane because he is such a good player, a world-class player.

I admit I have put up with things from him over the last six years, tolerated things from him in order to get the best out of him, and the team, on the field. That has to be done at times, for the good of the team and the good of the country. I made him captain as soon as I was appointed, even though there are players who handle some of the captain's off-field responsibilities far better with the squad. I have accommodated him at times because I know what he can offer us on the pitch. He is a great player who can make us a great team. I have even supported and defended him and seen the best in him over the last six years when others have raised doubts. When he was slaughtered by the media, I stood up for him.

What happens? He throws it all back in my face and now he is out of the World Cup.

I will be seen as the bad guy but my concern in all of this is for the team and its performance in Japan 2002, not for me personally. I have never worried about the public's perception of our relationship. I have never been close to him as a person but always believed we had a good working relationship. His performances in the green shirt have never given me reason to doubt that. And, anyway, I am not the manager of Ireland because I want to get Christmas presents from my players and go down the local for a pint with them every Sunday night. I am Ireland manager because I want to put this nation on the world football map and build a team that the Irish fans can be proud of. I want performances, not close relationships with my players. If that means putting up with the odd tantrum from Keane here and there as I have done in the past, then fine.

As a policy, it has worked. Look at what he produced for me and for Ireland in Amsterdam, in Lisbon and in Nicosia. He was immense in all those games so sometimes it pays to take the rough with the smooth. Not this time. He crossed the line last night, he went beyond the bounds of acceptability. And he has put our World Cup hopes in grave danger.

I hope people remember that when they look at this story in years to come. Here we had the Republic of Ireland captain, the role model for United and Irish fans across the world, attack his manager in front of the World Cup squad and call him everything from an effing c*** to an effing w****er. Are normal people prepared to accept that sort of behaviour from their top sportsmen? I hope not. I am not prepared to put up with it, not from Keane and not from any footballer in my charge. I hope the nation acknowledges exactly how he behaved when they come to analyse this story.

It is a tragedy for those on their way to support us at the World Cup. Some have packed their green shirts with Keane's name and number on the back and he won't be there next week, when they arrive in Japan. How will they feel towards me now? Will I ever have the same relationship with the Irish fans, the supporters who stood by me through thick and thin over the last six years? Can I fly into Dublin or Manchester or Cork ever again? Will the Irish people turn on me now?

I wonder all these things as I go down to an early breakfast before we leave Saipan but I know I have done the right thing. I took a stand last night, the stand any manager worth his salt would take. It is over now and we will move on. The finality of it almost brings a sense of relief. When Keane said he was staying on Wednesday, I asked him if he would blow up again, if we all needed to walk on eggshells. In hindsight, he might have done me a favour if he had quit, as he tried to, on Tuesday night after all.

I will not do a U-turn on this one. There is no pressure from the FAI to change my mind. Milo and John Delaney, back in Dublin, are both publicly supportive of my actions, which I appreciate. I am in charge of team affairs and if that ever changes I will be out the door after Keane. I made that point clear at the press conference last night and no one has a problem with it.

I do not want Keane back. I would love to get Colin Healy into the squad in his place but we have missed the deadline now and I can't see FIFA turning on that one. I feel for Colin in all of this, he wanted to play in the World Cup finals and he has been denied a late reprieve by a player who wants to go home.

There is a tangible feeling of relief around the place this morning. The players don't have to look over their shoulders anymore, as some undoubtedly did when he was around. They can relax now and they can get on with it. They joke about Keane on the bus to the airport, they stick an RIP sticker on his usual seat on the team coach.

And then the sing-song starts down the back.

> *We're on the one road, sharing the one road,*
> *we're on the road to God knows where.*
> *We're on the one road, it may be the wrong road,*
> *but we're together now who cares.*
> *North men, South men, comrades all,*
> *Dublin, Belfast, Cork and Donegal.*
> *We're on the one road, singing along,*
> *singing a soldier's song.*

In unity comes strength. The Saipan twenty-two are still with me as manager, they are clearly on my side as we check in for our flight direct to Izumo.

Keane is back at the hotel in Garapan as we board our flight, specially chartered by Massihiro Nishio, the mayor of Izumo, who is personally flying with us to his city. The FAI have booked him a flight home but their travel arrangements are no longer good enough for Keane. He has handed all responsibility for his flight home over to Manchester United so we leave him to his own devices and the handful of journalists and photographers who want to follow him off the island. He is no longer my player, no longer my responsibility.

Back on our plane, the craic is starting. There are only three rows of business-class seats and the management and officials nab them.

He's not even a day gone and already the players are moaning that they've been downgraded from flying in the big seats, or 'Roy class' as the lads call it.

Mayor Nishio has organised a special treat for the players. He gets the captain of the massive Boeing 737-800 to fly low over Saipan and give us one last look at paradise. The shadow of the plane darting over the island is quite something to behold as the captain goes so low that Taff, Packie and I try to spot the sharks in Tiger Bay.

Gary Kelly is not so happy with the detour. Since that incident at Stansted airport he has been a nervous flier. He shouts once to get the plane up and out of here. By the second shout, I realise Kells is serious and ask the hostess to tell the captain to get a move on. He accelerates and we are away from Saipan in a flash. Somehow, I reckon we will all hear about this little island again.

Our arrival in Izumo has been organised down to a T. Our bags are cleared for us so we head straight into the arrivals hall and an Irish-style welcome from our hosts. A quick sing-song with some local children, a rendition of the Irish national anthem and we are on the bus and off to the Royal Hotel.

So far I have managed to miss the barrage of cameras and reporters waiting for us in Izumo, a small agricultural city, to the southwest of Tokyo. The 50,000 people who live here have been waiting for months for our arrival. The mayor applied to act as an official host city for the World Cup a couple of years ago and was knocked back. So instead, he campaigned successfully for Izumo to become the host city for Ireland's training camp if we qualified. He has been writing to the FAI now for more than a year, even more confident than I was that we would make it.

The fact that he has eight million Shinto Gods on his side probably helps. They look after the famous Tachai temple and the city and they are now firmly on the side of the Irish. They helped us get past Holland last September, according to the mayor, and I pray they will help us through our latest crisis.

The players have the full run of the Royal Hotel for the next seven nights. It is the best hotel in town but the rooms are small, so small that they cannot share. This, believe it or not, causes a problem for some players. As footballers, they are conditioned to rooming together from an early age and they can get lonely, bless them. The only Irish player who likes to room on his own has already gone home. Some of the lads look to Ray Treacy for a switch to twins. It can't be done but that is the only complaint about the accommodation. Everything else about the hotel is top class, from the pool room to the notice board in the lobby which the players quickly start using for their own entertainment. We are barely a wet minute in town when a message is left for Jason to ring Kylie Minogue. Kells, meanwhile, wants anyone who sees the board to know that he is having a ball.

We adjourn to the town's new Hamayama Stadium for a brief training session. It will be officially opened tomorrow, thirteen months ahead of schedule, when we meet Hiroshima, a team in the J League, Japan's professional football league, in a warm-up match.

Oh, I forgot to tell you. There is a game tomorrow and we are playing in the World Cup finals next week. It is easy to forget such things in the middle of all this sensation.

After training, the mayor hosts a very brief and very special welcome ceremony in the town's magnificent sports dome. Local children present us with flowers, they sing Irish songs and I thank them for their endearing hospitality. The lads begin to get a sense of what the World Cup is really about now. Those who want to be here are in Japan to play for their country on the biggest stage of all and that is all that matters.

I adjourn to the media centre next door for the scheduled press conference. It seems appropriate that this building is normally home to the local Department for Disaster Prevention. I kid you not.

The press conference numbers are swollen. About forty more Irish and English journalists have arrived, caught en route between Amsterdam and Tokyo as the biggest Irish soccer story of all time broke in Saipan. Their desire to play catch-up ensures that Keane dominates the first ten minutes or so. The questions and answers are the same as the night before. There will be no change, I have no regrets. We will get on without him, starting against our opponents tomorrow. The questions must move on as well.

Back to football at last. We have picked up a few injury worries in the last couple of days in Saipan. Kenny Cunningham, Steve Finnan and Lee Carsley will all sit out the training game tomorrow but Jason McAteer is fit to play. Mark Kinsella will come into midfield in Keane's place. It's an ill wind, and all that.

SATURDAY 25th MAY

Republic of Ireland v Hiroshima

Roy Keane is on his way home to Manchester. Good luck to him. He slipped the press at Saipan Airport and he is out of my life. But not for long, I suspect. I have other things to worry about as he makes his way back to his family. I feel for them, knowing what my wife and children are going through back in England.

Brendan Menton has arrived in Izumo and we begin the day with a working breakfast. I have already outlined what happened over the course of the week to Brendan and he is fully supportive of my actions. The FAI is not prepared to let an Irish footballer behave as Keane did in Saipan on Thursday night. That's 1–0 to common decency. Brendan says he will announce as much at a press conference today when the FAI will formally appeal to FIFA for permission to replace Keane with Colin Healy, under the force majeure ruling. Neither of us is confident on that score but we will try.

It is good to wake up today knowing that we have a practice game in front of 11,000 fans this afternoon. I need to get back to football, and soon. The World Cup is only a week away now and I need to take stock.

Are the players as relaxed about all this as they seem? Is their nonchalance merely a front? Are they hurting inside, worried that their World Cup experience may not be all it promised to be when we left Dublin over a week ago as a united squad, on the surface at least? I need to know and today's exhibition game against Hiroshima will tell me.

The atmosphere in the dressing-room beforehand is strange; all is not as it should be. Concentration for a game like this is difficult when your world has been turned upside down in the previous forty-eight hours. The players seem as distracted as I am. It is hard to concentrate on anything, let alone worry about a game after everything we have been through.

Injuries mean Gary Kelly and Richard Dunne start in defence, otherwise the team is as expected with Shay, Stan, Hartey, Jase, Kinse, Mattie, Kev, Duffer and Robbie all favourites to start against Cameroon a week from now. It is made clear to the players before the game that performances today will colour my judgement. They won't convince me one way or the other but they will help me make my decisions. I tell the players not to take it easy this afternoon. I want all of them to show me they are worth a starting spot next Saturday. However, I do not want any more injuries, it is not intended to be that sort of game.

The players need to cross a white line and play a game again. They need a return to something approaching normality. They need to try out this new Adidas ball in match conditions, the 'keepers especially need to see how it reacts in game play. Martin Walsh, our doctor, and the medical team want to assess the squad's fitness after Saipan, measure how they are breathing and coping with the heat and humidity that the sun offers in this provincial outpost of Japan. Other than that, we will try some free-kicks and some corners in match conditions but this is merely an exercise, an observation. Or so I think.

We look leggy in the opening minutes, the lads seem tired and heavy in their breathing. It seems that events off the field have got to them.

Then disaster strikes. Jason McAteer breaks free in the opposition box, down to my right. He lets the ball slip ahead of him and races into a tackle from Hiroshima defender Bilong, a member of the Cameroon squad at the last World Cup finals, of all things. I can barely watch as Honest Jason flies into the tackle. He goes to ground straight away and my heart drops as far as his injured knee.

Physios Mick Byrne and Ciaran Murray are on the pitch before the Japanese referee has even called for them. I am stuck to the spot. Jason appears to be in agony. He is holding his leg and screaming with the pain. This was never part of the Carlsberg ad. The physios pull him off the pitch. Old habits die hard for Jason. He looks for the cameras and tells the snappers that he's f***ed.

The word is not good back on the bench as Steven Reid replaces the Sunderland midfielder. My players are still having a go at Bilong when the game resumes. They cannot believe that a fellow professional would commit a foul like that against a player on the verge of a World Cup finals appearance. They are still arguing a minute later as we concede a sloppy goal to Tatsuhiko Kubo but I care little. My only concern is for my injured player, currently lying prostrate on the Izumo turf. To lose a second midfield player, this close to the World Cup finals would be a disaster..

By half-time, Martin Walsh has Jase sitting on the medical bed in the dressing-room. There is damage to the knee and bruising on the joint. Only a scan will determine the full extent of the injury but Martin is confident that it is not serious. Jase, however, is distraught. He has already counted himself out of the World Cup finals and all but told Carlsberg to pull the TV ad. I try to reassure him that all will be well but I am not sure he is listening.

Martin Walsh has a more pressing worry. The players are not taking their fluids on board. They have practically ignored the Lucozade bottles scattered around the pitch and he is concerned. The lapse in concentration that was so apparent before half-time is, he believes, down to the fact that dehydration has set in. We remind the players of the importance of taking fluid regularly, reiterating the fact that a two per cent drop in bodyweight through sweat equates to a twenty per cent drop in performance. He has been weighing them regularly since we went to Saipan and he is concerned about their weight loss. Some have lost half a stone in a session.

For the second half I throw Andy O'Brien and Gary Breen on for Hartey and Richard Dunne. Stan moves to left-back, we get to grips with the pace of the game, sort our breathing out and everything is fine. Kevin Kilbane limps out with a foot injury on the hour but it looks no more than bruising and we are confident he will be right as rain by Monday or Tuesday. Duffer and Robbie Keane link well upfront and two goals from Robbie give the 11,000 fans an Irish win and something to shout about.

Even Jason is smiling again by the end of it. Bilong is waiting outside the dressing-room as soon as the game ends, wanting to apologise for that tackle. Quite right too, it was worthy of an apology but at least he was man enough to admit it.

At the press conference it takes me five attempts before the locals understand that I will not talk about Roy Keane. I want to move on, I am more interested in talking about Robbie and his goals or the way Gary Kelly and Gary Breen both impressed me today. They have both been flying on the training ground. Clearly, if the game today is anything to go on, they are not prepared to accept that their World Cup number equates to a place on the bench and that pleases me. They have given me another headache, a welcome one this time.

I have no worries about replacing Roy Keane in midfield. Just as the World Cup will continue without Stephen Carr and Gary Doherty, so it will carry on without Keane. Ireland will play Cameroon in Niigata next Saturday, no matter whether he is sitting in Manchester, Mayfield or at the heart of the Irish midfield.

I tell Kinse as much as we discuss the dramatic change in his World Cup fortune after the Hiroshima game. Keane's absence means Mark will now start alongside Mattie against Cameroon next Saturday, just as they played together in Iran. I tell Mark he should stick a coathanger in his mouth now to preserve that smile when he's asleep but I have no worries on his account. He has always played well for me, ever since I first introduced him as a late starter to international football in a friendly in the Czech town of Olomouc all those years ago.

New heroes will emerge over the course of the coming weeks and both Mattie and Kinse have the ability to rise to the occasion. They bring different qualities to the team than Keane but both are seasoned internationals, both are captains at their club and both know what needs to be done at this level. They will not let their country down. They have a week to think about the game plan for Saturday so I am confident that everything will come good.

My only concern about Kinse centres on his knee. Mark has had problems with it over the years and needs to protect it. We are not talking Paul McGrath-type knee problems here but he does need to be careful. There are days when Kinse will opt out of training as a precaution and I am happy to let him play the part of Captain Sensible on those occasions.

With Lee Carsley carrying a knock as well, we need to be careful. I cannot afford to lose another player this close to the big kick-off.

Republic of Ireland 2, Hiroshima 1

SUNDAY 26th MAY

Today I am due to leave the tent behind for a few hours. Cameroon are to play a friendly against England in Kobe and I will travel down by helicopter to watch our first World Cup opponents.

I fully expect the spectre of Roy Keane to loom on the horizon at some point this afternoon. He has told his side of the story in a Sunday paper and that can only spell more trouble. It is naive to think for even one minute that the story is going to go away, much as I would like it to. We do have the potential to bury it, at least temporarily, when the World Cup begins. Performance will count for everything then, performance will shift the focus of attention. Until then, however, I will have to put up with constant reminders of the Keane controversy.

I am not enjoying this World Cup experience. I knew coming here that it would be different to anything I have ever lived through before, as a player or as a manager, but the least I expected was some sense of achievement. Not so far. Instead, I have spent the first two weeks of this trip firefighting, and it is starting to get to me. I am beginning to feel isolated on the Keane issue and it worries me.

The distance between Ireland and Japan is a bonus in one sense. I have no exposure to the column inches and television hours that the Roy Keane story has dominated since Tuesday. By the same token, I have no idea what the public are thinking. Jack Charlton always told me that the public are the ones who decide when a manager should go, not the FAI. His insight has never seemed more pertinent. My fear is that the country, apparently 70-30 in my favour according to people I trust, will begin to turn as Roy Keane gets home and his PR machine kicks into action. If the men pulling his strings turn this story around, men who were nowhere near that room last Thursday night, then I have a real problem. I could lose the support of the nation before we kick a World Cup ball. If that happens I am in trouble, real trouble.

That thought is constantly at the back of my head. It makes it difficult to concentrate on anything else so it's a good job that training is a quiet affair this morning, a loosener.

The biggest job the medical staff and the rest of us face today is to raise Jason McAteer's morale. I saw him in his room last night and his Scouser spirit was visibly absent. There was no spark about Jase. In his own head the World Cup was already over. I had never seen him so down; it was almost as if he expected to go home before Saturday's game.

I tried to talk him around. He has time on his side and Martin Walsh is confident the damage to his knee is peripheral. The hospital is closed today but the mayor has asked the doctors to open the x-ray department and get the scans done as quickly as possible. They cannot do enough for us here in Izumo.

After training I leave for Kobe with Taff, Packie and a translator in tow. The helicopter ride down is brief, we will catch a scheduled flight back and must leave the ground early. That, at least, will keep me away from the English press today. They are sure to want to talk about Roy Keane and I'd rather not, thank you.

On our arrival in Kobe a Swedish FA official comes up to me, introduces himself and shakes my hand. He thanks me for doing football a favour and bringing the prima donnas of the modern game back down to earth. In sending Roy Keane home, he argues, I have sent a message to all the big-time Charlies who think they are bigger than the game and their national sides. Sweden have their fair share of such players, he says, and they will think twice now about stepping out of line. I had never considered my actions to be pioneering or deserving of any other nation's gratitude. His congratulations are as welcome as they are unexpected.

England coaches Tord Grip and Dave Sexton are also grateful for my week's work when we chat before the game. They are delighted that I have drawn so much press attention away from their team this close to the World Cup finals. I am glad that somebody is enjoying all this fuss. I am not, but at least I can go to work now and sit back and watch Cameroon for the next hour or so.

They impress me. I knew they would be better than the Nigerian team that beat us in Dublin a lifetime ago but I didn't think they were this good. Their physical power is impressive. So is their movement. They play a fluid 3–5–2 formation and they move the ball, at pace, across the pitch.

England, very cautious and clearly worried about further injuries after all their problems, can't cope with the structure employed by Cameroon. They have Wes Brown at right-back and Joe Cole in front of him and neither are experienced enough to know how to deal with Salomon Oliembe and Pierre Wome as they attack at pace and switch the play with ease. Oliembe is certainly the star of the show today.

Cameroon have two very impressive front players in Samuel Eto'o and Patrick Mboma. They like to turn defenders and play little one-twos in behind the centre-backs, something to note. I also like the look of Marc-Vivien Foe in the centre of their midfield. He sits in front of the three centre-backs and never moves. That allows the wing-backs to get on but it may also present a problem for Cameroon if we leave Duffer and Robbie upfront. England have a tendency to track back when Cameroon break and that allows Foe to dictate the shape of the game.

We are gone to the airport by the time Michael Owen snatches a late equaliser for England in a 2–2 draw. I have seen enough to know that Cameroon now rank right up alongside Germany in terms of potential. We are looking at a side that can win the group here. That said, England were cautious opponents. They stayed clear of potential injury all afternoon and never really expressed themselves in their final warm-up before the real action.

In my own mind the game bears similarities to the Holland–England match at White Hart Lane last August. The Dutch won that game comfortably and everyone thought they would just turn up and win in Dublin the following month. It was a false barometer for Louis van Gaal and I am sure this performance won't be too worrying for Sven-Goran Eriksson. He knows that this friendly will mean nothing next week. England will be better than this when the World Cup begins, but Cameroon clearly have the ability to be very good. The journey south has been more than worthwhile.

I arrive back at the Royal Hotel in Izumo in time for a late dinner. Firefighting is on the menu. The rumour mill has been rampant again in my absence. Word has come through from Dublin and Manchester that Roy Keane is already on a plane back to Japan. People are saying that the FAI have brokered a deal with Keane to get him back in time for the finals and he is in transit. It's news to me.

A number of players approach me about the story. They have spent the afternoon and evening living with this rumour, and by now their mood is mutinous. The players are furious that the FAI could even consider a return for Roy Keane after everything he said and did this past week. Several of them, and not all senior players, are adamant that they will return home if Roy Keane is imposed on us by the FAI. The squad will be decimated if he comes back.

The fact that Keane has criticised everyone again in two separate newspaper interviews today does his cause no good. Word has filtered through as to the nature of both pieces. I get it in the neck big-time, surprise, surprise. Boston is dragged up again and he repeats his silly claim that he wants to play for Ireland but not for Mick McCarthy.

He also launches an astonishing attack on the senior players who stood by me in the press conference that followed his World Cup dismissal. He brands Niall Quinn, Alan Kelly and Steve Staunton cowards. He goes so far as to express a wish that Niall and Stan both play against Manchester United next season. It is bizarre stuff and hardly the talk of a man on his way back into our World Cup camp.

I check the story out with the FAI and promise the players there is no substance to this rumour at all. I do not want Roy Keane back at any cost. I never want to see him again, never mind work with him. He is starting to ruin my World Cup and I won't have it. If he is on his way out here against my wishes then he won't be the only problem in the camp. I will have a major problem with any such development and so will the players. That is quite clear. If he comes out here against my will, I am going home. A few players immediately say they will go with me and I am heartened by their support. As it turns out, the rumour of his imminent arrival counts for nothing when I check it out with the FAI.

They believe that the Keane spin doctors are already at work. My fear now is that the hype to get Roy Keane back will gain momentum. Keane has a major advantage on his side. He is back in England and the PR machine behind him can orchestrate the media while all he has to worry about is when he should next walk his dog. In contrast, we are 7,000 miles from home and we have the small matter of the World Cup finals to worry about.

Thankfully, the media coverage of the story is not all one way today. Mattie Holland has a go in his *Independent on Sunday* column and I take Roy Keane to task for his behaviour in both *Ireland on Sunday* and the *Mail on Sunday*. Jack Charlton and Tony Cascarino, to name just two, are supportive in their newspaper columns. Brian Clough has even suggested he would have shot Roy Keane before he sent him home. That's a bit drastic but at this moment in time, as I sit in Izumo, I know exactly what he means.

MONDAY 27th MAY

Isolation is starting to creep in. I know the players and staff are with me. Their support has never wavered. They saw what happened in that room last Thursday night and they know I took the only course of action open to me. Some have said it publicly, others have backed me privately. Aside from them I need to know, in my own mind at least, exactly who is outside the tent peeing in with Roy Keane and who is inside, peeing out against the world. Where do some FAI officials stand on this? What do the fans think?

I need closure before this starts to eat into our preparation for the game against Cameroon in Niigata next Saturday. We said goodbye to Roy Keane in Saipan last Friday but the issue won't go away. There is no sign of the perfect storm abating.

The papers back home are full of more Roy Keane revelations. His spin doctors are at work, as I feared, and public opinion is swaying. If this degenerates into a Keane v McCarthy popularity contest back in Ireland, then I cannot win. The public will believe that Roy Keane the player is more important than Mick McCarthy the manager in the World Cup scheme of things. When it comes to achieving results, the public will see Keane as a bigger player than me if this spin continues to spiral out of control. If that happens, if the spin doctors manoeuvre a return for Roy Keane on the back of public opinion, then my position will become untenable.

Roy Keane and those inside his camp are playing a clever game, an orchestrated game. Today, he clearly states in print that he would love to play for Ireland again but not as long as I am in charge. Strange that only last Tuesday in my hotel room he announced that he was quitting international football no matter what once this World Cup was over. He confirmed that in two newspaper articles but now he wants to play for Ireland again, once I'm no longer in charge. Short memories are clearly the order of the day back home.

That sort of statement does me no favours. It twists the knife deeper and adds more pressure on Mick McCarthy the manager to get results in Japan. Lose the first game now and . . . you know the rest.

It is also difficult to judge how every one around me is handling the stress of all this. The players put on a brave face. They are still laughing, still joking, still leaving messages for Jason to ring everyone from Elle McPherson to Kylie. But the Roy Keane issue must still come up in conversation amongst them. They must talk about it, they must hear the news from home.

I know some of them are angry at the suggestion that Stan, Quinny and Alan Kelly are cowards. That is a horrible thing to say about anyone, particularly about a fellow professional who has been in the trenches with you for the last ten years. The attack on Stan is totally unwarranted. Keane has suggested today that Stan co-operated with some bizarre plot to get him removed from the World Cup in order to captain Ireland in Japan. Steve Staunton would never stoop to that level. No, only one person contributed to my decision to kick Roy Keane out and that was Roy Keane himself.

Funny thing is, back in 1992 I gave Stan, my room-mate then, a similar verbal volley to the one I gave Keane when he also arrived late for the bus in Boston, but it hasn't damaged our relationship. He doesn't bear a grudge over the incident ten years later. He has been a great player and a great friend since he first came into the squad back in 1988. I am proud to call him a mate and I am proud now that he will captain my team at the World Cup finals. He is everything a role model should be, on and off the pitch. The younger players look up to him in a manner that a captain deserves and I know he will act as an inspiration to them when things get really tough in the next fortnight.

I have had a couple of chats with Stan about the captain's role already. We must ensure that the players are focused entirely on the World Cup when Saturday comes. There can be no more distractions, however we manage to achieve that. I have to take the heat away from the players. I was the one who did the dirty deed in response to Keane's actions in Saipan last Thursday night, I am the one who should carry the can now, difficult as that is. The players must be allowed to concentrate solely on playing for their country and delivering in the Big Swan stadium.

At least the injury news is better today. Jason had his scans yesterday and there is no damage. His mood has lifted dramatically as a result and today he is out running, under the watchful eye of Martin Walsh. Happy-go-lucky Jason is back in town and talking about scoring the winner against Cameroon. It's a far cry from last Saturday night when he was expecting to fly home. I get Ian Rogers to video Jason running and tonight we will compare that with footage from last week's training to see how close he really is to full fitness.

Others do more as the big kick-off looms. Gary Breen and Kenny

Cunningham join in for the full training session while Lee Carsley and Steve Finnan are very close to normal service.

After training, the players go off to play golf or relax in the pool. And there is some personal light at the end of the tunnel when I get back to the hotel after the daily press conference. Fiona has arrived from London, four days ahead of schedule. She has been living through the hell of the past week on her own, wondering how I am and how I am coping with this unexpected spotlight. Eventually, it all became too much for her. She couldn't wait until Thursday to see me so she booked a flight on Saturday, flew out on Sunday and arrived this afternoon. Fiona needs to make sure that I am okay, just as much as I am grateful that she is around me now, there to offer comfort and support when it is needed.

People forget we have families at times like this. My wife and children have to live through this in London, just as Roy Keane's family have to get through it in Manchester and Cork. It is not easy for them, they suffer as much as we do. There are no winners in any of this; we all hurt. My family are just as isolated as I am. They wonder, as I do, if I will ever be able to walk down the street in Dublin again. They wonder if the country I have given so much to as a player and a manager will turn its back on me now.

Those worries are well founded. Fiona confirms that the newspapers in England have been dominated by my row with Roy Keane. They are, in the main she says, on my side. Back home in Ireland, it is a different story. Roy's people have organised a television interview for him with RTE tonight. He has been granted uninterrupted access to a full thirty minutes of prime-time television by our national broadcaster. No such offer has been made to me but what the hell. Roy Keane is welcome to his crocodile tears.

As I contemplate sleep, the do-gooders and the busybodies are starting to kick into action in Ireland, ahead of Roy Keane's interview with Tommie Gorman. The word on the street is that Roy Keane is about to apologise to me. All and sundry expect that such an apology will be enough to pave the way for his World Cup comeback. I have bad news for them, if they ever ask.

They don't, they are too busy sorting out my life without

involving me. That irks. I am well shielded from their good intentions but behind the scenes a whole posse of people seem to be arranging a deal with Roy Keane to facilitate his return. Politicians, FAI officials, solicitors, even journalists are all in on the act. Phones are buzzing between Izumo, Dublin, Manchester and London. Why?

Do these people seriously believe that Roy Keane's return would benefit this Irish squad after everything we have been through? Do they know something that I don't about my players and their attitude to Keane after his tantrum last week? It baffles me that these glory-seekers are sticking their nose into team business, my business. I am the only one in charge of team affairs with the Irish football squad. If Roy Keane ever comes back, he comes back on my terms and my terms only. Right now there is more chance of Mick McCarthy playing for Ireland at the World Cup finals.

I will repeat myself, I don't want to see Roy Keane in this World Cup again. The players don't want him back. Some of them have told me they will go straight home if he comes through the front door of this hotel. They are happy without him. The cloud has been lifted. They are getting on with life in a jovial and relaxed mood. They no longer look over their shoulders, they no longer wonder if their captain will growl or grin today.

If the busybodies back in Ireland and England ever bother to ask me, and it's easy to locate me on the phone out here, I'll tell them they are wasting their time. Roy Keane is history.

TUESDAY 28th MAY

Welcome to the worst day of my professional life. No, welcome to one of the worst days of my life, period. I am at a crossroads now. Roy Keane has been on television back in Ireland overnight and is winning the PR battle hands down. Only the tears were missing apparently, and even they were close, as the aggressor convinced the nation he is the aggrieved. Damage limitation is now the aim for Roy Keane and his advisors. They are slowly but surely cultivating the impression that Mick McCarthy and the FAI are to blame for the Manchester United captain's return home.

Those prepared to forgive and forget, and there are many, are conveniently burying the fact that Roy Keane quit on Ireland three times this night last week, that he hurled abuse at his manager in front of thirty-two other players and staff last Thursday. Decency is a victim in this propaganda war and I am losing heart.

All the talk from those pulling Roy Keane's strings suggest he will apologise and put the ball back into my court. I doubt it personally, I cannot see the Roy Keane I know backing down on this one but I have to listen to what Liam Gaskin, the FAI and the few friends I have left in this world are telling me. If they are right, if he apologises, the pressure is on me to be big enough and accept it, to act like a man and take him back.

I am heading into a no-win situation. If he makes that apology, the consensus is that I will have to take him back. The country will demand it. But if I allow him to return, some players will revolt, and personally I would have to consider my position in the future, when it is all over. I do not want him back in Japan, and if he is forced on me by the FAI, I may have to quit when this World Cup is over. Thankfully there has been no suggestion that the FAI would do that, their support has been rock solid and much appreciated by me.

By the same token, I have no intention of walking away from this job here and now and making life easy for those who want to bring Keane back. Why should I? I have done nothing wrong. I have only ever done what I felt was right for Ireland. Why should I allow this incident to bully me out of my job? Why should I be forced out of the best job in the world a few days before the World Cup begins?

I ring Liam in Dublin when I get up and ask if there was any apology issued on RTE television as I slept. His friends at the *Star* are getting us a transcript of the interview but it seems that Roy Keane went close to an apology a few times, but never close enough to force me into a corner. The ball is, however, back in my court. It is now early in the morning in Izumo and it's like feeding time at the zoo outside our team hotel. A posse of journalists has camped on the steps of the hotel. They still have time to make the late editions back home and they deserve a reply to the interview. Brendan McKenna arranges an impromptu press conference outside the front door and I am happy to talk to them.

The journalists suggest that Roy Keane has apologised. My information tells a different tale but I turn the tables anyway. I acknowledge that the door can still be opened to Roy Keane, but only on my terms, which must include a phone call direct to me, not dialogue through interviews or intermediaries.

We are, I explain, talking about two very strong-willed men. Two peas from the same pod, in many ways. I am as much a winner as he is. I want the best for Ireland even more than he does. The more this drags on, the less likely either of us is to make a conciliatory gesture. It has been allowed to develop into a PR war but I am prepared to open the door to Roy Keane if he makes the first move, if he apologises. I will listen to him if he makes the call.

In my experience, apologies are made man to man. They are not handed out on national television, they are not offered through the front or back pages of the national press. Sometimes in life you have to bite the bullet, you have to swallow your pride and say you are sorry if you really want to achieve something. My case is no different. If he apologises, I may have to take my own pride in hand, accept the wishes of the country and take Roy Keane back, no matter how much that would hurt me and go against my standards.

I am in charge of the Irish team but if the Irish nation tells me to pick Roy Keane, then I may have to pick him and consider my future afterwards. Likewise, if Roy Keane really wants to play in the World Cup, then he has to pick up the phone and ring the hotel. He has spoken to three and a half million people on television back home and told them there is a chance he could still play in this World Cup, even if it is an outside chance. If that is indeed the case, then surely we can have one more conversation on the subject, surely he can ring me. It will not hurt to talk to me again when he realises the value of the reward at the other end of the conversation. If Roy Keane really wants to play for his country, he knows where I am. He can get through to the hotel. A guy got through last night claiming to be Terry Wogan. All he has to do is make the phone call. He knows the score, he knows what's going on, what he needs to do. Let us see if he is big enough to pick up the phone and ring me.

Back inside the hotel, I read the full transcript of Keane's TV interview, which has been faxed through from Dublin. It does not make for pretty reading. There is no sign of an apology and little sign of remorse.

That's it. I have had enough of all this now. The endless debate on the subject is working against the one thing we came out here to do. It is eating into our World Cup and it is time to call an end to it. Let's forget about him and move on. Let's concentrate on the game on Saturday. I decide to call a meeting with the players before we go training. I need to put their minds at ease as rumours sweep through the hotel, again, that Roy Keane is coming back. The suggestion that we are a one-man team, that he got us here on his own, needs to be put to bed as well. More than anything, I want to know where they stand now.

I sit down with the twenty-two players and the staff and tell it as it is. I explain that, having read his transcript and considered his interview, I realise he has not apologised and, it appears to me, he has no intention of doing so. As a result, I do not want Roy Keane back, no matter what was said on the steps of the hotel this morning. If he comes back against my wishes, I tell them that I may walk. I cannot look any player in the eye and tell him that he will not play in the World Cup because Roy Keane is coming back.

It has moved beyond what was said in Saipan last Thursday. I now believe that the squad is a better squad without Roy Keane, that the players are happier, more content and even more determined than ever to do well without his influence around the place. He was prepared to walk away from those same players last week before I eventually sent him home. He has said nothing on RTE about wanting to play for them or with them. He has offered no sign of remorse with this 'poor boy harmed' routine.

Any Roy Keane return would, in my opinion, shatter morale within this squad now. We might as well pack up and leave him to play the World Cup on his own. I tell them I may find it impossible to work with Roy Keane, even if he apologises. I do not want to sit in the same room as that man, never mind work with him. I sent him home and I don't want him back. If the players feel otherwise, however, I will listen to them. If they tell me they are prepared to forgive Roy Keane for the sake of the World Cup, then I will accept their judgement and abide by it. If they tell me we are a better side with Roy Keane in the team, then fine, I will go with them. I may have to rethink my own situation after the World Cup finals if that is the case but I will do whatever they feel is best for Ireland.

I lay my position on the line and tell them I need to know where they stand. They were in the room in Saipan, they saw what happened and heard what was said. In my mind it was unacceptable and I ask the players whether they are prepared to accept that kind of behaviour. And then I leave the room, taking the staff with me. All twenty-two players stay behind to decide exactly what they are going to do. Their meeting takes about twenty minutes, delaying the start of the training session.

We depart for the training ground and some of the players work on a statement for the media, down at the back of the bus. By the time we get to the ground, just five minutes up the road, they have a press release ready which they ask me to approve. I am delighted, and surprised by the statement, which reads:

> Regrettably the manner of Roy's behaviour prior to his departure from Saipan and the comments attributed to him since have left the staff and players in no doubt that the interests of the squad are best served without Roy's presence.
>
> The players bear no malice towards Roy on a personal level and are looking forward to a successful World Cup with the complete support of our loyal supporters, both home and abroad.

The door which I had appeared to open to Roy Keane this morning is now, it appears, closing rapidly. The players also want to bring this to an end, they have backed me, shown the world that they are behind their manager on this. You have no idea how good that feels. I know the storm this hard-hitting statement will kick up but it is, I believe, indicative of how we all feel right now.

We train, very well as it happens. It seems that the football pitch is offering the players real sanctuary from the furore and they are relishing the two hours of escape every day. Jason McAteer, Gary Breen, Kenny Cunningham, Steve Finnan and Lee Carsley are now fully involved. All the players who want to play in the World Cup are fully fit. The players have smiles on their faces. Every so often one of them will go down in a heap, pretending to be at the centre of another training ground bust-up. Apparently Quinny and Robbie came to blows last week but I missed that one.

Some of the players are flying now, four days before our first game. The two Garys, Kelly and Breen, are pushing hard for a place in the starting team. Jason's fitness is okay but Steven Reid is on fire. He is so strong, mentally and physically, and he hits the ball like a rocket. David Connolly is also hitting the mark on the training ground. He has taken a shine to this new ball and is scoring for fun. At least I have something other than Roy Keane to think about, however briefly.

Of course, that issue soon comes to life again. I have no idea when the player's statement will be released. It was written on the back of the bus on the way to training and they have it typed up while we are working. The plan, I believe, is to release it after I update the media on my reaction to Roy Keane's television appearance, now that I have read the full transcript, but nothing goes to plan today. My press conference is delayed to allow Brendan Menton to get back from a FIFA meeting in Seoul in time to add his presence to the podium. I go back to the hotel as the players' statement is released, prematurely, to the press. FAI media officer Brendan McKenna is left to carry the can as accusations of player power rain down on the top table.

As strange as it seems, having previously blamed me for the whole sorry episode, some are now accusing me of kowtowing to the players. The accusation is so far removed from the truth. The players only voted against a Roy Keane return after I outlined my opposition to any such move. They feared that Roy Keane would be forced back on me by the FAI and wanted to back me up. They wanted the world to know that the Irish players are as opposed to his return as the manager. They, like me, want to bring an end to this issue.

The staff and players head off to visit some children in a local hospital after lunch. My press conference is delayed again but Niall Quinn, well aware of the furore that the players' statement caused this morning, decides to face the media on behalf of the squad to explain the vote and the stance they have taken.

More than anything, Niall wants to make it clear that the players have acted in my defence. He outlines the timetable of events behind the statement and the level of support for me as manager that exists within the squad. Their statement was a public gesture of that support.

Quinny goes on to say that the squad want to do what is best for Ireland. If that means bringing an end to the conflict between Roy and me then, despite everything that has happened today, Niall would gladly act as peace broker, no matter what his former captain said about him over the past forty-eight hours.

Niall reveals how the issue is affecting certain players, how he is struggling to sleep at night, how David Connolly approached him here in Izumo and asked his attitude to a Roy Keane return. Quinny has spent serious time on the phone with Michael Kennedy, his solicitor as well as Roy Keane's, and believes the two sides can be brought together if Roy Keane is prepared to apologise. He also says that everything will become much clearer when I hold my press conference, now put back until after tea-time as we await Brendan Menton's arrival from Seoul.

Ireland's World Cup campaign must look like a total mess to the outsider. Cameroon must be rubbing their hands in glee. I am sure they worried about Roy Keane when the draw was made. Little did they know his actions would play into their hands like this. Back at the hotel, I drag my heels with Fiona in tow. Half the world, it seems, is attempting to broker a deal to get Roy Keane back without talking to me. It is amazing that all these diplomatic efforts are being kept from me.

Niall comes to see me on his return. He wants to clarify some issues that arose at his conference and re-iterates the depth of support for me within the squad. They are worried that public opinion will turn against me, that the nation will look for Roy's return no matter what the cost is to me. The players do not want to see me hung out to dry. If the nation want Roy Keane back, the players want to ensure that Mick McCarthy is still the Irish manager, that any deal protects my position even if that means they have to backtrack on their earlier vote.

Big Niall and the players are prepared to back any plan that can benefit everyone, even Roy Keane, so long as it protects my tenure as manager. He spends forty-five minutes with me, endeavouring to find some way to work things out to everyone's satisfaction. He has been on the phone constantly to Michael Kennedy since this morning's vote and still believes a deal can be done for the good of the country.

I feel sorry for Niall. He has been dragged into this and all he really wants to do is what is best for the squad and what's best for Ireland. I am still not sure exactly what that is, what the best thing is for Ireland's World Cup. He wants my blessing to make one last call to Kennedy and see what can be done. I tell him to make that phone call but remind him that Roy Keane must apologise. I can't see it working but it's worth his time making the effort. I will do anything now to try and end this.

Eventually, Brendan Menton returns and we head back to the Dome for the worst press conference I have ever been involved in. The knives are out big time as Brendan Menton, Brendan McKenna, Taff and I take to the podium. The conference is relayed back to Ireland on live television and the presence of the cameras kick-starts some of my most ardent critics.

Did I put a gun to the players' heads this morning? No. I did not force any decision on them nor was I even present in the room when they discussed their strategy before their vote. I had made my point at that stage and left. I merely wanted to know exactly where they stood as I had outlined the content of Roy's television interview and the lack of any attempt at an apology. I wanted closure on all this before it jettisons our game against Cameroon on Saturday.

I did open the door to Roy Keane on the steps of the hotel but I was led to believe by the media, at that stage, that an apology had been made. Not directly to me, of course. There is a protocol for apologies in the real world and that has not been followed in this case. When I read the full transcript after that initial briefing, I realised no apology had been made and none looked forthcoming. Brendan Menton had informed me this morning that he had it on good authority from Roy Keane's people that he would apologise last night but that promise was not kept. I have to move on here. We have a game on Saturday, the first game in the World Cup finals that we all worked so hard to reach over the past two years, that's why I called the meeting with the players.

This story has long fingers that are reaching out and touching a lot of people and a lot of lives and it needs closure now. Aware of the efforts that Niall is making behind the scenes, I know that an apology may yet be forthcoming but this is not up for discussion now at this press conference.

I am asked how all this will influence the fans and my relationship with them. That's a question I do not have the answer to, unfortunately.

How will the players feel if Roy Keane apologises since they voted him out of the World Cup this morning? If an apology is made, I will discuss it with the players and the staff, the only people who were in that room last week, when Roy Keane lost his temper with me from the moment he opened his mouth – a fact that seems to be forgotten now.

Did I accuse Roy Keane of feigning injury, as he has alleged? No, when I asked him if friendlies were beneath his dignity he said yes, so I asked him did he pick and choose games and he said yes, he did. He said friendlies were not for him. Iran was mentioned in terms of picking and choosing the games he played in, after he had told me on the Saturday night that he would travel, and he did refer to a 'deal with his gaffer' but I am not going down that line in this press conference. The Iran game is not on this agenda as far as I am concerned.

More and more questions, and thinly veiled accusations are hurled at me. Some of the anti-McCarthyites within the media are using this whole thing as a lever to get at me and they are having a field day. The venom and the vitriol in the room is incredible. They are like animals in for the kill. It's a frenzy.

My backside is out the window here, big time, I am completely exposed to the media's onslaught. Brendan Menton pulls me out of the conference, almost drags me away. Perhaps I didn't do myself any favours leaving like that but it is a good job I got away. I am seething with rage. I will never forget how some of those journalists have treated me today.

The pressure on me to lower my standards, to go against my convictions on this issue, is really getting to me. Despite the visible support for me, I still feel alone, isolated and exposed. The FAI are behind me, the players and staff are behind me but so much is going on behind the scenes that undermines my position as Irish manager. The busybodies are working away to get Roy Keane back. Some misguided idiots still believe his return will serve Ireland well when the World Cup kicks off for us in Niigata on Saturday. Some are even prepared to get me out in order to get him back. I am gripped by siege mentality now and it is not getting any easier as the day drags on.

On my return to the hotel, Quinny comes to see me again. He is still working away in the background and wants to know how it went at the press conference. I cannot paint a pretty picture as I sit in the team room upstairs, over a dinner that feels more like the last supper, with Fiona, Liam and Brendan Menton. Taff and Packie are there as well and Mick Byrne pops in from time to time to keep my spirits up.

Niall explains, as he had done earlier, that the players are concerned that I am about to be shafted in all of this. Their worry is that Roy Keane will be forced on me and I will be hung out to dry. They are also of the opinion that I may be left with no choice but to take Keane back. Niall believes that Keane will call and will apologise. He assures me that the squad will stand by me, no matter what I do. If I have to give ground and let him return to Japan, they will abide by my decision even though they have stated publicly earlier today that they don't want him back. An emotional Quinny is literally in tears as we throw the debate backwards and forwards. Niall makes it clear to me once again that the players' statement this morning was an attempt to show the world that their allegiance is to Mick McCarthy and not Roy Keane. It is good to hear such support from my players. I need it.

Events take another twist when Brendan Menton is told that Roy Keane will apologise in the morning, Japanese time. It is definite now, according to Roy Keane's advisors in their negotiations with FAI officials. Taff goes to see the players downstairs and tells them the news. If I want to bring him back, they will support me.

I don't. I still have no desire to work with Roy Keane again at this World Cup but if he apologises, I realise now that it is something I will have to consider. If the Irish people want him back, I have to accept their wishes. What do I do then? Do I quit three days ahead of the World Cup, give up everything I worked so hard to achieve? No chance. Come hell or high water I will go through these World Cup finals no matter what happens now. I have earned the right to be here, the players and the staff want me here and I will not walk away from them. After the World Cup is a different matter but we will cross that bridge when we get to it.

Brendan tells me to expect a call from Roy Keane in the morning. I am shattered, dead on my feet. I need to sleep. I tell Brendan to get him to ring at ten a.m. local time, two a.m. in Ireland.

It appears Roy Keane is on the way back.

WEDNESDAY 29th MAY

I slept soundly again last night but when I wake at eight o'clock I am still tired. This business is really getting to me, it is getting to all of us.

Today is judgement day. Today, I will know where I stand, where Roy Keane stands in all of this. He is due to ring in a couple of hours' time. All he has to do is say 'I'm sorry' and he could be on the way back to the World Cup, with just enough time to play against Cameroon on Saturday. I believe he is about to apologise.

But is he? A note is waiting under the door, left by Brendan Menton around three hours ago. Roy Keane has issued a statement through RTE in Dublin. He is not coming back.

His statement reads:

> In the interests of all genuine supporters of Irish football I believe that the time has now arrived when I should bring to a conclusion the continuing speculation with regard to my participation in the World Cup and for the players to concentrate fully on their preparations for the competition free from all further distraction.
>
> Whilst I appreciate all the support which I have received and all the efforts which have been made by a number of people on behalf of all the parties involved in this unfortunate matter, I do not consider that the best interests of Irish football will be served by my returning to the World Cup.
>
> The damage has been done. I wish the team and the management all the best and they will have my full support throughout the competition. I urge all the people of Ireland to give their entire support to the team. I do not feel that any useful purpose will be served by my making any further comment.

The nation expected two words and he has given us 167. I feared an apology, instead he is finally out of the World Cup and wishes the management the best of luck without him! I am ecstatic.

It has taken Keane eight full days to finally do what he tried to do in Saipan last Tuesday night and quit the World Cup, international football and the green jersey. He has tortured and tormented so many of us in the days and nights since then, perhaps even himself. He has made my World Cup a misery so far. He has put my family, and probably his own, through hell. He has split the Irish nation. He has walked away from the players he captained. And still he is a hero in some people's eyes, still there are people out there who will lament his World Cup exit.

Keane clearly feels he has nothing to apologise for. He maintains that he was right and proper to speak to me the way he did, in front of my players and staff, last Thursday night.

What baffles me now is the finality of this latest twist. As I went to bed last night, I was led to believe that Keane would make a call and apologise this morning. I had prepared myself for that call, I was ready to accept his return on the back of the apology and then work out my own post-World Cup strategy. That is what I believed the Irish people wanted but now Keane, and Keane alone, has taken the final decision in all of this. It is down to him that he is not on his way back today, no one else can be blamed for that one. I was prepared to move, despite everything, if public opinion wanted him back, if my players wanted him back.

Now, I wonder if Roy Keane ever intended to come back. Maybe his truest actions came when he quit in Saipan over a week ago. For whatever reasons, he did not abide by that retirement decision then. Instead, he has engaged in eight days of limiting the damage to his own public image while doing his best to destroy mine. I am not the aggressor here, yet his PR machine has won the battle, hands down. They have depicted me as a monster who has forced Keane out of the World Cup. His torment may be over but mine will continue. This has been the worst week of my football life, without a shadow of a doubt. I am a stronger person for it, but it has been difficult. I would not wish this experience on anyone, friend or foe.

Somehow, I have put a brave face on and struggled through it. The first person I have had to motivate every day in order to keep the train on the tracks was myself. That was not easy. When you are told you can't manage, you can't coach and you can't make a decision by the best midfielder in the world, self-doubt is bound to creep in. I have had to fight through all that and attempt to prepare for a World Cup finals.

The last week has left me feeling drained emotionally and physically. I have been through every emotion possible but I have had to keep up my morale and that of the team. I have had to work bloody hard to ensure that the team spirit and camaraderie we have built up over the last six years is not destroyed by the actions of the man who came out here as Irish captain.

I regret the incident. I am sorry it ever happened in the first place but I do not, for one second, regret anything I have done in the past week. I have nothing to be ashamed of. All I have ever tried to do, as player and manager, is the best for my country. I think I have done a bloody good job as it happens, on both acounts.

I was never trained to handle a crisis like this. I don't think any football manager can be prepared for something of this magnitude. What happened in Saipan came along to test me and everyone else involved with this Irish squad.

Now, at last and at least, I hope we can move on. This is not what the World Cup is about. The young players who dreamed of such an occasion when they watched Italia '90 and USA '94 did not deserve this. They must be wondering why they have come to Japan, asking themselves if the World Cup is really worth it. That is the biggest tragedy of all this. It has robbed the players of the feeling of enjoyment that should go with the greatest achievement of their professional careers thus far.

It has robbed the nation of World Cup joy as well, so far. We must all unite now, we must march down the one road. I do not care what the people think about me, for the moment at least. Some will support me, some will back Keane. The only important thing between now and Saturday is the team. The team needs the country behind it more than ever.

I have got to get these players up for the game, get them focused on Cameroon. We are going into the World Cup without our best player, the legacy of that will be decided by events on the football field come Saturday. If ever an Irish team needs a big game, it is now. The players can diffuse all the heat and all the pressure if we get a result against Cameroon. I tell them as much at training this morning and I can see they are champing at the bit.

They heard the news about Keane this morning, Niall even earlier than I did, and the players too are glad that we have finally reached finality on this issue. Training is lively and bubbly. Jason is now fully active while Mark Kinsella sits out the session as a precaution. I just want Mark to play on Saturday. What he does between now and then is irrelevant as long as he is fit for the match.

Back in the hotel, I lie down on my bed with a book and fall asleep for two hours. It is most unlike me and is indicative of the stress I have been under. I am woken in time for the press conference.

Some of the English papers have suggested overnight that I will quit the Irish job as soon as the World Cup is over. I certainly considered a lot of things this past week. If Keane had been forced on me, I would have been out the door and on a plane back to London. Even if he had apologised, I may have considered my options after the tournament. My position may well have been untenable in those circumstances. But my relationship with the FAI is stronger than ever now. Brendan Menton says as much publicly at this press conference, John Delaney and Milo Corcoran have said it to me personally. They have stood by me and I am grateful for their support. I have no reason to consider my future now.

Tonight, I unwind with a few beers with some of the staff. We end up in a Karaoke bar around the corner from the hotel. Someone plays U2's 'With or Without You'. Even I manage a smile at that one.

THURSDAY 30th MAY

Roy Keane is still a part of the Republic of Ireland World Cup squad. FIFA have finally turned down our appeal to bring in Colin Healy as a replacement. They faxed the decision through to the FAI overnight and we must enter the tournament with twenty-two players, one fewer than in the other thirty-one countries' squads.

I am not surprised. It is not the end of the world, it is hardly an issue in light of some of the problems thrown at me in recent days. But I am annoyed when the decision is made definite this morning. My anger is based on regret, the regret that Colin Healy has missed out on the chance to join the Republic of Ireland squad at the World Cup finals. I feel for him right now. I feel sick that I didn't call him in last week and let Roy Keane go home when he first said he wanted to.

I know I left Colin out of the original twenty-three-man squad when I named it in May. I felt at the time that he was a great bet for the future, but I did not believe for one second that Keane would not play in Japan. Now, after Keane's expulsion, Colin has been denied an immediate chance to sample the World Cup atmosphere. God knows what that might have done for his career.

He was not going to come out here and go straight into the team, he knew that as well as I did when we spoke on a very crackled line from Saipan. Mattie Holland, Mark Kinsella and Lee Carsley were ahead of him in that queue but World Cups throw up new heroes from the most unexpected sources. Maybe this could have been Colin's chance. We will never know now but it irks me still.

Keane knew I could bring the squad back up to twenty-three players when he attempted to retire from international football that Tuesday evening. He said then that he did not want his country to go to the World Cup with just twenty-two players. And here we are, a day away from our flight to Niigata for the opening game, with a twenty-two-man squad.

Anyway, to hell with it. I have more important things to worry about. I am two days away from kick-off in the biggest game of my life and only now can I get around to thinking about team selection. What a week.

The real test is only beginning for me now. I am not stupid, I am not as green as I am cabbage-looking. I know that the football world, never mind the entire Irish nation, is waiting to see what happens in the Big Swan stadium come Saturday afternoon. My career, my judgement, my management is under the microscope now like never before. If Ireland win or get a draw, I will be a hero. I will have risen above the crisis and inspired these Irish players to one of their finest hours in the wake of incredible drama. If we lose, I am a goner. I will be blamed for assassinating Ireland's World Cup hopes when I sent Keane home. I will be cast aside as the leper who let his country down when I took a stand against my captain.

The players will escape censure if it all goes wrong on Saturday. They will not be blamed because their manager will be seen as the one who did the dirty deed and exposed them to the pressure that has followed us from Saipan to Izumo.

I seek solace from the Shinto gods. Mayor Nishio has invited me to the Tachai temple this morning and the trip is a resounding success. It is so peaceful and calm as I mingle, metaphorically speaking, with the eight million gods. The mayor assures me his gods are on my side. He says they guided us here through the Group of Death and they will guide us into the second phase of the World Cup finals. I want to believe him. Mayor Nishio arranges for my fortune to be read and it says we are going east, which represents good luck. I enquire if South Korea is east of Izumo as I pin my fortune to one of the trees in front of the temple.

My spirits are high after this trip to the temple. Izumo, despite all the controversy surrounding one player, has been good for Ireland. I tell Mayor Nishio as much as we head for the only closed training session of our week in Izumo. All along, the people of this city have done us proud. In any other set of circumstances, they would be heroes of this story. They have welcomed us with open arms, they have come out to cheer us on in training sessions, they have become more Irish than the Irish themselves. They have placed Irish flags all over their city, they have arranged Irish exhibitions, they have even put draught Guinness on offer at a stall in the shopping centre. And they have made us feel so welcome.

Today, I have to close the doors to the Hamayama Stadium to our new Japanese friends. I need to work on corners and free-kicks away from the glare of the cameras. I need to ensure that some of Ireland's World Cup preparations are kept from Cameroon eyes at the end of a week when everything to do with Irish football has been exposed.

I also need to decide on a team. There are only two issues in my head, providing that Jason McAteer is fully fit. He is laughing again, always the barometer with Jase, and he is putting himself about in the training sessions. I think he will be fine but I am going to nail the issue when we train at the Big Swan on Friday afternoon. I want him to play, I want him to start the World Cup but I will ask him to test his fitness to the limit tomorrow and see if he can take the rigours of a World Cup match. Right now, I believe he will play.

That leaves me with two questions to answer, Gary Kelly or Steve Finnan at right-back and Gary Breen or Kenny Cunningham in the middle of the defence?

The first decision is made after training today. I pull Kells and tell him he is playing. He has worked his way into the side on the back of his performances, in matches and in practice, ever since we gathered in Sunderland almost a fortnight ago. It is a tough call on Steve Finnan but Gary deserves his chance and he deserves to know about it now.

I have no worries about Gary's playing ability. He was first choice at the start of the season when Stephen Carr got injured and only that red card against Holland, and the suspension that followed, cost him his place in the team for the rest of the qualifiers. Who knows what might have happened if he hadn't been sent-off for that foul on Overmars. Nobody would even have questioned the decision to start the World Cup with him if he had played the full ninety minutes against the Dutch.

Gary's demeanour and morale have also helped his case. He has been a giant within the squad over the past ten days, he has kept heads and spirits up. His attitude has been exemplary ever since it all went off in Saipan. I will tell Steve the bad news when we train tomorrow but Kells is in on merit for this game.

Gary Breen is also very close to the team. He was a little aggrieved when he received the number fourteen shirt for the Nigeria game but I did tell him then that he could play his way into the side. I have a feeling I am about to be true to my word as far as Gary is concerned.

Everyone else is fine. Mark Kinsella trains today after resting his knee yesterday, Ian Harte sits out the game as a precaution. He has a blister on his heel but that will not be enough to put his World Cup place at risk. There is a great buzz about the squad as we train for the last time in Izumo. The players are looking forward to Cameroon.

It is around this time before a match that we start to really focus on the game and get into the zone. We will play our usual 4–4–2 against their 3–5–2 but the players are well used to such tactics. I remind the front men to stay up when Cameroon break and put pressure on their midfield players to stay back.

Central midfield is not a worry for me. Kinse and Mattie both know the score, both have the bit between their teeth now. I back their abilities at the press conference, back beside the Dome. New heroes will emerge on Saturday. New stars will take to the World Cup stage. We have sent our biggest name home but this is not a one-man team. Not by a long shot.

Damien Duff, Clinton Morrison, Steven Reid and Mattie Holland follow me into the press conference. Duffer admits that the Keane affair has taken some of the gloss off the World Cup for the younger players. I am not surprised to hear that they have struggled to enjoy the whole experience so far. It will change come Saturday, the game will overtake everything. Duffer acknowledges as much and talks about the determination to do the country proud, now more than ever.

He is followed onto centre-stage by Clinton. The guy is pure entertainment. He has the press eating out of his hands and laughing all the way back to their downtown hotel. Kells look out, there's a new joker in the pack.

Tonight, we say goodbye to Izumo. The mayor has organised a going-away ceremony in the Dome and a city wishes us well on our World Cup voyage. I thank the people for their hospitality and tell them I will be back someday. I will keep that promise.

Back at the hotel, I go to see Jason. I am still uncertain about his fitness and I want to hear what he has to say on the subject. I ask him to give me an honest answer to an honest question. Can you play on Saturday? Yes, he says. And I believe him.

Later again, President Mary McAleese rings the hotel. She wishes us all well on behalf of the Irish nation ahead of Saturday's game. See, it is good to talk.

NINE

31 May–1 June, Niigata

FRIDAY 31st MAY

Niigata is the start of the real World Cup. The players realise that as soon as the plane chartered by JAWOC, Japan's World Cup Organising Committee, arrives in town. Welcome to officialdom. We are whisked off the plane and straight onto the coach as soon as we land at the airport. There is an air of formality about the proceedings that was missing throughout our time at the training camps in Saipan and Izumo. FIFA take control at this point. They dictate what time you can train at the stadium, when you can talk to the media.

We are scheduled to see the Big Swan for the first time at 4.30 this afternoon. I can sense excitement in the air as the coach departs the Hotel Niigata for this brand-new, purpose-built stadium. This is finally what it's all about. This is why we are in Japan, why we worked our backsides off for the past two years. It is a proud moment for us all as the bus pulls into the cavernous tunnel underneath the stand and we disembark for the first time as World Cup finalists in a World Cup stadium.

There is something special about today. The lads can feel it, touch it, as they stroll through the dressing-rooms and out into this masterpiece of modern architecture. Hartey, not normally a man of words, stands on the pitch and declares that he finally understands what the World Cup is all about. He is not alone. We are global players now on the biggest stage of all. Millions will turn on their television sets tomorrow to watch the Republic of Ireland play Cameroon on this very pitch. People who wouldn't normally dream of watching a football match will switch on to the World Cup. This is what it is all about.

I am a proud man as the players warm-up behind closed doors on that billiard table surface. This is my team, this is my moment. No one can take this away from me. Some have tried to ruin it for me in recent days but they are forgotten now. There were times in the midst of the crisis when I wondered if I would ever see this stadium, ever stand on this pitch less than twenty-four hours before kick-off.

The players go through their paces. I pull Stevie Finnan and tell him I am going with Gary tomorrow. He is unlucky. Stevie was voted the Premiership's right-back of the season on merit and he is a world-class player. He has had his problems with injury over the last few weeks but he was very close to this team. My gut instinct is to start with Kells and I explain why to Stevie. His response is measured. I have yet to meet a player who is happy to be told he has been dropped, but Stevie is a complete professional and accepts the decision with dignity.

Likewise, Gary Breen is in ahead of Kenny Cunningham. It is a tough call on Kenny, one of the most consistent performers with Ireland since I got the job back in 1996. Gary is the man on form right now though. He has been driven and focused since the squad met up and he is the man to partner Stan against Eto'o and Mboma tomorrow.

The rest of the team is as expected. Shay in goals, Hartey opposite Kells, Gary and Stan in the centre at the back.

Jason has done enough to start on the right in midfield. I push him hard before the training session. I take him down under the stadium and introduce him to a wall. First, I block tackle the wall. Kick it and the ball, just to show him what I want him to do. Then I get him to block the ball hard against the wall four or five times. No problem to him, thank God. Back on grass, I get him to twist and turn under pressure and he seems fine. I want him there tomorrow and he will start. I have put my faith in him to deliver now and tell him as much as I run through the team selection with each of the lads.

Mattie and Kinse were always going to play in the middle once I sent Roy Keane home. Likewise, Kevin Kilbane, or Killer as the lads call him, offers no surprise on the left side of midfield.

Duffer and Robbie are upfront, the worst-kept secret in world football. I remind them that they must stretch Cameroon and put pressure on their 3–5–1 shape. That is going to be a key tactic for us tomorrow. Michael Owen did it for England in Kobe last Sunday and I just know the tactic can work for us against Rigobert Song, Raymond Kalla and co.

We throw the session open to the photographers for the last fifteen minutes, then it's into the official FIFA press conference. For some reason there is no specific room for the managerial press conferences in use at any venue in this World Cup finals. Instead we all exit through an area dubbed the mixed zone because the players must walk through the press to get out to the coach, and can stop to talk as they feel fit. It is not the answer for either the teams or the media but we have to get on with it. Today, I stay for a little over ten minutes. I am asked to name the team and refuse. Let's see who can get the eleven names right in their preview.

I am a happy man now, or so I make out to the press. I talk of the immense pride I felt when we walked onto the pitch for the first time this afternoon, how this is my team and my World Cup. I am up there now as a World Cup manager with Jack Charlton, a mentor and one of my best friends in football. The proudest moment of my playing career came when I captained Jack's team at the quarter-finals back in 1990, but this achievement means more to me now, especially after everything that has been thrown at me over the last ten days.

Can we reach the last eight again? I am optimistic about our World Cup chances but I am only looking to get out of the group at this stage. Cameroon impressed me last Sunday as a side that can match the Germans in this competition. They will be our toughest opponents because they are our first opponents. We need to get through tomorrow's game without a defeat. If we can take anything out of this game, then we have a real chance of progressing. That is as far as I am prepared to look at the moment. Yes, we must regard this as a league rather than a knock-out but the first game is vital. I want to win it but I do not want to lose it, at any cost.

Back at the hotel, the team sponsors Eircom have laid out a book of well wishes from back home, messages that have been sent to the players via their World Cup website and by fax. I know that someone has censored this collection of e-mails and faxes because there are no references to a former player but they do make for great reading and offer a welcome release so close to kick-off.

Robbie is the big hit of the tournament before a ball has even been kicked, if the message book is anything to go by. I lose track of the number of girls who want his number. Others want to have his baby. It is quite amusing, for an oldie like me at least.

One of the best faxes comes from Danny Lynch, PRO for the Gaelic Athletic Association which runs the sports of hurling and Gaelic football back home. He wishes the team well on behalf of all the members of the Association. That one means a lot to me and to the lads. Many of them are staunch GAA fans.

The goodwill towards the players from the nation is immense. They want the team to forget what's happened and give them a performance to be proud of. I know that feeling is reciprocated by every one of the twenty-two players in this hotel tonight.

The travelling fans have arrived in Niigata as well. As ever the numbers amaze me but I am a little uncomfortable in their presence, I have to admit. I feel isolated as we make our way through the crowd in the hotel lobby and up to our dining-room tonight. There are plenty of slaps on the back for the players, plenty of 'Do it for Ireland!' shouts at the lads, but there is no great warmth towards me. I am not getting paranoid nor am I insecure but I am uneasy with the fans.

I wonder if many of the ordinary people of Ireland have been turned against me back home. The people want the team to do well at the World Cup but some have little faith in my ability to deliver after the Roy Keane affair. The opinion polls may suggest that I am a good guy again, since Roy Keane refused to apologise, but there appeared to be little evidence of that support from those fans tonight. I feel for them, they must be finding it hard to believe that Roy

Keane is not here. I suspect that they are all rallying behind the team now but are unsure about me. If the fans in the team hotel tonight are anything to go by, they want the players to feel loved now more than ever before but there is very little of that passion coming my way. That disappoints me. I have to stand my ground but it is hard tonight, just hours before the game.

Here I am in a busy Japanese city, surrounded by thousands of my fellow countrymen and yet I am lonely. I am out on a limb. More than ever, I need to motivate this team tomorrow. I need to motivate myself. I have to get a performance from this team that will put this whole sorry affair to rest.

The squad are in the zone now, less than thirty-six hours to kick-off and counting. The outside world is just that, left outside.

We run through the schedule at a brief meeting tonight. We remind the players of exactly what is expected from us tomorrow afternoon, what the World Cup means to the fans, those who will travel out here at great expense and those who will get up very early tomorrow to add their long-distance support from home.

For half an hour or so, we talk through the World Cup, what it took to get here, what it will take to make this an enjoyable experience at last for everyone. And then we familiarise them with the tactics that the African champions will employ, tell them who to pick up on corners, what to watch out for on free-kicks. We already know how we will play the game ourselves. Today is about recognition, about ensuring there are no surprises awaiting us from the Cameroons tomorrow afternoon.

We know how they will play and whom they will play. Their side will be the team that started against England last Sunday. It would be silly of Winfried Schaefer to change anything at this stage. I may surprise him tomorrow with one or two faces in a couple of positions but not with the make-up of the team. International sides do not change their shape or their tactics as a rule.

We must deliver against Cameroon. We must march together.

SATURDAY 1st JUNE

World Cup First Round, Group E

Republic of Ireland v Cameroon

Today is the first day of the rest of your life. How often have I read that and thought 'what a stupid notion'. Not today. Today is the first day of the rest of my life in more ways than one. My backside is about to go into the bacon-slicer, big time. The Republic of Ireland is about to take to the World Cup stage and my future is on the line.

I am nervous this morning as I try to relax ahead of our ridiculously early departure for the stadium. Senegal's win over France in Korea last night hasn't helped my digestive system. That was a big win for African football and a big boost for Cameroon ahead of the first game on Japanese soil.

Our game will kick-off at 3.30 p.m. local time but FIFA want us in the Big Swan a full two hours before kick-off, just to be sure, no doubt. Traffic is as big a worry in Japan as it is back in Dublin but today there are no jams. We sail through to the stadium and arrive well ahead of schedule. The Green Army are in town in huge numbers and the locals, it appears, have decided to nail their colours to an Irish mast this afternoon. The green shirts line the route to the Big Swan.

The early start to our journey is not as big a nuisance as I had expected. The players have time to take a stroll around the pitch and soak up the atmosphere. In some ways, I envy them as they take it all in. They are cheered onto the playing surface by the fans, they know they are still loved, still wanted by those supporters. And they have only the game to worry about, they need only concentrate on their own jobs and their own opponents this close to kick-off.

Privately, I feel I am on a different planet to the players and the fans as I stand here on the pitch. I cannot isolate the game from events that have gone by, even this close to the kick-off. I am still nervous about the reception I will get from the fans, still worried about the consequences if it all goes wrong today. I do not want the World Cup to flop for anyone today. I want it to work for the players,

Saipan and the worst week of my life. Announcing Roy Keane's World Cup departure, at a hastily arranged press conference, was the saddest moment of my World Cup.

Leading the team in thanks to our hosts at the spectacular Izumo City Dome.

The picture that says it all.

HERMANS
BAKERY

It is good to get back to football and this is the big one. Steve Staunton leads the team out.

Robbie Keane leads the celebration as Matt Holland equalizes.

The Packie jig.

A draw. This means so much to us all. The celebrations continue in front of the Green Army. I stay on the field. I am not ready yet to risk the bosom of the crowd.

Ireland v Germany 5 June 2002

Bloody hell, we must have scored! We are level with seconds to go.

The final whistle goes and we invade the pitch to share a group hug, and celebrate 'the best 1–1 win' in world football history.

The handstand! Robbie Keane celebrates the greatest goal of his life.

Ireland v Saudi Arabia 11 June 2002

The netbusters. Robbie Keane and Damien Duff enjoy Ireland's third goal.

The number one. Shay Given celebrates as the fans start singing, all the way to Seoul.

Gary Breen salutes the crowd as he emerges the patron saint of our unsung heroes in Japan.

Ireland v Spain 16 June 2002

Robbie Keane tries a little flamenco dancing with Casillas.

United we stand. The lads wait to take their penalties and no matter what happens now, they have so much to be proud of.

There are no regrets as we leave the field, no regrets at all. We gave it our best shot. No one can ask for any more than that.

A hundred thousand fans welcome us home from the Far East.

The response at Phoenix Park proves to us all how much the Irish football team has achieved.

for the supporters, for the country. I know that anything other than a positive result will leave us all open to ridicule and not just from our people. We will be a laughing stock across the globe if we blow it today after sending our best player home. And I will be the one to carry the can if it all goes wrong.

I have no idea what the result of the match will be but I know full well what will happen if it all goes against us now. This is the biggest game of my life, there is no doubt on that score. The one certainty is that I can trust my team, I have one hundred per cent belief in those twenty-two players.

As I am about to go back to the dressing-room, I manage a smile at last. The stadium screen has flashed up a shot of Cameroon's German coach Winfried Schaefer. Then they split the screen with a live shot of the UTV cameraman Albert Kirk, standing with his tripod behind one of the goals. They look like identical twins, long blond hair streaming over their shoulders like the guitar player from Status Quo. Albert, and his presenter Adrian Logan, have been with us since Izumo. They are a great crack, a pleasure to work with and a credit to their station. Even now, this close to the first game of the rest of my life, Albert makes me laugh. I like that in a man; I appreciate it at this moment in time.

Back in the dressing-room, the lads are relaxed. Some head for the warm-up area but they have to be careful. Every ounce of energy spent in there could cost us on the pitch once the game begins. We remind them that a two per cent drop in bodyweight relates to a twenty per cent drop in performance. They are sick to death of hearing it, sick of listening to the need for fluid consumption, but they know it makes sense. We have water and Lucozade waiting for them all around the perimeter of the pitch and they must take it on board at frequent intervals.

The players strip to their playing kit, then head back to the grass for their final warm-up as the sun beats down on the Big Swan. This is the loneliest time for me as an international manager. The ground is filling and you are stuck in the dressing-room, many feet below pitch level, alone with your thoughts and your fears.

I know we can get a result against Cameroon. I know that Damien and Robbie can run their defence into the ground if we get the ball to them. I also know that we must compete across midfield and at the back. Cameroon are slick and fast, they will cross the field with the ball and they will play neat one-twos in front of our central defence. They are not here to make up the numbers.

In previous World Cups, even in 1990 when Roger Milla inspired them to the quarter-finals, you never knew which sort of Cameroon side would turn up. They were so good at going forward, so bad at going backwards. This team is different. Schaefer has instilled some typical German doggedness into their play and they are the better for it. They have learnt how to defend at international level under his leadership and they are a force to be reckoned with now.

I think of these things as I sit in the dressing-room, waiting for the players to return, waiting for the invite to join the party.

They come back and the atmosphere builds. Taff and Packie have stuck a big smiley face on the message board and a simple message – 'No regrets'. This is the theme for the day, the theme for the tournament. We must not come into this dressing-room in two hour's time with the slightest hint of regret.

The air is buzzing with anticipation now. You close your eyes and you hear the shouts. 'Get stuck into them!' 'Give it a go lads!' 'We didn't bust our balls to get here and then lie down!' 'This is it, this is the World Cup!'

Stan is brilliant. He quietly gees the lads up, gets them motivated. The subs are telling the team to get at Cameroon from the kick-off. We are on the brink of the World Cup finals. The sense of achievement is almost as tangible as the anticipation.

Then the knock comes on the door, exactly thirteen minutes before kick-off, bang on schedule. The Japanese referee is ready and wants us out. We hug, we wish each other well. I remind them it is the biggest stage of all, the biggest game of their lives. Make sure you come off after ninety minutes with no regrets. Give your all.

Stan leads them out. The reception from the Irish fans is incredible. Once again, they take us by surprise. I hoped we'd get 5,000 with us this far from home but there could be treble that number in green shirts as I take my seat in the dug-out. The Green Army is up and singing 'Walk on' and it has never sounded as good. We have hope in our hearts like never before; this team will never walk alone. That means so much right now.

We stand for Amhrán na bhFiann. I sing the anthem in Irish, having learnt it phonetically. I stand beside Mick Byrne every match and sing with gusto. I am proud of my country, proud of the song, proud to sing it in our native tongue in a Yorkshire brogue. We stand shoulder to shoulder on the bench as the team faces the flag.

Before the game begins, Stan pulls the players in for a Celtic-style huddle. It is something we planned a few days back. I want the team to unite, to play for each other like never before. He gets them together, tells Breeny to shut up as he is shouting and dominating the huddle and Stan gets them raring to go.

The Green Army are in full voice as the game begins. I am still uncertain as to the whereabouts of Mick's Army but I have no doubts about the guys out on that field. They will do me proud, I know that.

Ireland starts the World Cup in nervy fashion. Our defence looks like it has never played together before, we are giving the ball away too easily and it is costing us. Stan and Breeny are at sixes and sevens at times and that is most unlike them. We have to tighten up, we have to start winning the individual one-on-ones that are so crucial in a game at this level.

Mboma breaks free on nineteen minutes but Shay is equal to the challenge and makes a great save. A minute later Jason drags Salomon Oliembe back and the referee books him, rather harshly if you ask me. Jase is struggling but I give him the benefit of the doubt, for now.

We begin to settle into the game and in the twenty-third minute Robbie goes close with a header. But still the African attack is making life uneasy for me on the bench. I told the guys to watch the Cameroon front two like hawks. They are all over the frontline, they are moving at pace and we are giving them chances.

Real Mallorca's Eto'o puts one wide on thirty minutes and then, nine minutes later, Mboma does the damage with a goal that threatened to turn my hair the colour of Winfried Schaefer's or Albert Kirk's. It is Eto'o who creates the chance. He gets by Stan on the byline and pulls the ball across the face of goal for his partner. Mboma steers it home as Mattie Holland and Kells try to aid Shay Given to no avail.

We are a goal down six minutes before the break. There is never a good time to concede a goal. I am angry, but I am not unduly worried. I know that I can rework the shape of our play in the dressing-room at half-time, I can close the gaps between the defence and midfield and between the midfield and the forwards.

Before we get in for the break, Ian Harte tests Cameroon's defence with a free-kick which Song almost turns past his own 'keeper, Boukar Alioum. I take that as an omen into the dressing-room with me. It is time for diplomacy and gentle words, not tantrums. This game is here for the taking. We are a better side than Cameroon, not on the evidence of the first-half, granted, but we are a better side. Individually, we can lift it a gear, and I feel I can get more out of the side tactically. The Cameroons have scored but they did nothing in that half to frighten me. It is all down to how we react now.

I tell the players they have to start competing in their one-on-one situations, they have to face down their man and nail him. Defensively we have to pull together and play as a unit. We are not solid down the field, we are not playing in those two blocks of four that I have come to expect from my defence and midfield. That too can only improve. The game is passing us by and that has to stop. We have to get to grips with the heat of the battle and start forcing the pace of the match. If we stop giving them chances, if we raise the tempo through the middle then we have a chance. We need to keep Duffer upfront with Robbie and get them the ball.

I have to think about making changes as well. I am concerned about the left side of midfield but decide to give Killer some time to take my speech on board. I know Kevin is a better player than the first-half suggests but maybe the week gone by has taken it out of him. He can do better, he has to. If that improvement fails to materialise, Quinny will come in alongside Robbie with Duffer pushed out to the left.

Jason is a different story. He says he is okay as he lies on the treatment table but he has not looked a hundred per cent in the first-half. To make it worse, he has been booked and he had an ice-pack on his knee when I got into the dressing-room. That confirms it for me. He is coming off, Kells will switch into midfield and Stevie Finnan will play at right-back. I tell them to make the switch work as the team goes back out. I ask them once again to ensure they finish this game with no regrets.

And they do just that. We look like a settled side in the second-half. We are on the front foot from the off, playing as a team, looking like a cohesive unit. Stevie and Kells link like old hands down the right and all of a sudden we are the ones dictating the pace of the game and causing most of the problems for the opposition. Only two minutes into the second-half and a Hartey cross is headed just wide by Killer. This is better. Hartey almost lets Geremi in on goal moments later but we are in control now, we are the better team.

We confirm that five minutes later as a Killer cross from a great run down the left opens up the Cameroon defence and Kalla knocks the ball out with half a clearance. It falls at the feet of Mattie Holland. He lets fly, a carbon copy of his goal in the Stadium of Light against Portugal. The ball squeezes through the narrow gap between Alioum's desperate hand and the post.

We are level and I am up on my feet with the rest of the bench. Elation once again, the stadium is erupting. Mattie runs to celebrate in front of his wife, his two boys and his dad, high in the Big Swan stands. The Green Army dance and sing for joy, 'Walk On', 'The Fields of Athenry'. We are a nation once again. We are back on that one road, North men, South men, comrades all.

We deserve that goal and we dominate the game from here on in, bar one more scare at the feet of Eto'o. Another chance created by an Irish mistake, by the way. There is nothing fortunate about the chances that come our way. We are playing as a unit now, the gaps between our three outfield lines have disappeared. Duffer is causing havoc and we look like scoring again.

Mattie and Mark have taken control in the middle of the field. I am not trying to be malicious here but Matt Holland, in our new central midfield partnership, is my man of the match. He stepped up to the plate like the pro I know he is today. He is showing the world how good he is in his own right, without Roy Keane beside him. And he is not alone, this is no one-man team. Killer is flying down the left, Stan and Breeny are outstanding at the back. We are the only force in this game.

Killer produces another top-of-the-range cross for Breeny in the sixty-second minute. His header strikes Song's hand on the line as Robbie waits to pounce. No penalty. Well you can't win them all.

Legs are tiring now so I throw Steven Reid on for Hartey with fifteen minutes to go. Kells goes to left-back and Reidy announces his arrival with a clattering tackle on the first Cameroon player he meets. Welcome to the World Cup, son.

We are in total control and our stamina looks far stronger than Cameroon's. Saipan must have worked because we are doing all the running, we are creating all the chances late in the game. The best comes when Robbie curls a shot off the woodwork in the eighty-first minute. Then Reidy almost makes it a fairytale debut when Kells tees up a late, late free and Steven's rocket shot is somehow pushed away by Alioum. We almost win the game at the death.

The final whistle arrives. I race onto the pitch and hug the players. This means so much to us all. We have come through the toughest test we will ever face; we exorcised a ghost out there today. We have given the squad and the nation a huge lift. Now we have a display full of commitment and fervour and no little skill to talk about, we have a dream to realise. We always knew we could play at this level, now the world knows it as well. I feel relief more than any other emotion as the players celebrate in front of the fans. It is almost the perfect end to a bad week. Only a win could better this.

The performance and the result settle some things. They prove what I have claimed all along, that Saipan was the right place to take this team for their humidity conditioning. They were the stronger out there, they were the better prepared. We got it right and sod the begrudgers. I take immense personal satisfaction out of this point gained.

And I know I was right to do what I did last week. This performance, more even than the result, proves it. If anyone ever again wants to question my ability as a coach or as a manager, then just look at the video of that second-half performance. I have not lost the players; I have not lost their confidence. Look at how they performed for Ireland and for Mick McCarthy in the second-half today. To manage a team that played like that, to lead a team that turned the game around in that manner, is a matter of enormous pride for me. I know my family are sitting in the stands, Fiona and Anna and Katie and Michael and my sister Catherine, enjoying this moment. I know that my friends Glynn, Tommy and Marion, Mike and Sandra, and Woody, Liam and all those close to me are glad for me now.

The celebrations continue away to my left, in front of the Green Army. I stay on the field, I am not ready yet to risk the bosom of the crowd. I am delighted with the result, thrilled with the manner in which we played the game, but I am not brave enough to question the fans' loyalty to me, not yet anyway. Maybe after the next match, if the German result goes our way. I am not prepared to have my heart broken, I do not want to hear one dissenting voice, so I stay away from the crowd. They were a hundred per cent behind the team today, which is the most important thing, but I am still not sure if they are a hundred per cent behind me.

As I enter the dressing-room, I realise this could be the turning point. I have a new focus now, a new starting point. There will be no calls for Roy Keane to come back immediately after this result. The demands for the guillotine to fall on my head will subside, at least until the next match on Wednesday night. It is a relief to close the door on all that, I need some positivity in my life. I am not a wall with a solid brick heart; I do care, I do bother about what other people think. This whole Keane affair has affected me deeply. But it is fading now, thanks to that Matt Holland goal and a great performance.

As the singing starts in the dressing-room I understand what this means to me and to mine. We can move on, we can begin again, we can forget, for a while at least. Now I can enjoy the World Cup. Other people can talk about Roy Keane but we have other items on the agenda now, for at least the next ten days.

The pressure is on to qualify for the second phase. The pressure is on to get a result against Germany. Great, bring them on. That kind of pressure has never bothered me.

Republic of Ireland 1, Cameroon 1

TEN

2–11 June, Chiba and Yokohama

SUNDAY 2nd JUNE

Today is family day. Some of the wives and children were waiting for us at the New Otani Hotel in Chiba City when we flew from Niigata to Tokyo late last night. More will join us today in this five-star luxury on Tokyo Bay, our base for the next twelve days or so.

It is great to see them. Any manager who tries to ban the players' families from an occasion like this is, I believe, making a mistake. We had family days in Italy back in 1990 and they went down a treat. It is crazy to suggest that having your wife and kids stay with you the night after a game will make any difference to your performance in the next match. I personally believe it can only help. When the players are on duty with their clubs in England, they stay in their own beds every second Friday night and play home games in the Premiership the next day. Does it affect them? Does it heck.

The lads have been away for twenty days now and need a break from staring at each other and staring at me. Just to talk to someone different, just to discuss something other than the World Cup can make all the difference at a time like this. And much as I know the wives will find this hard to believe, we miss them just as much as they miss us.

In this instance, the wives and the girlfriends have had their problems as well and have plenty to talk about when they meet up with their husbands and boyfriends. Some have experienced travel difficulties. Those had nothing to do with the FAI but the Association has done its best to help them over their problems.

Today our families will eat with us and relax around the hotel. First though we have a light training session at the Inage Park sports ground before all the fun can begin. There are thousands of Japanese fans waiting to cheer our every move as we work on another perfect pitch. Their enthusiasm is as immense as their welcome. It is hard to believe that they are here just to witness a training session.

It is not even an elaborate session at that. The players who played yesterday are free to do as they wish, I take those who weren't involved against Cameroon for a workout which I try to make as light-hearted as possible. We do some one-on-ones, two-on-twos, some sprints and some ball work. The players who stayed on the bench against Cameroon need to keep their fitness levels up just as much as those who played. We don't know who we will need or when in this tournament.

I know that watching from the bench and waiting for a chance to play is hard on the players who have yet to feature. I cannot play all twenty-two players and some will go home without kicking a ball in the World Cup finals at all. How these players respond and react to the others is vitally important when a squad is away for this length of time. We need them as vibrant and as happy as those guaranteed a place in the team and that is not always the easiest thing to achieve. Thankfully, I am blessed with twenty-two great guys in this squad. They root for each other to such an extent that today the guys who played are egging the others on in training, keeping their spirits up and ensuring that they all feel involved.

One man is in trouble today. Jason's knee is clearly not right. I knew that at half-time yesterday and his lack of involvement in even the jogging today just confirms it. I am not going to rule Jason out of the Germany match on Wednesday night but he will not be in the starting line-up.

It is less than twenty-four hours after the Cameroon result and I have already decided the team to face the Germans. We will go into that match with the side that started the second-half in Niigata yesterday. If they can perform as well as they did over those forty-five minutes, then we will be fine on Wednesday night. If they can better that, then the Germans are in for some trouble.

Rudi Voeller's side dominate the press conference today. As we were flying from Niigata last night, they were putting eight goals past Saudi Arabia in their opening Group E game, three of the goals coming from Kaiserslautern striker Miroslav Klose. It was an impressive start to their World Cup campaign; it was also a dangerous start as far as Rudi Voeller was concerned. It has raised expectation levels about this German side; they will be seen as world-beaters now, as potential champions. That puts pressure on Rudi and his players to deliver but the result doesn't do us any favours either.

If we get a result against Germany we will then be expected to run in a bagful of goals against the Saudis. Even though I have only seen the goals from the match last night, I cannot see them playing as badly again. It looked to me like the defending was non-existent. Klose was unchallenged for his headed goals and the Saudis appeared to sit back and let the Germans swing uncontested crosses in at will. My only promise at this stage is that the Germans will not get it as easy against us on Wednesday, just as we won't find it as easy against the Saudis in Yokohama next week.

After training I go back to the hotel with the team. There is an official opening ceremony awaiting us at the Irish Village, a tented area erected behind the New Otani where fans and players can mingle freely.

The reception here is as warm as it has been throughout our time in Japan. Italy were also due to use Chiba as a base but I think the locals are quite glad that they can concentrate all their attention on the Irish. And we're happy about it too.

After dinner with the wives and children, I settle down for a few drinks as I watch England draw with Sweden in their opening game. It may cost ten euro a pint but for me it was worth every cent, thank you. It's been another long week.

But, as they say, all's well that ends well.

MONDAY 3rd JUNE

A few months ago I was hoping for a glamour game in the World Cup finals. I wanted the Republic of Ireland to face Brazil, Argentina or Italy in Korea or Japan. Those teams represent the romance and the intrigue of this great tournament. They have a swagger and an aura about them, a magical quality that ignites opposing fans and teams with the same desire to play them and beat them.

When the draw was made in Busan back in December we did land one of the big guns. While Germany will never be as attractive an opposition as the likes of Brazil, they are one of the stalwarts of World Cup history, a team with tradition on their side. We have only made it to three World Cups in the history of Irish football, they have won the tournament three times. That is the reputation they will bring with them to Ibaraki on Wednesday night.

It doesn't bother me that they have the record books on their side, though. Nor am I that worried that their team is packed with players with Champions League experience. They will only play eleven men in their team at the Kashima Stadium, no more and no less, and they are not going to put out eleven World Cup winners against us. They are not going to parade Beckenbauer and Muller and Netzer and Klinsmann on Wednesday night. We will face the current German team, a side that has never won the World Cup. We will come up against eleven Germans tasting the World Cup experience as a team for the first time, just as we are. Yes, some of them have been to European Cup finals, European Championships even, but they have never played in the World Cup finals as a team.

The eleven we will face in Ibaraki are not invincible. That is the lesson I begin to preach as we get back to normal service at our training ground outside Tokyo this morning. My players have a big job on their hands against Germany but this is not Mission Impossible.

The draw against Cameroon has set us up nicely for the rest of the World Cup but it is only a start. Lose against the Germans and we are back to square one. Even with a win against Saudi in the final game, four points will not be enough to get us through to the second phase. That is why our attitude is so important going into this game. We cannot believe for one second that we are inferior to Rudi Voeller's team, we cannot imagine that we are playing the great German sides of the past. They are no better than Holland or Portugal, neither of whom managed to beat Ireland in the qualifying series that got us here.

It's similar to the manager of a mid-table Premiership side going to play at Highbury or Old Trafford. His players will know all about the history and the pedigree of Arsenal and United but he cannot allow that to consume them. They have to go to those grounds believing that the eleven players in their team are just as good as the current eleven players lining out for the Gunners or the Red Devils. As a manager you cannot allow your players to face history and tradition and reputation as well. If you do, you are wasting your time turning up.

Anyway, I am not all that convinced about this current German team. I didn't watch them lose to England last September because I was having a pint and celebrating our hectic win against Holland. When I left my room at the airport hotel to go to the bar, Germany were a goal to the good and had just missed a great chance to make it 2–0. I reckoned they would win the match so the end result was a bit of a surprise. We've watched that tape since and the video of their play-off win against the Ukraine when they impressed me and looked more like their old selves.

Since then they have flattered to deceive a little bit with results that are better than their performances merited. My scouts Seamus McDonagh and Gerry Peyton have both been to see them live and they have offered me encouragement as we prepare to play them.

Calling the Saudi game a football match was a misnomer, if you ask me. I sat down to watch the video today and gave up after twenty minutes. It bored me to death. There was no opposition and nothing to gauge the German performance against. It is easy to score goals with your head when neither the cross nor the header is contested by the defender. Saudi Arabia were so poor that I will just get the goals edited together and let the lads watch that before Wednesday. There is no point subjecting them to the full ninety minutes of that match.

German attention has, of course, turned to Ireland now as well. Their media are all over today's training session and I am sure they are curious about the yellow jersey on Jason McAteer's back. The shirt is worn by the worst performer on the training ground the previous day and is called the 'I had a Macedonia' jersey after that painful experience in Skopje. At the end of the each session the players have a vote and the winner, or loser I should say, has to wear the yellow shirt the next day out. It is never washed, by the way, but I am glad to report that a new shirt was introduced for the World Cup.

Jason has seen it a few times. The younger lads do tend to gang up on the older members of the squad and they also use it to bring players back down to earth. Anyone developing an ego around here soon sees yellow, if you know what I mean. Likewise, newcomers to the squad can be voted in very early in their international career, just in case they have ideas about themselves.

Have I worn it? Of course I have. I was framed.

Jason is struggling with his injury today. I know he is busting a gut to prove he is up to Wednesday night's game but I have already decided he will start on the bench.

I have other players to worry about. Gary Breen, capped more times than any other player since I became manager, is struggling again but expects to be ready by game time. Stevie Finnan and Shay Given are also carrying knocks so their training is restricted today.

Today's press conference is busier than usual with all the Germans now in tow. Albert, the UTV cameraman, entertains them with a spot of magic before we begin but it is down to the serious business when I arrive.

I am asked about Germany, about their result against England and about the player back home. I praise Rudi Voeller and his side, question the Saudis' effort against them on Saturday and refuse to read anything into that 5–1 England game last September. I tell their media that I am more interested in how they played against the Ukraine in the play-offs. That tape gives me a truer insight into Rudi Voeller's mindset.

Do I regard this as our toughest test in Japan? With Germany's history it should be, but circumstance dictated that the Cameroon match was the toughest game of my life. If I could survive that, I can survive anything.

That topic comes up in conversation later today when the former Celtic and Aston Villa manager Dr Jozef Venglos comes to see me at the team hotel. Dr Venglos is working for FIFA at the World Cup, analysing how managers and coaches are coping with the stresses and strains of a big tournament. He is a fascinating man whose presence on both sides of the managerial fence gives him a unique insight into his subject.

We chat at length. I explain that the World Cup has not been as pleasurable as I had hoped so far. I always knew it would be hard work but I wanted to get through this tournament with a perpetual smile on my face. That has not been possible, not at all. Sending your captain and best player home doesn't help, I know, but the pressure of living in a goldfish bowl has really affected me.

Of course, bringing a party of thirty-three people to the Far East for anything up to six weeks was always going to present problems. You cannot juggle that many plates in the air without one of them smashing down on your head. I just never expected the whole experience, the media attention, to be this overwhelming. I never expected the walls to come in on me as they have.

Dr Venglos knows where I am coming from. He has listened to managers with similar stories throughout this World Cup. None have been thrust into the spotlight to the same extent as I have, not yet anyway, but many of their complaints are along the same lines.

Some years ago, when we failed to qualify for Euro 2000, I read an article that questioned why the FAI had extended my contract ahead of such failure. The article pointed out that fifty per cent of the managers at France '98, which we failed to make, had been sacked or resigned within a month of the tournament's conclusion. I had always thought that statistic was frightening and possibly unbelievable. Not now. Now I can see exactly where it is coming from. Some of the stresses and strains presented to the thirty-two coaches and managers here in Japan and Korea are unlike anything I have ever encountered in club or international football. It is little wonder that fifty per cent of us will be out of a job this time next month.

TUESDAY 4th JUNE

It is time to end the game of cat and mouse with Steve Staunton. My World Cup captain played his ninety-ninth game for his country when he led us to that 1–1 draw with Cameroon on Saturday. He is one game away from the century, the first Irish player to make the ton. If he plays against Germany tomorrow night he will make history. If he plays.

I was asked the question at yesterday's press conference and refused to confirm or deny his presence in the team for our second Group E game. Today, Trevor O'Rourke and John Givens have organised a special Eircom Ireland shirt with the number 100 on the back and below the crest on the front. I had better settle their nerves – and Stan's – and let him know that he is playing.

I tell Stan the good news at training, after I have diffused a row between Jason and Gary Breen. They are arguing over the merits of a pass from Jase to Harty. Spirits are running high and they need to come down a peg or two.

Back to Steve's news. He feigns surprise. He will win his hundredth international cap fourteen years after his first when he played alongside a certain Mick McCarthy in a Lansdowne Road friendly win against Tunisia. This is an incredible achievement for an Irish footballer. I know we play more games nowadays and players start at this level younger than they ever did in my time, but to play a hundred times for your country takes some doing.

I started playing international football at twenty-five years of age and managed to make it to fifty-seven caps. Steve started at nineteen and could go on for some time to come. I suspect he won't, though. He hasn't told me as much or even discussed the subject, but I have a feeling he will retire after this World Cup. I can understand why. The demands on international footballers are huge now and he has played at the top for club and country for a long, long time.

Stan was telling me the other day that his youngest son is two this week – and he has never been home for his child's birthday. International duty meant he was in Estonia last year, Japan this time around. I know a two-year-old won't remember his birthday but it is a sign of the sacrifices that these players make for their country. People tend to forget that when they criticise players, when they take them to task over events on the pitch.

At least if he does retire, Stan will go out on a high, with the hundred caps safely deposited. Nobody deserves it more than Stan. He is a genuinely decent bloke, always has been. Jack first introduced him to the squad before Euro '88. He was starting to make a name for himself at Liverpool, and was brought along to train with us at Finnstown House before we departed for Germany. He didn't make the trip but did make an impression and later that year he played his first game for Ireland.

Stan's progress was meteoric. Within a few months he was the left-back on the World Cup team, the teenager in a very mature side. He kept Chris Hughton out of the side in Italy as we went all the way to the quarter-finals and then moved into midfield as Kevin Sheedy's replacement by the time we got to the USA in 1994.

Now he's a centre-back. And I have to admit I never saw him in that position when we played together for Ireland all those years ago. My criticism of Stan then was all to do with his heading. I never considered him dominant enough in the air to see him as a central defender. He has clearly worked on that element of his game. His presence of mind and his speed of thought make him an excellent contender for the position now and he proved how good he now is in the number five shirt in the second-half on Saturday.

Stan is also a good captain. I know some people have claimed that he backed the decision to send Roy Keane home because he wanted to lead Ireland in his last World Cup but that is an absolute insult to the man, absolute nonsense. He stepped into the breach after Saipan and I could not ask more of him. He is a measured leader who lets his actions speak louder than words . His presence within the squad cannot be underestimated. Like Quinny, he has done so much for team spirit and for the sense of togetherness that you need within a group of this size.

Stan, like Niall, can read situations off the field very well too. Before training yesterday, he asked me if there was any need to go to Ibaraki today, to train at the stadium where we will play Germany. It's at least a sixty-minute bus ride away and the players would rather miss the traffic, train in Chiba and see the stadium at first-hand tomorrow afternoon, when we get there at the designated time of two hours before kick-off. In the past we have always gone to the match venue on the day before the game, but I had no problem with his suggestion. Why spend two hours stuck in traffic when we can train here in Chiba and relax afterwards? Little things like that can make a difference to the players.

Steve's experience is going to be vital against the Germans. This is as big a game as we have played as a team, as big a test as anything that Croatia, Yugoslavia, Holland, Portugal, Romania, Iran and Belgium have thrown at us over the last six years. I take solace from the fact that we have stood up to be counted in situations like this. We are no pushover against top-class opposition, if anything the underdog role is one that we thrive on. We have never, for example, lost any competitive game by more than one goal in all my time in charge.

I have no intention of losing this one. We have to take something out of the game to keep the World Cup alive, and we can. If we lose, the next six days between now and the Saudi match will drag. They will become a nightmare. There may be no way back for us if that next game is rendered meaningless by events tomorrow night and on Thursday when Cameroon play the Saudis. If we lose and Cameroon beat Saudi Arabia, we can be squeezed out. A draw between Germany and Cameroon in the final series of games would then be good enough to see them both through, no matter what we do against the Saudis.

I am confident however. People go on about the camaraderie and togetherness in this Irish camp but they are not the only qualities that have got us this far in the World Cup. The Irish fighting spirit is something that we love to project but we have some good players here as well. We can pass the ball, we can play direct football when necessary and we can create chances. After Saturday's second-half performance against Cameroon, we know now that we can play on the World Cup stage.

Look at the way Duffer and Robbie played in that second-half. They ran Cameroon ragged and that will give them so much heart as they face up to a very resolute German defence. I expect a lot from Duffer tomorrow night. It took him forty-five minutes to adjust to the pace of Saturday's game. Like a lot of our players he struggled when the sun was at its strongest in Niigata. This will be different. We are playing at night so the humidity and heat will be the only factors to worry about. Duffer, Robbie and Killer won't have the sun beating down on them as they did in the first-half on Saturday when it was very strong down the left-hand side of the pitch before going down in the second-half. I have told them to stay forward more, to wait for the ball to come to them and then to run the German defence. That is when Damien and Robbie are at their most dangerous, not when they have to go back looking for it.

We have the first game out of the way, nerves are settled now, emotions are calm. We have got past the first hurdle unscathed; we are still alive in this group. Someone asked me today how we can deflate German confidence tomorrow. The answer was simple, beat them.

WEDNESDAY 5th JUNE

World Cup First Round, Group E

Republic of Ireland v Germany

Lunchtime on match day. I can see the headline take shape before my eyes. 'Footballers show emotion shock.' Yes, it happens from time to time, on and off the field.

Today, I witness one of the nicest things I have ever seen in all my years with the beautiful game. As we lunch at the New Otani Hotel ahead of the trip to Ibaraki, a hush descends on the room. Steven

Reid, the youngster player in the squad and barely out of nappies when Steve Staunton played his first game for Ireland, stands up to say a few words. He talks about the pride he feels making this speech as the youngest member of the squad, how privileged he feels to make a presentation to one of the oldest. Then he thanks Stan for his contribution to the Irish team over the last fourteen years and presents him with a Cartier watch on behalf of all the players and all the staff to mark his hundredth cap later tonight.

Stan is gobsmacked. He had no idea what was going on when Reidy stood up, no inkling of the whip-round for this presentation. He is genuinely moved by the moment, so moved that his response is almost muted. He thanks the lads for the gesture then mutters something about getting out there and beating the Germans.

I am touched myself. One of the great things about the Irish team that made it to the quarter-finals back in 1990 was team spirit, but this lot have surpassed that already. We were old men back then, coming towards the sell-by date in terms of our effectiveness as a team, but these guys have so many years together ahead of them. It is almost frightening to look around the room and realise how young they are.

Packie always talks about the fact that we were a settled team in 1990, that most of us were family men with kids back at home. Many of this squad, in comparison, are still kids themselves. They have grown up together, they have lived through the hard times and the good times together and they are maturing rapidly. The experiences of the past few weeks have brought them closer. As I look around this lunch table I know that the future can only be bright for Irish football.

How do the Germans feel as they enjoy their pre-match meal right now, I wonder. Certainly, Rudi Voeller will know all about the potential in this squad. We may not have the Champions League experience that is within his group of players but we have youth on our side and we have players who can play the game. That, I tell them as we discuss the game for the final time after lunch, is the key tonight. We must play the game, we must have a go at the Germans and believe that they are just as worried about us as we are about them. They have tradition on their side, we have potential. That is the way to go into this game. And remember the golden rule – no regrets.

I am, at last, cool and relaxed and in charge of this World Cup experience. All the anxiety and the stress have vanished in the days and hours since that draw with Cameroon. I am clear in my own head as the bus leaves Chiba for the hour-long hop to Ibaraki and the Kashima Stadium that is home to the Antlers, the club that enticed the Brazilian star Zico to Japan.

Spirit is everything again today. The kids are growing in confidence by the minute, the likes of Duffer are developing at pace in this World Cup. Duffer has come out of his shell over the last fortnight, he has lost the inhibitions and the awe of some of the senior stars around him. He is a player in his own right now, on and off the field. He is standing on his own two feet away from the pitch and that is clearly helping him on it. He even sang on the bus going to the hotel after we landed in Tokyo on Saturday night. I could barely believe my ears as he stood up, down the back, and rattled off 'Leroy Brown'.

The songs are back today, though there is more of a traditional nature about them. Barely has the bus left our current home when the sing-song starts from down the back. The lads rattle through the old reliables as we charge down the motorway. 'Sean South from Garryowen' is saved for the final bend, arms punching the air as the stadium pulls into view.

We are Irish, we are alive and we are up for this one. Really up for it.

Again, the fans amaze us. They have come from every corner of the globe, not just Ireland, and they never cease to amaze me. Only yesterday I met two-month-old Jamie Brett with his parents Enda and Monica. He practically went straight from Holles Street* to the airport to add his cry as Ireland's youngest supporter on tour. Incredible.

Those fans give us hope but not before FIFAdom raises its ugly head again. We first run into trouble at the ground when somebody

* National Maternity Hospital on Holles Street in Dublin.

from FIFA cops on to the presence of Seamus McDonagh and Gerry Peyton on the team bus along with our spiritual advisors Monsignor Boyle and Father Paddy. My two scouts are decked out in team gear, official members of the party as far as I am concerned. The same goes for Father Liam and Father Paddy. But they are not accredited for the dressing-room area because we only have thirty-three accreditations for the players and staff. So they shouldn't be on the bus, or so FIFA say when they make an official complaint to the FAI later on. Give me a break.

Then the flags draped around the stadium run into trouble. For years now, Irish fans have brought their tricolours with them across the world, proudly telling all and sundry which football club they belong to or support back home, or which pub they drink in. One flag in Ibaraki even proclaims 'Good Girl Sharon', a reference to Roddy Doyle's *The Snapper*, no doubt. That is not the offending tricolour, however. One of the official FIFA types complains to Joe McGlue from the FAI about the flags bearing the names of public houses. They are, he says, in violation of the FIFA sponsorship deal with Budweiser. Joe spends an hour and a half arguing the case with FIFA. They want the flags taken down, he explains that every pub in Ireland sells Budweiser. Eventually they agree to let the flags stay.

I am in no need of a Bud as I sit on the bench. The players are having a look around the pitch, waving to the fans already inside this impressive, traditional style football stadium. I am at peace with the world, sat here in my suit and tie, taking it all in.

Conall Hooper, one of the docs, takes my photograph. He remarks how relaxed I look. I tell him I have no worries at all. I know what we need to do to stay alive in this World Cup and how we are going to do it. Calm is the essence of the day, as I tell the players in the dressing-room preparing to face their next test. There is no need to panic, no need to feel in awe of the opposition tonight. Keep our shape, leave the frontmen upfront and we will be fine. Concentrate and give it your all. No regrets.

The knock comes, thirteen minutes before the kick-off again, and the team are out the door. We follow them, link arms on the bench and salute the fans who are sending warmth in my direction at last.

This is better, this is more like it. I can sense a belonging again as the anthem is played and we win the singing contest by a Johnny Logan margin. We have clearly outnumbered the Germans off the pitch, it is time to outplay them on it.

We start well. Duffer has a chance after just two minutes and Christoph Metzelder nips in to clear. Then Carsten Jancker tests Shay Given, to no avail, before German captain and 'keeper Oliver Khan sets his stall out with a fifteenth-minute save from Robbie, set up by Duffer. Klose then plays for a penalty off Stan but Danish referee Kim Nielsen is having none of his play-acting.

I am happy enough until disaster strikes in the nineteenth minute. An Irish attack breaks down on the right-hand side and Michael Ballack sweeps a great ball forward. Klose, the dangerman on Saturday, nips off Stan's shoulder and in between my captain and Hartey. The finish is world-class and we are a goal down.

I am seething on the bench. The Germans will regard this as a great goal but our defending was poor. We should never concede a goal like that.

It is time to sink or swim now. Once again, we have made life difficult for ourselves at this tournament but I have faith in the character of the Irish side and my faith is well founded. We are a goal down but we are playing well. We do not panic, we do not lose sight of the bigger picture.

Duffer is flying upfront, thriving on the service that Kinse and Mattie are providing through sheer hard work in the middle of the field. He goes close a minute after the goal but Khan does what Khan does best and denies him. We finally beat the 'keeper a few minutes later when a Breeny flick falls for Mattie but this time his shot, a similar effort to the goal on Saturday, flies just past Khan's right hand and his post.

There is no need to worry just yet. We have weathered the German storm, we have Stan and Breeny in commanding form at the back and we are more than capable of controlling the remainder of this game. When Duffer hits one off Thomas Linke's head right on the break, I know the balance of power is with Ireland.

I have one sneaking doubt, however. For all our possession and all our beautiful play in the final twenty minutes of the half, I wonder where the goal is going to come from. There is nothing to be gained from a 1–0 defeat at this stage of the World Cup. Nobody will thank us for that or remember the style of our play if this result contributes to our elimination from the tournament.

I have a plan B in my mind. If we are still a goal down after twenty minutes or so of the second half, I will throw caution to the wind and Quinny at the Germans. I prime him for this possibility in the dressing-room at half-time, tell him to be ready to lead a three-man attack in the final quarter with Robbie and Duffer alongside him.

I know we are playing well but I need to see a goal, I have to see a goal coming from somewhere. My half-time spiel is simple – do not play Germany off the park and come back in here with a 1–0 defeat to your name. We do not deserve that on the way we have played so far so don't let it happen. We will see what happens for twenty minutes, then make the change if necessary.

Again we start well. Germany are on the back foot again and I think we have scored when a Killer flick puts Duffer through on the 'keeper in the fifty-sixth minute. It takes a great save from Khan, who else, to deny Damien his first goal in the World Cup finals. I really thought we had that one.

Robbie tries to beat Khan a couple of times before I decide to go for broke in the seventieth minute, throwing Quinny and Steven Reid in for Hartey and Kells.

I switch to 3–4–3, leaving Stevie Finnan, Breeny and Stan at the back. Kevin Kilbane can add his weight to the left when necessary. My need for a goal is more important than any worry about conceding another. I'm taking a chance but I cannot see the Germans scoring a second, without a mistake on our behalf, so it is a risk worth taking as far as I am concerned.

Duffer is told to stay up, push out to whichever wing takes his fancy and play off Quinny. We are going to hit diagonal balls off Niall and I want Robbie and Duffer to be ready for the pickings.

The ploy works. Germany are at sixes and sevens now, they are arguing with each other and one Jancker chance aside, they create little or nothing for the rest of the game. We are full of running, full of drive, full of stamina as the game ticks on. Quinny makes a huge difference as he tears the Germans apart with his presence, and sets up chances for Duffer and Robbie before scooping a chip onto the roof of Khan's net.

We are creating chances now but we still need a goal. Kenny is on for an exhausted Stan, time is running against us and I will be criticised for making the biggest tactical error if we don't score soon. People will want to know why I changed from a 4–4–2 that was working reasonably well to a 3–4–3 that still couldn't produce a goal. I believe we had to do something, we had to take a calculated gamble. It is a fine line we walk at times like this.

I am on my feet as the clock counts down. Full-time approaches and no goal. Extra-time begins and still no equaliser. And then it happens, the breakthrough comes and salvation arrives in the shape of Stevie Finnan, Niall Quinn and Robbie Keane rolled into one in the ninety-second minute. Added time is running out when Stevie floats a long ball from the right wing, just inside the halfway line. Quinny is already rising as the cross comes his way. I am craning my neck to follow the flight of the ball.

As Niall rises above his man and connects with the cross, Robbie has started one final run. His intuition is perfectly timed and the ball falls into his path, just inside the box. He takes it forward, hits it with his right foot and Khan gets a hand to it. We are denied again, or so I think, as the ball heads for the left-hand post. S**t, it's going back out.

Then the crowd behind the goal erupt. I am stunned, shock tattooed across my face as they celebrate and Robbie throws his hands into the air before running to the corner and flipping, the trademark Robbie Keane goal celebration.

Bloody hell, we must have scored. The ball must have gone in. Khan has been beaten after all. We are level with seconds to go. We have done a Macedonia on Germany, we have managed to score a late goal as joyful as that equaliser in Skojpe all those years ago was painful.

I cannot believe it. This seems too good to be true. We have scored. As the bench erupts, I look down to the corner-flag at those players celebrating and I am ecstatic. We have done it. We have scored and we are within touching distance of the second phase of the World Cup finals. The performance has finally got the goal it deserved, we deserved. There is no time left for the Germans to get back into it. They were seconds away from a certain place in the next round when Robbie pounced and they are sick. Their faces tell it all as the final whistle goes and we invade the pitch, celebrating the best 1–1 win in world football history, as Quinny later describes it.

I am still in shock as the players drag me into their celebrations. The Irish fans in the stand away to the right of the dug-out are on their feet, singing and dancing and waiting, like me, for someone to tell them it is all a dream. There must be an offside flag waiting somewhere for us, there must be a man in a black jersey waiting to tell me to sit down and realise that the goal was disallowed. But no, this is as real as it gets. This is as good as it gets. I am dizzy with emotion and I am at one with the supporters again. I am sucked into their corner of the ground by the naked emotion of it all.

The Green Army is Mick's Army once again. We are re-united. We are as one again.

Republic of Ireland 1, Germany 1

THURSDAY 6th JUNE

There are so many thoughts, so many emotions that fill your head at a time like this. It is the very early hours of Thursday morning and I am sitting in the ballroom of the New Otani Hotel, family at my side and beer in hand. Some of the players are still around me, others are downstairs in the bar with fans and FAI officials. Nobody is in a hurry to go to bed tonight. John Delaney has thrown the bar open at the FAI's expense downstairs and it is going to be a very late and a very special night.

Stan is the centre of attention on the floor below me and rightly so. It is not every night that you win your hundredth cap for your country, not every night that you play like that when your team really needs you. He is the epitome of what this World Cup is all about for Ireland. He is the role model now and his team-mates know it. Richard Dunne, Quinny, Duffer, Kells, Hartey and Robbie serenade Stan in song, with the assistance of Ireland youth team coach Noel O'Reilly, Duffer's younger brother Jamie and a cast of hundreds.

It is Stan's night, Ireland's night, the best night of my managerial life. We haven't just taken a point off Germany in the World Cup finals, we haven't just moved within touching distance of Korea and the second phase, we have also produced one of the greatest Irish performances of all time. That's what gives me the greatest pleasure right now as we party upstairs and downstairs in this hotel. This team, my team, the Irish team has come of age.

The past few hours have been a bit of a blur, I have to admit. The fans wanted to keep us on that Ibaraki pitch forever, or so it seemed. They have been faithful to the team throughout this tournament and the players repaid them in full last night. For me it felt like I was back in the fold after Robbie's goal. They took me to their hearts again, they wanted me to be a part of their joy. That was the greatest feeling of all.

I am delighted for others as well. I knew Quinny had something to offer this World Cup, told him as much last February when I asked him to stay fit and stay involved for just four more months. He will hang up his boots when this World Cup is over. I knew that coming out here but I always wanted him with us in Japan. He has such a role to play for me, both as a player and as the senior squad member. The youngsters look up to him, wait on his every word and his every move. He can lead by example in a way few professional footballers can ever hope to emulate. He is vital to the development of these young players. Niall has also been a constant contact between me and the players throughout this tournament and he deserves an award for the way he has handled himself through some very testing times.

He can still play a bit, as he has just proven against the Germans. They were quaking in their boots when they saw him warming up and rightly so. Niall got stuck into their big centre-backs as soon as he went on, he showed he wasn't afraid to put his head where it hurts and that really unsettled their defence, more than I imagined possible. He opened the game up for us and I am just so happy that he made a very positive contribution at the end of what has been a hard year for him. Niall didn't come out here just for the ride. He wanted to make an impact after a difficult season when he has had his back problems but still featured in over thirty games for Sunderland. Now he has made his mark on the World Cup as well, his final World Cup. Even if he doesn't feature again, it is a great way to go out.

Robbie Keane has many more World Cups ahead of him if last night was anything to go by. We can build the team around him now, confident in the knowledge that he will score goals and create goals for us for many years to come. Keane Og, the younger Keane as the fans call him, is a better player than many people give him credit for. He will smash Niall's goal-scoring record into oblivion very soon, I have no doubts on that front. And the goal against Germany will be the making of him. It has catapulted Robbie into the realm of Irish folk hero and he will thrive on that. It will also erase the memories of the recent past for him and give him the confidence to look to the future with club and country.

We asked so much of Robbie when he burst into the Irish team as a teenager. We expected so much when he took to international football like a duck to water. His full debut against Argentina in 1998 was sensational and he followed that with a move to Coventry, then to Inter Milan. He scored our first goal in this World Cup campaign in Holland and we all relied on him so much, too much in my opinion.

When it didn't happen for him in Italy, the fall from grace was as sensational as the rise to fame. People who praised him to the heights, knocked him to the depths. The hype that surrounded Robbie when he first played for Ireland did him no favours on the other side of the fence.

It will be different now. He has age on his side and he has this World Cup experience to back him as well. I believe he can improve, he will work on his game and he will get better. Robbie has this incredible instinct that will not go away. We saw that in the way he read Niall's flick last night and his finish was pure magic. Okay, so I thought Khan had saved it but he had saved everything else we had thrown at him for the previous ninety-one minutes so allow me that mistake.

The game proved to me how far we have come as a football side. Back in 1990 we were very good at closing teams down but we struggled at times to open the lock. That was never more evident than in the scoreless game at the Italia '90 finals against Egypt. I am still convinced that had Liam Brady been fit for that World Cup, we would have opened them up with ease and won that game. It is different now. We have creativity throughout the side, we have players who are comfortable going forward. We showed that when we had Germany on the back foot for most of the second-half last night. Kevin Kilbane, Jason when he's fit, Gary Kelly, Sparky, Stevie Finnan and Ian Harte can all open up defences with their crosses. Duffer and Robbie can make those chances count for something.

I know people will look at Duffer's second-half and argue that he should play wide against Saudi, that I should start Robbie and Quinny as the front two. That is not on my agenda, I am afraid. I believe that the left-wing role restricts Damien too much in the way I want the game played at international level. I rely on two solid banks of four behind the frontmen, I need the midfield to protect the defence when we are on the back foot. Kevin Kilbane does that job exceptionally well and, for now, Robbie and Duffer are my best strike partnership.

Damien is an attacker, a free spirit. I do not want to curtail his freedom of expression, the role of striker gives him a licence. I want him to link with Robbie, to run at defenders and frighten them. I would hate to take that carefree element out of his game.

I know he has stirred the debate with that performance but it is not about one player when you sit down to pick the Irish team. I have to select the eleven players and the balance that I feel is best suited to the way I want Ireland to play. Right now, that means playing Duffer and Robbie upfront with Quinny on the bench. I saw nothing to make me change my mind last night.

I am not going to switch away from the starting 4–4–2 formation when we play Saudi next Tuesday night either. Yes, I took a gamble with twenty minutes to go last night and went to three at the back but I had no choice at that stage. We had nothing left to lose. There was no sign of a goal coming for all our possession (we ended up with fifty-eight per cent of the possession, by the way), and a 1–0 defeat was no use to us in the greater scheme of things. If we had lost, I would be cast as the biggest plonker of all time right now. But since we pulled the game out of the fire, I am a hero. Thin line.

The way we played the game was more satisfying for me than the praise that follows my gamble. We left the recovery as late as possible, we made it as dramatic as possible, but nobody can deny we deserved that draw. It was a mature and measured performance. I told the players not to panic, even at half-time, and they responded royally. Our passing was never short of sensational, our concentration levels were spot on and once again we were full of running as the game progressed into those final magical minutes. I reckon I am getting something right as I head off to bed in the early hours of the morning.

Today is Disneyland day for the players and their families. They are taking our Michael with them to the theme park just down the road from us here in Chiba but his daddy has World Cup business to attend to. I pass up Disneyland in favour of Saitama and a spying mission to watch Cameroon against Saudi Arabia, a game that is now of critical importance for us. We can still win the group but only if Saudi beat the African champions. I don't expect them to be as bad as they were against Germany but I can't see that happening.

The FAI have already given me my tickets when news comes through from FIFA that they have VIP tickets awaiting collection at a hotel near the ground. This turns out to be a bad idea. The hotel is miles off our planned route and we eventually get into the ground with only five minutes to spare.

I am right on both counts with regard to the game. Cameroon fail to rise to the occasion as they did in the opening game, Saudi lift their performance substantially from Saturday night's embarrassment. Yet Cameroon eventually get a win thanks to a sixty-fifth-minute goal from Eto'o, set up by Geremi. They scarcely deserve it. Saudi striker Al Temyat is the best player on the field but they couldn't have scored if they were still there now.

I think of my old friend Miroslav Blazevic, the Iranian boss we met in the play-offs, as I leave the ground. He is probably still talking of killing himself back in Tehran after we ended his World Cup dream and he must know his side should be here and not the Saudis. Iran were a much better team on anything I have seen from the Arabs so far. It is well worth seeing the Saudis at first hand but little has changed in my own head concerning our game with them next Tuesday night. I always knew that we would have to beat them and that is still the case. Nothing other than a two-goal win will do now but I am confident. Win by two and we cannot be caught by Cameroon if they draw with Germany. That would leave us both on five points with second spot in the group, behind Germany, going down to the respective Saudi results. There wasn't anything to frighten me out there tonight.

Back at base, I head out for a family drink with my daughters Katie and Anna. The girls are left to look after Daddy tonight and we end up in Always, a Cheers-type bar in one of Chiba's many shopping precincts with screens playing tonight's match. I am watching the end of the France–Uruguay game when the players and their wives arrive, en route from a very enjoyable day at Disneyland. They hire the karaoke room upstairs and Joanne Staunton, Steve's wife and an old friend, invites me up to join them on the condition that I sing. Much as I love them all and have a great relationship with them as their manager, I do not want to cramp their style. This is their night and I do not want to spoil it. The players see enough of me as it is and I am sure they would prefer the company of their wives and girlfriends right now. Nothing to do with the fact I can't sing, of course. I make my excuses and leave.

A couple of hours later, I am enjoying one of those ten euro beers back at the hotel when the players arrive. Jason presents me with a pint, a peace offering of sorts after he disagreed with my decision to leave him out of the team last night. It isn't necessary but I drink it all the same.

Then Robbie approaches me in the bar and says he has something he wants to give to me. The lads saw it earlier and they just had to buy it. They have chipped together and nominated him, as goalscorer the night before, to act as the master of ceremonies. He apologises in advance as he hands me a plastic bag with a bottle of something or other inside it. I open it. It is a bottle of Scotch. Dunphy Scotch. I laugh at that one. I laugh a lot.

FRIDAY 7th JUNE

There are some sore heads in the hotel this morning. Some belong to players, others to fans. Some proponents of the modern game will frown at alcohol intake in the middle of a World Cup. Some will slam it as traditionalist, a relic from a bygone age. Rubbish. There were no question marks raised against my players in the ninety-second minute of the game against Germany. They deserve to let their hair down after a big game. We don't play Saudi until Tuesday so there was nothing wrong, in my opinion, with the lads having a beer or two or three last night. Nothing wrong at all. We are not a pub team but we are a team that knows how to enjoy itself when the time is right.

We are also happy to enjoy ourselves in the company of the fans who have paid good money to follow us to Japan this week. That has always been a trait of the Irish team and I don't want that to change as long as I am involved. We have a special bond with the fans, a bond that should never be broken. As I said before, we don't do back doors and we don't hide. We are out there when results go our way and you can always find us when we lose. I have been upfront with the fans at the best of times and the worst of times. Like the players, I don't run away when things go wrong.

I know the real fans are right back behind me as well as the team now. And we stand a great chance of moving forward, of taking this team into the second phase of the World Cup finals. That was my aim coming out here and it is all I am prepared to look towards now, even if these finals are proving to be perhaps the greatest leveller in football history. France, my tip to win the tournament, are almost out. Other big guns are struggling to find their form. We are in a better state of mind now than some of the biggest names in world football. It means little in real terms but it does offer some satisfaction as we discuss the changing face of the World Cup over lunch before this afternoon's training session.

It will all count for nothing of course if we lose to Saudi next Tuesday. I am a little annoyed that the game is so far away. The four days between Cameroon and Germany was just right, the same again before the Saudi match would be perfect. Instead, we must kick our heels for another five days and keep the players focused on the job in hand until kick-off in our final Group E fixture. That presents its own problems.

Training can become repetitive in such situations so today we try something different. Robbie has been on at me all week to play a game of Gaelic football so today is his lucky day. Robbie is gifted at this game as well by the way. He looks good enough to play for the Dublin Gaelic football team in their Croke Park home and scores some cracking points as the lads get stuck in, much to the bewilderment of the Japanese on the sidelines. I just hope the Saudis are taping this session.

Clinton Morrison takes to the game with a vengeance. He winds the lads up something rotten, telling them all the time that he is a natural. He says he'd love to play the game for one of the big teams in Ireland. Quinny points out that the players don't get paid. 'I'd do it for the love of the game,' replies the Palace striker, with a straight face.

Duffer has a problem with my interpretation of the rules during our GAA experiment. He constantly calls for free-kicks, I consistently refuse to give them. He asks me if I know the rules. I say no, I don't think there are any rules. Quinny gives me a crash course but I ignore the rules anyway and continue to give Duffer a hard time.

Training ground ref, incidentally, is the worst job in Irish football. It is bad enough with football when I know the rules so I am not taking any chances when it comes to the GAA and the interpretation of their rules. They can tackle Duffer any way they want so long as they don't hurt him. I discover afterwards that Duffer doesn't know the rules either.

Today's training session is mostly light-hearted. The players have all the stamina they need in the bank now. The two games so far have confirmed that I was right to bring them to the heat and humidity of Saipan. They do not look leggy two games into the World Cup. They look ready to run all night.

Not everyone in the squad is a happy camper today, however. Jason has had a hump on ever since he was left out of the team to play Germany. He was very upset by that decision and it has clearly affected his normal, happy-go-lucky demeanour.

I went to his room on Tuesday night and told him he wasn't in the side. I did not feel he was fit enough to start but I thought he would be fine as a sub. On Wednesday night he didn't want to strip with the other subs. He didn't think then that he was fit enough to be a sub if he wasn't fit enough to play but I explained that we are all in this together. I wanted him on the bench, he's better off there with the rest of the squad than up in the stands on his own. Jason then spoke to some of the senior players, some of his closest mates within the squad, and he saw the sense of my wish.

I can understand that Jason's nose is out of joint. He scored two of the most crucial goals that got us here and I stood by him in the qualifying tournament, even when he was rotting in the reserves at Blackburn. This was probably meant to be his best World Cup, the World Cup finals that dreams – and ads – are made of. Instead, he got injured in the final warm-up game and taken off at half-time in the first match. He has seen Gary Kelly take his place on the right-hand side of our midfield and he is not happy about it. I wouldn't expect him to feel any differently but his response to being left out disappoints me.

I wanted him to play in every game in these finals. I wanted him to score the winner in the final itself, just like the ad promised. I was so desperate to see him on the field that I picked him for the opening game even though I had doubts about his fitness. So I don't think I deserve this kind of reaction from him now.

I pull Jason after the session and ask him how he is feeling. How he would rate his fitness on a scale of one to ten? He is honest with me this time, he has come off the painkillers and the anti-inflammatories and he is struggling. I'm sure he will be fine, given time, but the bad news is that he will not start against Saudi Arabia on Tuesday.

I don't admit as much at the press conference today, but already I know the team that started against Germany is the one that will go out against Saudi Arabia. I have no fears about changing it if I have to midstream, but the same eleven will begin the match. I am not one for muddying the waters anyway. We have created chances throughout this tournament even if we have only scored twice so far. I don't like making changes for the sake of it, so I won't.

Some German media are still around. Their final game against Cameroon took on a whole new complexion when Robbie got that goal and they now have more than a passing interest in our showdown with the Saudis. A two-goal winning margin for Ireland will be enough to see us through no matter what happens in the other game. The scoreless carve-up I once feared between Cameroon and Germany cannot happen now. And the Republic's arrival as party poopers seems to have upset some of our continental cousins.

One German journalist even asks me if Ireland's World Cup progress is a fairytale. Firstly, I am not so sure about the fairy bit. Did he never see me play? And no, it is not a fairytale. We came here expecting to do well and believing we could. None of us were scared of playing Germany and aside from the first fifteen minutes or so, we were the better side on the night.

The fact that we had more than fifty per cent of the possession backs that up. I also felt we were the better team overall against Cameroon, so it is not a fairytale. Maybe it is a case of good players, good coaching, good management, good staff and good preparation. Maybe we are not a bad outfit after all, maybe that's the reality of it.

As I leave the press conference, FAI general secretary Brendan Menton announces an enquiry into the Association's handling of the World Cup thus far. He issues a brief statement which reads:

> Irrespective of the outcome of the team's remaining participation in World Cup 2002, the officers and general secretary of

> the FAI are recommending to their board of management that an independent external review of the Association's organisation and involvement in World Cup 2002 be undertaken upon our return to Ireland. The report will be made public when completed.

The announcement is taken by some as the first steps into an investigation of the Saipan affair. I don't give a flying if people see it as an investigation into me because I know it is not. I was assured as much when the FAI told me about the enquiry. It has nothing at all to do with the football side of the World Cup so I am happy to go along with it and happy to make any personal contribution they feel will be of use to whoever undertakes this investigation.

The announcement could have been better timed, say in July when the World Cup is well and truly over, but I am not in the least worried by it. It will not affect the team so it will not affect me. It is not an issue right now as far as I am concerned.

SATURDAY 8th JUNE

You know the story with the tent my team live in. You are either outside the tent peeing in, or inside the tent peeing out. There is no middle ground. If you are one of the residents of my tent, then I will defend you to a fault. No matter what other people say or do to you, I will be there backing your name and your cause.

Today, Ian Harte is up for persecution. A journalist wants to know if I am surprised that Ian is getting some stick in the media back at home. I am not going there. I will not criticise my players in public nor will I discuss criticism of them. I never have. I don't like it when they are singled out like this and I will defend them to the last. Step on one set of toes and you step on us all.

I am getting tired of certain players being singled out for criticism. Some are media heroes and can do no wrong, some are not and can do little right. It is a fact of life with the Irish team but it still annoys me. Ian is today's victim but others have been there before him, Lee Carsley, Gary Breen, David Connolly and Richard Dunne will all know what I am talking about. As for Hartey, two years ago he was the Premiership's left-back of the season in the PFA awards. Six years ago he was good enough to play centre-back for me at just nineteen years of age when I first became Irish manager. He is a good player, a very good player. He is the best left-back available to me and he is a constant in my team on merit, because I believe in him. If I think Ian is not doing the job required of him, I will take whatever action I feel necessary. I will, however, make that decision on my own, thank you, not on the recommendation of someone who has never played the game at this level.

Today, I am asked my reaction to those who have made Ian a scapegoat in recent days. I reply that it is sufficient to say, 'It begins with the letter b and ends in s.' Too many people are prepared to look at Ian's so-called shortfalls. They don't see what he brings to the party when he turns up to play for Ireland and that gets on my wick, it really does.

Hartey isn't the only one set to make headlines in tomorrow's papers. There is a bizarre rumour going around that Jason wants to do a Keane and go home. Some of the papers are ready to run this non-story, some journalists believe Jason will say as much in his *Sunday Independent* diary. But a couple of the staff have already seen that diary piece, due to be published tomorrow, and have told me there is nothing inflammatory in it, so I'm not concerned.

Jason did speak to the medical staff about his injury and he did ask them if there was any need to send him home because of his knee. They said no straight away. That's as far as the 'going home' line went, aside from a scene in his room when he suggested to Stan and Mick Byrne that the injury would force him out of the squad. He did not throw a tantrum, he did not threaten to storm out at any point as far as I know.

We did talk on Tuesday night, when I let him know he was not starting, and then again on Wednesday before the German game when I told him I wanted him stripped and on the bench. He complied with my request eventually and he seems fine to me right now. He is training again and it looks like that storm has abated.

His mood swings in recent days have been noticed by the other players, however. When he stepped out to train today, Stan welcomed him back and asked Jason if he had had a good break, had he gone anywhere nice when he was away. The players even sang 'Welcome Home'! Footballers can be a cruel lot. He hadn't been anywhere, of course. He was still around, but they felt his mind was elsewhere and they let him have it now.

He is not the only one to return to training. Shay, Stevie Finnan, Breeny, Stan, Mattie Holland and Kinse are all back at full pace as we go through our drills four days before our next game. The session is routine enough until Kevin Kilbane goes over on his ankle and my heart stops. He is back on his feet in no time but we take no chances. Killer sits out the rest of training but he will be fine by Tuesday night.

The six-day gap between the second and third games is a bit ridiculous. So is the fact that we have already played two games while some teams have just finished their first. Time is starting to drag now for all of us, including the Irish press. Still, it leaves time for other subjects to come to the fore, for others behind-the-scenes to get some attention.

Take Noel O'Reilly for example, Brian Kerr's coach with the Ireland youth teams and one of the men responsible for our great success at that level in recent years. Noel, a super singer and guitar player incidentally, has been with us since Izumo and has done great work on behalf of Irish football here in Japan, taking coaching sessions with local kids wherever we have gone. At any other time, he would have been splashed all over the Irish papers by this stage of our trip. Other events have kept him off the sports and feature pages this time around and that is a shame.

It is heartening to watch Noel at work. He has the kids enthralled on the training ground here in Chiba as he passes on his passionate love for the beautiful game. In years to come a Japanese Maradona or Robbie Keane will emerge from Izumo or Chiba City and give all the credit to the Irishman who started him down the road to fame and fortune in World Cup year 2002. Duffer and Robbie swear by Noel and are the first to admit his part in their progress to this stage. A good guy.

Another story emerges later today, after I have sent the locals into a frenzy by leaving the training session on a mountain bike and cycling back to the hotel. That threw them, I can tell you. They didn't expect to see a World Cup manager on a bike in Chiba.

Back at the media centre, the FAI, in particular president Milo Corcoran and general secretary Brendan Menton, have been talking about another new deal for Mick McCarthy. Two weeks ago I wondered where my life was going, it seems that I am now a wanted man.

I have yet to sign the two-year contract we agreed back in February. The paperwork wasn't complete until the Nigeria game and everything was too rushed and hectic to sign it then. Instead, I gave it to my advisor Liam Gaskin, asked him to run it by my solicitor and to bring it out to Izumo with him. Liam did just that and I will get around to putting pen to paper any day now. In the meantime, it appears that I am flavour of the month again with the FAI, which is great. I have appreciated their support over the past fortnight and I am happy that they are now talking in terms of extending my contract to run up until the 2006 World Cup in Germany. Some are even talking about me being in charge of an Irish team in Dublin for the 2008 European Championships if our joint bid with Scotland to host the championship is successful.

That is a nice vote of confidence to receive just two games into the 2002 World Cup finals but I am a realist. I know that results mean everything in the world of international football. The performances in this competition so far have been special, there were times when we played Cameroon and Germany off the park, but the results also went our way. People back home, and out here, celebrated the way we played because they had something to celebrate on the scoreboard. If we had lost those two fixtures, 1–0 say, who would remember the performances? Very few. And who would want to keep Mick McCarthy in charge for another two years? Fewer still. No matter what happens now, the World Cup has seen Ireland get results but a new competition starts in September when we begin our European Championship qualifying campaign in Moscow. The pressure will be back on then, contract or no contract.

Tonight, I am back in Ibaraki. We go to see Italy play Croatia, just in case we meet one of them in the quarter-finals. It is good to look down on that pitch again, to see where I stood in disbelief as Robbie's goal went in on Wednesday night. I feel a real World Cup buzz tonight as Croatia shock the Italians with a 2–1 win.

Italy's two disallowed goals didn't help them much. I was already on the way home so I missed the second one, late in stoppage time from Inzaghi. So did the linesman as it happens!

SUNDAY 9th JUNE

It is hard to believe we met up in Sunderland a month ago tomorrow. So much has happened in that time, so much that has changed all our lives forever. It would be too easy right now to dwell on the impact the past four weeks has had on me and on my former captain. Instead, I look around the breakfast table this morning and I ask myself how these twenty-two players have responded to the challenge thrown down to them in Japan.

They have surprised me, I have to say that. I never doubted their ability to compete at this level but their resilience and their spirit has surpassed all my expectations. And I am not just talking about the players who have performed on the park. As I said before, those sat on the bench for the last two games and those who will sit on the bench on Tuesday night are just as important. The attitude of those who don't play can do more for squad morale than that of those in the team. I remember that from 1990, which is one of the reasons why I try to keep everyone involved.

By and large, we have got on like a house on fire. There are players who thought they were about to play in the two games so far, only to be disappointed. I nearly threw Quinny on for Kevin Kilbane before he crossed for Mattie Holland's goal against Cameroon, although the big man did get his chance last Wednesday. Others have yet to feature. Their faces may show their disappointment from time to time but they have never made an issue of it and I appreciate that. We need to keep this ship stable and content as we go forward now.

It helps that all eleven players not picked in the team get to sit on the bench. If ever FIFA made a good decision, this is it. I know it was a nightmare for Jack when he could only pick five subs from eleven players not in the starting line-up back in 1990. In '94, the players not on the bench used to call themselves the Muppets. World Cups can be a great experience, even as a squad member, but it takes real guts to keep going, to keep smiling, when you know you won't make the team.

Newcastle defender Andy O'Brien has typified that attitude thus far. When we were in Saipan, he said he was going to walk around with a smile on his face for the duration of his World Cup journey. He knew coming out to the Far East that Stan, Breeny and Kenny were ahead of him in the centre-back queue but he had no problem with it then and he has no gripe with it now. He is still smiling and his chance will come. Maybe not now, maybe in the Europeans, but he will get his day in the spotlight. We will see the best of Andy over the next few years and this World Cup will stand him in good stead then.

Steven Reid is the same. He has already played out here and nearly scored against Cameroon. When you consider how young he is, he has so much to offer Ireland in the future.

That youth offers me real hope. The European Championship was the making of Jack's team back in 1988. We built on that experience in the World Cup two years later and I know the same logic will apply with this team, no matter what happens against the Saudis. Experience counts for everything at this level. Once the players have tasted the big stage, and accepted that they can compete on it, they will want more of the same. More than that, they have enough skill and enough time on their side to start really competing at this level. Qualification will not be enough in the future.

That Euro bid is on my mind today. After training I am going to Yokohama to watch Japan play our European Championship opponents Russia in their second Group H game. But first, we train. Jason is flying now and the walking wounded have all made full recoveries. Mattie has a slight problem with a rib injury but it is nothing serious.

We start to talk about the nitty gritty of the game on Tuesday and the implications of the favourites tag we will wear in Yokohama's International Stadium. This is uncharted territory for us in the 2002 finals. We were underdogs in both the games so far and that suits our Irish mentality. We like the opposition to have an air of authority about them, it seems to suit our rebellious nature. Favourites – now there's a different proposition altogether. All I can do is prepare the team properly for the game and ensure that we take nothing for granted on Tuesday night.

The Saudis will not lie down and die for us, that's for sure. They will make us work bloody hard for the winning margin we need. I wouldn't want it any other way. If I was their manager, hanging around for six days waiting for a game of little or no consequence, I would repeatedly beat the pride drum. They have to do themselves proud on Tuesday night, they have to restore their reputation back home after two defeats, one of them horrendous.

We are sitting on a different fence altogether. Someone pointed out in today's press conference that no Irish team has ever scored more than one goal in a game at a World Cup finals, nor have we ever finished on five points in the group before. Negativity. More bloody negativity. So what? This team have never been to a World Cup before so the history books mean nothing to them. We could easily have scored more than once against Cameroon and Germany, we could very easily be looking at winning this group with three points against the Saudis. I get tetchy when people bring up things like this. I am a football man and I live in the present, not in the past. We will qualify for the second phase if we win by two goals or more on Tuesday. That is the only stat that concerns me. Forget history until we make some.

I am reminded that we won all the games when we were cast as favourites during the qualifiers. Again, this is not something I took any note of. I look at performances rather than results in situations like that and the performances have been good, very good, over the past two years. The way we played in those games augurs well for the Saudi match, much more than any set of results.

I leave the statisticians behind and head for Yokohama, venue for

Tuesday night's match and host stadium for tonight's clash between Japan and Russia, our Euro 2004 opponents. The pitch looks superb although the running track that encircles it means the players are away from the crowd. It is a less traditional football stadium than Ibaraki, but I like it.

I enjoy the game as well. Russia are beaten by a goal from Arsenal midfielder Junichi Inamoto and the home crowd go mad.

Our Euro opponents don't make much of an impression on me, I have to admit. For a start, they have all shrunk. Whenever I played against the USSR, each player was a Soviet bloc in his own right. Even when they provided the opposition for my first game in charge of Ireland back in 1996, they looked bigger than us. Not any more. Maybe we have grown but they certainly looked smaller and weaker tonight. I don't know how valuable this exercise will be come September when they will probably have a new manager and some new faces but at least I know one thing. We won't be pushovers in Moscow. Not against the weight of this lot, anyway.

MONDAY 10th JUNE

Old habits die hard. Back in 1990, Niall Quinn made a fortune on the training fields of Malta, Sardinia, Sicily, Genoa and Rome. The routine was simple. He stood in goal at the end of every training session and all comers were invited to shoot penalties at him for a fee, a fiver for three attempts. Miss one and he kept the money, score all three and you doubled your stake. We all had a go, even David O'Leary who must have found it handy when it came to taking a certain penalty kick against Romania a few weeks into the tournament itself.

Niall is up to his old tricks again on the training ground in Chiba today, our last session before the Saudi game and our final workout in this baseball-mad city. It is not the first time Niall has tried his penalty routine on this trip but still he finds gullible souls willing to have a go. Today, he has lined up nine penalty takers at 5,000 yen a go. That's about five euros a shot or £3 sterling, which means penalty kick inflation has run quite high since 1990.

I am not so sure about this. The Brazilian captain Emerson, has missed out on these World Cup finals because of an injury picked up when he tried to play in goal during training, so I voice my concerns towards Quinny as he welcomes all takers. He assures me he will be fine. He reckons the 2002 version of Niall Quinn is more supple than any Brazilian captain so he gets on with it. Anyway, it's been good practice for the lads from the spot throughout this trip. Or so I think.

Guess what? Only Alan Kelly and Mark Kinsella get their money back today. Quinny is quids in and promises to buy the drink when we qualify for the second phase tomorrow night.

His optimism is to be found throughout the squad. We are positive about this game without being cocky. The players know that Germany's 8–0 win over Saudi was a fluke, they know they will have to work bloody hard to make that flight to Korea on Wednesday morning. But, as they say at closing time in Ireland, we didn't come out to go home. We didn't travel all this way to bow out at the first hurdle.

My players keep a fairly even keel about themselves going into most games and this is no different. They will prepare as if they were playing Portugal or Germany in Yokohama. They are not going around the place boasting about the second phase or the implications of a 2–0 win. They are not even talking about the game that much, to be honest. That will change when we watch a video of the Saudis before dinner tonight but for now it is business as usual.

Training is lively. We are ninety minutes away from the second phase of the World Cup finals and everyone wants a part of the action. They all want to be involved tomorrow, they all want to play their part. We are close to the dream now, close to the initial target I set when that plane left Dublin for Amsterdam all those weeks ago.

Robbie's late goal against Germany ensures that our fate is in our own hands now and that is as much as I could have asked for. I'd have settled for this coming out here, no doubt about it. We were underdogs coming into this group but now we are in a great position to finish second and take another plane to South Korea on Wednesday. We can determine what happens now, unlike so many of football's big guns as they enter their final group games. Call me smug, but I am sure the likes of France, Argentina and even our old friends Portugal would swap places with us right now. I am sure they would love to know that a 2–0 win tomorrow night would see them safely through to the second phase.

As always, we will go for that win. It is against our nature to play any other way. Coming here, I even said we would try to win the World Cup. That was not a ridiculous statement, it was merely the natural intent of any Irish side. We play to win and we give it our best shot.

The team won't be made public until tomorrow night, an hour before kick-off, as per my rules. Some journalists think I play this waiting game just to annoy them. I don't. I like to keep the opposition waiting, although the make-up of this team will come as no great surprise to anyone.

The players learn the team today. Gary Kelly will start on the right side of midfield again, even though Jason is now fully fit and itching to get back into the team.

I cannot drop Kells or Stevie Finnan at this stage. Their partnership has been one of the highlights of this tournament for me since they came together for the second-half of the opening match. Jason has to be patient and wait his chance. He's long enough in the game now to know the way it works. And there will be more games, I am very certain on that front.

FIFA are seemingly not so sure. Today, they present each of the players and staff with a beautiful gold medal to acknowledge our participation in the 2002 World Cup finals, just in case we are thinking of leaving town and going back home tomorrow. It is a nice gesture on the part of the powers that be and we all appreciate it.

We will either fly to Seoul on Wednesday or back to Dublin, via Amsterdam, on Thursday. Certain arrangements have to be made for either eventuality so the staff have some work to do in advance of the Saudi game. I let them get on with it. Eddie Corcoran and Ray Treacy have already been to Seoul to check out hotels and other arrangements and report no potential problems if we get through. I am so confident that I may pack my bags for Seoul tonight. I am not tempting fate but I have time on my hands this evening and why not?

Hopefully a few thousand fans back home will be getting ready to pack their bags for Korea as well. I know that many of those already with us will travel on for the second phase and I am sure the credit unions back in Ireland are bracing themselves for a wave of loan enquiries. Long may it last.

My advice to the fans at today's press conference is borrowed straight from the Boy Scout's rulebook – be prepared. I believe we will go through as second in the group and will probably meet Spain from Group B in Suwon next Sunday night. Have your money in order and be ready to roll on Wednesday.

I fancy Germany to win the other game in Shizuoka tomorrow night and the group. Cameroon disappointed me with their application against the Saudis last Thursday and the Germans will be eager to bounce back from their Irish disappointment. They really thought they had booked their passage to the next round when injury time went up on the board at the end of the match. Little wonder then that Rudi Voeller asked me if I was still smiling when I met him in the mixed zone, some fifty minutes or so after the final whistle. Robbie knocked the smile off his face, but I am still laughing, I can tell you.

Rudi has it all to do now, but he will have no worries getting his side past Cameroon. The one bonus for Ireland is that Germany have to play now, they must come out of their shells and beat Cameroon to guarantee qualification. I genuinely feared a scoreless carve-up in their game with Germany if we had lost last Wednesday and both teams needed only a draw to guarantee their qualification for round two.

That's impossible now so maybe it explains why I am very relaxed tonight as we sit the players down and show them a brief video of the Saudis in action. I isolate Al-Temyat, show the lads how he drifts between the forward and midfield areas and comes off his marker. I also remind them that we have already beaten Iran to get this far and there is no way the Saudis are as good as our old friends from the Arabian gulf. We have beaten better teams to get here and we can beat this lot.

Personally, I am a happy man tonight, as happy as I have been at any stage of this trip. The worst is over for me now, there is nothing this World Cup can throw at me anymore, there are no surprises left. I feel invincible, untouchable almost, on the eve of one of the biggest games of my life.

I was probably a bit blunt with my old friend Chris Davis of the *Daily Telegraph* when he asked about the significance of this match earlier today. He enquired if this is my toughest test yet as Ireland boss. No, not at all, I answered. I explained to him that nothing will ever surpass the Cameroon game in terms of personal or professional significance but I was not prepared to go into detail on that one this afternoon. That can wait until we are back home and in reflective mood.

I just want to get this game under way now. In international football, even more than at club level, the next match is the most important. That's why the World Cup feels so right at last. I have been together with my players for over a month now, I have worked with them on a daily basis for every one of those days away. I have just spent four weeks on a training ground and you have no idea how good that felt. I have always said that the one element of a club job I miss is the day-to-day involvement. This is as close as I will get to that without returning to the asylum and I can't get enough of it, to be honest.

I want this World Cup to go on forever now. I want to wake up every morning in the knowledge that I will be working with these great players again. I want to wake up in Japan for the final time on Wednesday knowing there is another story to come from Ireland at these finals.

At last I am enjoying my job and the World Cup again. Sweet dreams . . .

TUESDAY 11th JUNE

World Cup First Round, Group E

Republic of Ireland v Saudi Arabia

The demons are always there. Once you have lived through Skopje and that late, late goal from Mr Staverevsks, they will never, ever, go away. You know in your heart and soul that your team is good enough to win this match, you know your players have worked hard enough over the last eighteen months to deserve the result they need to go through. You look at the names in your squad, Robbie, Duffer, Mattie Holland. Big names who deserve the big stage. You compare them with a Saudi team that has conceded nine goals in two defeats so far in this tournament, two results that have rendered this game meaningless for them. It all pointsto an Irish win, to at least the two-goal victory that will spark a scramble for seats to South Korea. Yet still the doubts remain as you wake up on the morning of the match.

What if the Saudis score? What if we get just one goal? What if the banana skin this Irish team has so far avoided in the World Cup, all the way from the qualifiers to the finals, suddenly slips us up in Yokohama? What if we implode? There it is, the real danger when we take to that bowling green pitch in the International Stadium tonight, the host venue for the 2002 World Cup final. Only Ireland can deny the Irish a place in the second round of the World Cup finals now. We are the only ones who can kill the dream at this stage.

And that's the secret. If we keep our heads tonight, we will be fine. If we keep our shape, dictate the pace of the game and force the Saudis onto the back foot, then we will win this match and book our place in the second round. That is the theme of discussions in the early part of the day.

We breakfast in Chiba then get on the bus for an hour or so, travelling across Tokyo's grey concrete skyline towards Yokohama Bay and the Sheraton Hotel. Lunch and a couple of hours' sleep follow before the Green Army send us on our way again. They have packed the foyer of the hotel to wish us well. The fans are clearly as excited about the night ahead as the rest of us.

The players get their first look at the Yokohama pitch as soon as we throw our bags down in the dressing-rooms. Tonight also heralds our introduction to the Japanese rainy season. The air is moist and the humidity high as we look around the huge stadium for the first time and count the Irish through the turnstiles. Once again, they are here in their thousands, spread out at either end of this 65,000-capacity ground.

They are ready to party, so are we. The lads make their way back to the changing-rooms, their determination yet to explode in any noisy outburst. They are quiet and focused as they strip for the warm-up. There is no shouting yet, no visible sign of nerves. It is all cool, calm and collected. These players know this is their chance to make history.

As they head back out the door with Taff and Packie, I gather my thoughts. This is it, the big moment. I need to keep my focus just as much as the players. I need to be ready to react if all does not go according to plan on that pitch tonight. We are too close now to blow it.

My final Group E team talk is remarkably relaxed. I talk them through the effort they turned in to get here, the sacrifices they have made along the way to Yokohama and the game that will make or break our World Cup ambition. We are on the brink now and we are more than capable of reaching out to that second phase. Keep your shape, keep it tight and remember the golden rule – no regrets.

Shay sums it up when he says we haven't been cooped up for four weeks to blow it now.

The big sermon centres on the need for a positive start. The previous games against Cameroon and Germany have seen us jittery in the opening stages and we conceded the first goal in both games. That was not done on purpose, even if the shock brought out the best in this team. We cannot afford a repeat tonight. We must be bright and bubbly from the off.

We are. There are only seven minutes on the clock when Steve

Staunton fashions a brilliant ball from left to right out of defence. His pass sweeps upfield to Gary Kelly, on the run from the right of midfield.

Kells reacts with speed as he gathers the ball in the corner, times his cross to perfection, scoops it goalward and Robbie hits it first time, on the volley. I am on my feet before the ball hits the back of the net. This is just what we ordered. Robbie fires a bow and arrow salute and embarks on his customary flip as he becomes the first Irishman to score two goals in any World Cup finals. We are on our way – but not for long.

Instead of signalling an all-out assault from Ireland, that goal sends us back into our shells. We go on the back foot, we lose our shape and our rhythm. We start to chase the opposition as individuals, not as a team.

I cannot believe what I am seeing in front of my eyes. The Saudis discover they can play the ball through us, they can pass their way through midfield and our defence with some very pretty patterns. This gives them new hope. It also gives Al-Temyat a licence to thrill which he gratefully accepts. They start to look like the team in the ascendancy, not the plan at all. They make the real chances as Khathran tests Shay with a long-range effort on twenty-two minutes.

Then Shay has to come to the rescue again, saving at the feet of Al-Shahrani after a good through ball from the overlapping right full-back Al-Jahani. We are giving this guy far too much room and we are paying Al-Temyat far too much respect. I cannot understand what is happening here. Kinse does well to block Al-Yami and Shay denies Al-Jahani, Al-Temyat and Khathran as the first-half comes to a close.

I am livid. Agitated is too kind a word for it as we head for the sanctuary of the dressing-room and some very straight talking. We have forgotten the golden rule, we have just produced a first-half full of incidents worthy of regret. We were fragmented, we were chasing them all over the park and we were in constant trouble down the left side.

Time for change. Hartey picked up a bang on his foot in the

first-half and irritated a long-standing injury. I decide to take him off and throw caution to the wind again. We will push Duffer out wide left, bring Killer back to left-back and throw Quinny in with Robbie upfront. It was something I had thought about before. I knew Kevin would be more than comfortable at left-back in this sort of game and Niall had already made an impact as a sub against the Germans.

He had told me before the match that Peter Reid sometimes waits for five minutes or so after half-time before throwing him into the fray. He likes the crowd to get excited when they see Niall warming up and reckons he makes more of a dramatic entry once the second-half is underway. Nice idea but no thanks, not tonight. I want my impact and I want it now. I need to show the Saudis who's the boss around here once again and quickly.

We are not going to chase them any more. We will revert to two solid banks of four and invite them on to us when they have the ball. Let's see if they can play their way through us when we have our shape under control. Let's see how good they really are.

The plan works. Quinny makes his impact and gives us something to aim at. Duffer starts to rampage down the left and the Saudis have no option but to kick him by foul means or fair, mostly foul. They concede one such free-kick in the sixty-first minute. Stan is the victim of a silly yellow card from Senegalese referee Falla Ndaye for alleged time-wasting but when he does take the free, he makes it count.

Gary Breen, a player who adds an ariel threat to our side, had been working on free-kicks and corners with Taff ever since we left Dublin. I like his height on dead-ball situations, like the fact that he gives us another target to aim at on these occasions. Normally, we expect Gary to get his head onto the end of the cross, this time it is his magical right foot that steers Stan's ball into the corner and past a helpless Mohammed Al-Deayea. Brilliant.

At last we are in control, not just of the game but of our own destiny. I have no idea what is happening in the other game between Germany and Cameroon and I don't care. I know the two goals will do us. There is no way the Saudis are going to score now, they had their chance in the first-half and they blew it. We are solid and we are comfortable. We are finally playing with freedom, when the referee allows us to that is.

He is a bit finicky. He annoyed me in the first-half when Kells was off the pitch briefly for treatment and he wouldn't let him back on. I was shouting at Gary to track back when I realised he wasn't actually on the pitch. Now, the ref gets on my goat again as we try to get Jason on for Kells with twenty minutes or so to go. He is having none of it in scenes reminiscent of the famous Aldo row at the '94 World Cup in Florida, when he tried to get on against Mexico and the linesman kept delaying him. Jack got banished to the stand for the next game over that one.

I am seething but the game is over now as a contest. Duffer is playing with them out on the left and finally gets the goal his performance deserves with a piledriver just three minutes from time. Actually, I'd like to say it was a piledriver but it wasn't. Duffer let fly from the edge of the box alright but the 'keeper let it through his hands. I told Duffer afterwards that I reckoned Al-Deayea had money on 3–0 and he broke his backside laughing. As soon as Damien's goal goes in, Johnny Fallon tells me that Germany are 2–0 up in a very ill-tempered game in Shizuoka. It's great news, in the event of a German victory any win would have seen us through. I know I said I didn't want to hear the score but he could have put my mind at rest a little earlier!

We play out time. Lee Carsley gets on for Kinse and another player gets to say he played in the World Cup finals. I am delighted for Lee, he has kept his head down and worked hard all trip without as much as a single moan. If only all professionals were like him.

The celebrations explode with the final whistle. Mick Byrne leads the charge onto the pitch. The fans are singing now, all the way to Seoul. The lap of honour seems to take as long as the game itself. We cover every inch of this stadium, salute every Irish man, woman and child who has taken the trouble to travel out here and support us. This is their night as much as ours. They had faith and today that faith was repaid many times over.

I am smiling now. Satisfaction is replaced by a sense of vindication as my overriding emotion. I have disproved so many criticisms since we first met up in the North East of England. Someone reminded me the other day of the scene in *The Quiet Man* where an old dear hands John Wayne a stick to beat Maureen O'Hara with. I know how Maureen O'Hara must have felt. There are plenty of media pundits out there who look for sticks to beat me with. They reckon I can't make tactical changes. I can't analyse opponents. We're a pub team. I can't manage and I can't coach. Really?

The Irish team has taken its place in the second phase of the World Cup finals and, for once, I can take the credit. We have achieved the goal we set ourselves on the way out here. We have done it in a professional and entirely appropriate manner with players who wanted to play in the World Cup for their country. My tactics have worked, my substitutions, my team talks have all passed the greatest test of them all. I have been to a big tournament now and I have come out smiling. We are through to the second phase and damn the begrudgers. They are welcome to their narrow minds.

I have been to hell and back in this World Cup and here I am, standing on the pitch in Yokohama and celebrating a famous Irish win tonight. I have learnt from everything this tournament has thrown at me and I am the better for it all. I have made the decisions, the tough ones as well as the easy ones. All this will make me a better manager and a better person, I have no doubts on that front. I will do a better job for Ireland in the future now on the back of everything to do with the World Cup, the good and the bad.

I watch as Duffer and Robbie milk the applause for all they are worth. They deserve this moment in the spotlight. Duffer was magical again tonight, a superstar in the making. I look at him and I see a player who can be anything he wants to be. He can be the Irish Ryan Giggs, the Irish David Beckham. He can be a superstar after a World Cup that has beamed his talents into so many millions of households across the globe.

Robbie is guaranteed folk hero status back home after his two World Cup goals. He deserves all the credit that will come his way but first comes a tap on the shoulder from a FIFA drugs tester. They want to take Robbie to doping control once again, the second game in a row he has been tested. He is livid and I can understand his frustrations. He missed the dressing-room scenes when his goal secured that late draw against Germany the other night. He was stuck in the doping centre for a good two hours after that game and we end up waiting for the bus. Tonight, his name has been picked from the hat once again. He cannot believe his luck but he has no choice.

I have been in this situation myself. I was picked after the win over England back in Germany in 1988 and it took me an age to fill their bottle. I had ice bags on my stomach trying to induce the feeling but nothing would work for me, not even when they offered me some of their non-alcoholic beer. I said I preferred the water but even that didn't work for an age.

People don't realise how hard these drug tests are on players. Modern advice says that players need carbohydrates inside them at least half an hour after the final whistle to compensate for all the weight loss, particularly in this heat and humidity. Those tested are denied access to food, they won't even provide them with as much as a sandwich inside the doping centre in case it has been tampered with. And even the decision to take blood samples, a simple procedure, this year hasn't helped. They still insist on a urine sample as well so God knows when we will see Robbie next.

FIFA officials lead him off as we depart for the chaotic scenes in the dressing-room. It is one for all and all for one as the singing begins and the craic flows with the ease of a bottle of bubbly. I interrupt the celebrations with a simple request made to the lads who have just played in the game that has secured our place in the second phase.

Many years ago, I was a novice international sitting on the bench when a Michael Robinson goal beat Russia in a famous World Cup game at Lansdowne Road. I was only a bit-part player then, out of the picture really and about as useful as an ashtray on a motorbike.

I felt I didn't really belong as the dressing-room celebrated a famous Irish win. That feeling always stayed with me, the 'us and them' that arose between those who had played and those who were left on the edge of it all. I do not want a repeat performance tonight so I call the lads together and ask those who played to show their appreciation for those on the bench. The applause that followed may have meant nothing to the lads on the periphery of it all but it meant something to me.

That one road is very important you know.

Republic of Ireland 3, Saudi Arabia 0

ELEVEN

12–17 June, Seoul

WEDNESDAY 12th JUNE

Another day, another vote of confidence from the FAI – apparently, we're talking about a new six-year contract again. Great, keep them coming. As long as they're happy, I'm happy.

That will come as a disappointment to the man from Saudi who asked me after last night's game if I'd be interested in managing their team. I am always flattered by such questions but I explained that they have a manager and I have a two-year deal with the FAI that I am very happy with. I know you should never say never but I had to decline his approach. Meantime, I really must get around to signing that FAI contract and giving it back to my employers.

At the breakfast table, Gary Breen is making the most out of the unemployment line. Gary is currently without a club. He left Coventry when his contract expired before the World Cup began but I can't see him having any problems getting a new club as soon as he goes home. He was immense against the Germans and after last night's goal he has fully vindicated his selection. If anything, he has emerged as the patron saint of our unsung heroes here in Japan. And we have had a few unsung heroes down the years.

I have seen great club players who have flopped at international level and good club players who have gone on to become great internationals. Gary is one of those players who have never let me down. No matter what is happening for him on the club front, he steps onto the international stage and he is inspired. Maybe now, at last, he will get the credit he deserves.

Gary has milked every interview for all it was worth with his claim to have hit the best goalever scored by an unemployed footballer at the World Cup finals. It's not a bad story, to be fair. Nor is his revelation that his granny Mary Lynch back in Clare prophesised from her sick bed that he would score against the Saudis. She even told him to put some of his dole money on it!

I must ring Mary today and see if she has any insight into who will be our opponents in Suwon next Sunday night. Spain play South Africa in their final Group B game tonight with Paraguay up against Slovenia in the other game. Slovenia are the only team who can't win the group so it is still up in the air. I should also compliment Mary on the fine grandson she has sent out to play for Ireland, here in the Far East. Gary has been a stalwart of this World Cup campaign, at great personal cost it has to be revealed.

We had a real problem with Gary's insurance before the Nigeria game. Since Coventry had released him when his contract expired at the end of the Nationwide season, some three weeks earlier, we couldn't insure him for the value of his Coventry contract. And since he has yet to sign a deal with another club there was no new contract we could insure in the middle of May. And there was no transfer value to insure because Gary is available on a Bosman free. The insurers wouldn't place a value on a contract that has yet to exist and refused to value the contract that had expired. Gary never made an issue of it, but it was a concern. We eventually got him covered for the Nigeria match but for nothing like the value of a four-year contract under a Bosman transfer. If he had been seriously injured in that game, and it is always a possibility, then Gary would have been left severely out of pocket in the name of Irish football. It is important that people know that, know the sacrifice he was prepared to make to play in a World Cup finals. His loyalty was demonstrated by another faultless performance last night, highlighted by that goal.

I look forward to the day when Gary renews his partnership with Kenny Cunningham at the centre of my defence. I am not trying to push Stan out the door, he has yet to confirm or deny that he will quit once this World Cup adventure comes to an end, but I know that Gary and Kenny will be just as effective as Breeny and Steve have been over the past fortnight. And when Stan does go, is Breeny a contender for the captaincy? Wait and see.

Robbie is still fuming when the lads get up, earlier than normal, ahead of the coach journey to Haneda Airport this morning. It took him almost three hours to have a pee last night and he is no longer amused. The craic was almost over by the time he got back to the hotel and he really feels cheated on this one. Once bitten, twice shy. The fact that he got pulled in for a dope test late in the season at Leeds doesn't help his humour in this instance. I assure him that it is a random thing and point to the fact that Niall Quinn and Richard Dunne were tested after the Cameroon game, even though neither played any part in the match.

Robbie wonders why the blood sample isn't enough. I have asked the same question of Martin Walsh but he tells me it will take time before FIFA agree to that. They want blood and water, if you know what I mean, and we have to put up with it. Taff reckons they could blood test all twenty-three players before and after each game but I suppose they won't agree to that either. That might not be the answer but it beats having a player held back for two or three hours after a game, twice as in Robbie's case. I just wonder where the famous FIFA Fair Play comes into it when a player is kept back, without food, for almost three hours in doping control. Robbie's stomach still isn't the better of it and his anger is fully understandable in the circumstances.

His unhappiness sets the tone for the day to come. We arrive at Haneda to discover that KAWOC, the World Cup Organising Committee in Korea, have sent the wrong plane. I am told they expected Cameroon to qualify from our group and got Ireland. As a result, they have sent a plane that is way too small for our needs. Cameroon travel with a smaller delegation but we are struggling with this plane. The journalists have to leave their luggage behind, cameras and all, and the whole procedure delays take-off for Seoul by a couple of hours.

When we eventually get airborne the breakfast tray, consisting of bread and jam and tea or coffee, is a little meagre considering we are now well into lunchtime. The flight itself is hit with heavy turbulence and we bump our way from Japan to Korea. I know the French team, who went out of the competition yesterday, would give their right arms to swap places with us right now but I do not enjoy the flight one bit.

When we disembark, it appears that Seoul has forgotten we are coming as well. The Japanese fans who made us so welcome are a memory now. Instead, armed guards hidden beneath black berets and dark shades greet us in the arrivals hall and escort us out through customs. The transport for the skips is too small, the bus just about fits the players and staff. It is all a bit farcical this side of the World Cup finals. Korea 0, Japan 1.

Matters improve when we arrive at the Westin Chosun Hotel. It's in the heart of the city, right beside the plaza where Korean fans gather in their hundreds of thousands to watch the matches and enjoy their communal World Cup experience.

The hotel is top class and I tell the players we will meet downstairs in O'Kims, a curiously named Irish theme bar of all things, to watch the Spain–South Africa game over a few beers. As they depart for their rooms, I head off to find a training ground with Brendan Menton. Three official venues are on offer in Seoul but Turkey are already housed at the Olympic Stadium and China have the run of the second-best facility.

I go to see the third. At first glance it looks great, but only at eye level. The pitch is awful and it is just not good enough. Now I know why they wouldn't let Eddie Corcoran and Ray Treacy see it when they were here last week. KAWOC were most unhelpful then, in contrast to our Japanese hosts who couldn't do enough. World Cup life clearly moves at a different pace in the two host countries.

There is one more potential venue available to us, at the Sanggok-dong Military Sports Fields. I can't get to see it until the morning so I head back to O'Kim's and the Spanish game.

The lads have a free night tonight, in all senses. The wives have gone back home after the first phase and Gary Kelly reckons they can have a rest now they don't have to worry about their better halves. Like the rest of the lads, he relaxes over a game of pool and a spot of darts as we keep an eye on Spain's very impressive victory over a plucky South African side, whose 'keeper gifted Spain their first goal.

Spain are slick and fluent as they win the group and go through to a meeting with the Republic in phase two, as expected. For once they have lived up to their hype in a World Cup finals and I am more than impressed. In fact, our potential opponents look so good that Mattie Holland asks me, midway through the second-half, if it is wise for us to watch them play at this pace and level. I point out that their coach Jose Antonio Camacho has made eight changes for the game from the team he played against Slovenia on Saturday. In effect, this is their reserve side!

I look for weaknesses in the Spanish play and they are few and far between. With France and Argentina out of the equation, we could be looking at the next world champions here. That's how highly I rate the Spaniards at first glance. Seamus McDonagh, the former Irish 'keeper, is at the game scouting for me so I am looking forward to reading his report tomorrow. Maybe he spotted a flaw or two.

THURSDAY 13th JUNE

Up and at it nice and early, before Ireland has even gone to bed. I travel some forty minutes out of town to see the military training ground and it is the answer to all my problems. The grass is a bit long at the moment but the pitch is excellent. They can't cut it until tomorrow but we will train here today and the locals are quite chuffed. They had been knocked back as a potential World Cup training site so our endorsement is most welcome. One problem out of the way.

By the time we train, Dean Kiely has gone off in search of a dentist. He needs a tooth removed before he goes any further but he declines the offer, made by several of the lads, to knock it out for him.

Packie decides it is time to start talking about penalty shoot-outs with the 'keepers. He is, of course, an expert on the subject after the Genoa shoot-out with Romania in the 1990 finals when he famously saved from Timofte and we won through to the quarter-finals and a game against Italy. He begins to prepare Shay and Alan Kelly for the prospect today. The lads have been firing penalties at Niall ever since we left Dublin so we will have no worries when it comes to looking for volunteers to take them if it comes to that on Sunday.

Shay, in his Donegal innocence, asks Packie if he can take one if we go to spot kicks on Sunday. Packie, polite as ever, tells him to concentrate on stopping them and not to be worrying about who takes them. Or words to that effect.

Stan (thigh), Robbie (groin), Kevin Kilbane (ankle) and Duffer (knee) all sit out training but everyone else is fine. Hartey has recovered from the knock he picked up in the first-half on Tuesday night and is eager to get back into the action. He knows he has yet to play as well as he can in these World Cup finals and he is desperate to make amends.

Some of the press reckon his performance has not been all it should be too. Welcome to a bad day at the office, otherwise known as a bad day at the press conference. We meet for our daily chat in the ballroom of the Westin Hotel. The media numbers are increasing dramatically by the day so several new faces will leave the room this afternoon thinking I am a grumpy so-and-so.

My mood is not helped by the tone of the first question. Someone has got wind of the story that I turned down a training ground last night and has blown it out of all proportion. According to some reports back at home, I have even complained to FIFA about the standard of the training facilities. Absolute rubbish. I hadn't even turned the first one down yet this morning in case the alternative wasn't up to scratch. Yet here we are, days away from a World Cup second round match against Spain and only hours after the win that saw us through to the last sixteen, discussing a non-story about a training pitch.

Give me a break, please. Of course I am tetchy. Can we not talk football here? Can we not discuss how well my players have performed for Ireland in this World Cup, how their achievement in reaching the second round deserves recognition? No. We will try to make a mountain out of a molehill once again and get bogged down by the standard of pitch at a training ground that I eventually turned down. The fact that I have located a more than adequate venue, and trained on it already, seems irrelevant.

By the time the media start pussyfooting about the place on the Ian Harte issue, my patience has snapped. I know what they are all trying to say about Hartey without any of them actually saying it. What they want to know is whether or not I will drop Ian based on his performances so far, only nobody asks me the question out straight. It always amazes me that some journalists never ask a question at all, unless it is in print, whilst others beat around the bush to try and find out what they really want to know. Today, they all try to get an answer about Ian Harte without actually asking the question. I know what they are after so I refuse to play ball. I will not name the team until Sunday, an hour before the kick-off. Anyone who thinks otherwise is off their rocker.

I am also amazed by the suggestion that we have achieved our World Cup goal now and might as well pack up shop ahead of Sunday's game against the Spanish and accept that the tournament is over for us. What a load of manure. Yes, my initial aim coming out was to qualify for the second phase and move on to Korea but that is not the end of my team's ambition by any stretch of the imagination. We are well aware that the fans, here and at home, are celebrating the fact that we have made it through to the last sixteen but nobody is accepting that as the end of it all.

Spain looked good last night, very good. But are they a bigger threat than Portugal in Lisbon or Holland in Amsterdam? I don't think so. Yes, they have Raul and Fernando Morientes and a handful of world-class players who can win this game on their own but so what? We have played against big names before and we have beaten them. Will they fancy marking Duffer or Robbie? I doubt it. Stop asking me how we will stop them. Ask them how they will stop us. How they will end the momentum that has seen us through the games against Cameroon, Germany and Saudi.

I leave the conference in a huff. I came into this room in good humour. I have borrowed that coat hanger from Mark Kinsella and will wear it inside my mouth to protect my grin for as long as this World Cup adventure continues but sometimes this negativity does my head in. Today is one of those days.

FRIDAY 14th JUNE

Jose Antonio Camacho is saying very nice things about me this morning. Good man. He tells anyone who will listen that this Ireland team will present Spain with real problems in Suwon on Sunday night. He is talking up Duffer, Robbie, Mattie Holland and Quinny. He is even talking up my ability as a centre-half which stops me in my tracks for a second. I didn't think many Barnsley matches were shown live on Spanish television but there you go.

I played against Camacho once, apparently. I do remember playing against Spain on that great Flower Lodge pitch in Cork back in the mid eighties, but I have absolutely no idea who their centre-backs were. I only ever remember centre-forwards and there are times when I can only remember kicking them!

Camacho doesn't stand out in my memory but I know he was a tough number five who took no prisoners. My kind of guy. He is also, clearly, my kind of manager judging by the compliments he is paying all things Irish right now. I like that attitude in an opposition manager. I have never understood those who engage in open warfare with other managers or teams before an international game. There is nothing to be gained by slagging off the opposition, all it does is wind people up. The best thing any opposition manager can do for Ireland is slag us off. That really gets the lads going.

Italy discovered that to their cost back in 1990. I remember the way they talked themselves up and Ireland down before that quarter-final. In their own minds, all they had to do was turn up and they were into the semi-finals. I know they were playing to a home crowd with their talk but they showed absolutely no respect for the Irish team. Ultimately that worked against them. We were spitting blood in our hotel outside Rome by the end of that week. When we stood in that tunnel in the Olympic Stadium, waiting for the call to the pitch, I did not see eleven arrogant or confident men. For all their talk, I stared straight into the eyes of eleven frightened and nervy footballers. They were big men in print, not so big when push came to shove. They won the game but we were a lot better than any of their disparaging remarks. It was no walkover. We ran them close and they knew it.

Football matches are only decided over ninety minutes on the pitch, not on the back pages as the 1990 experience with Italy proved to me. That story will come in handy between now and Sunday, even if the Spanish are falling over themselves to be nice to us. I can see through that too. We won't get fooled into complacency by their nice words. They want to win this game as much as we do but their manager knows there is nothing to be gained by winding us up before a ball is kicked in anger. Camacho is playing it cool by paying us compliments, just as I was nice about them yesterday when I stated publicly that they are potential World Cup champions, that there are no weaknesses in their side. In fact, I would struggle to find something negative to say about them! It is all a game of cat and mouse and it will mean nothing come the big kick-off on Sunday night.

Camacho has guided Spain to their best World Cup start in fifty-two years and the pressure is on him to deliver on that early promise. With so many big names gone, I am not the only one who believes they can win this tournament and that sort of expectation brings its own problems. We were favourites last Tuesday night against the Saudis and that does change your emphasis before the game. This time around we are back in the role of underdogs and that suits me just fine. I won't need to motivate the players or lift them for this one. If you can't raise your game for a match against Spain and a place in the quarter-finals of the World Cup, then you really shouldn't be here.

I always fancied we would end up against Spain in round two and the fact that this is the hardest possible tie-up available to us just makes the potential reward all the greater. This is as tough a game as there is at this stage of the World Cup, particularly when you see some of the teams that are already out of the tournament, but it is a fantastic game for the players and for the fans.

On paper, Spain are the favourites but I never go down the road of judging it player by player, man by man. I have faith that my team can compete with anyone over 90 minutes, or 120 minutes if the game goes to extra-time and even penalties. I don't believe it will though. There are too many scoring options in both teams to see this one going to the wire. We have created chances and scored in all our games so far, the Spaniards have been even more prolific on the scoreboard.

The players practise penalties at training again today, just in case. Shay Given, who seems desperate to take one if it goes to a shoot-out on Sunday, has a go but shaves the post. I tell him once more to concentrate on saving them, not taking them like some. Jose Luis Chilavert does a good job for Paraguay and is known as a bit of an international goal-scoring goalkeeper so there is nothing to suggest that Shay wouldn't score if it came to it, but we have enough good strikers to push him down the pecking order.

I have not thought about the five penalty takers in a shoot-out. I don't see the point. I could pick five players now and three of them could be off the field by the end of extra-time on Sunday night. I also believe in the power of the players at times like that. You have to ask for volunteers if it goes down to a shoot-out, you have to see who feels right in their own mind about taking one in the cauldron of emotion. It is one thing to beat Quinny from twelve yards on a training pitch, quite another thing to beat Shay, Dean or Alan Kelly and completely different to do it in the last sixteen of the World Cup.

Duffer is a classic case in point. When the lads were taking their penalties today he admitted to me that he was nervous, hitting a penalty on the training pitch. Then he shaved it off the upright and into the top corner, way beyond the 'keepers reach. I explained to Duffer that it is big and ugly centre-halves who have every right to be nervous taking a penalty, not a player with his skills.

I was nowhere to be seen when Jack went looking for volunteers back in Genoa all those years ago. I didn't want to know but only because I knew there were better strikers of the ball available to Ireland. If it had come to last man standing then I would have taken one but I didn't fancy it. I had missed one for Manchester City and for Celtic in a previous life and the omens were not good.

Duffer should have no worries on that score. He can bend the ball any way he wants but the fact that he was nervous on the training ground is interesting.

Today's press conference is a far more civilised affair than yesterday's. We talk about football mostly and that eases my mood for the duration of a twenty-minute chat.

Outside the hotel, Seoul is preparing for tonight's big game between South Korea against Portugal, the match that will decide who makes it into the last sixteen. My thoughts are with my old friend Joao Pinheiro at Prainha in the Algarve. A passionate Benfica fan, Joao is also a devout Portugal supporter. He cannot be a happy man right now. One poor Portugal team lost to the USA in their opening game out here, a very good alternative hammered Poland in their second match. I wonder which of those two sides will turn up tonight.

Our Seoul base is right beside City Hall Plaza and already the atmosphere is building, four hours before kick-off. Thousands of fans are lining the streets in their 'Be the Reds' tee-shirts and I know it is going to be very noisy, with an estimated 400,000 people gathered outside by kick-off time. I tell the lads to enjoy it. We don't play until Sunday so I don't see the noise as a major problem and anyway, 400,000 Koreans are hardly going to do what I tell them if I ask them to keep it down!

Before the Portugal game, we manage our own bonding session with the fans. RTE's Tony O'Donoghue has organised for some World Cup footage from Ireland to be sent out to us by satellite, and TV3 have sent out tapes as well. The players spend an hour or so watching everything from the scenes in the Submarine Bar to video footage of Apres Match, the RTE television comedy sketch show. I actually think I am listening to myself until I realise it is one of the impersonators.

The lads love this tape. I remember the great Con Houlihan

writing back in 1990 that he missed the World Cup finals because he was in Italy. That line always stuck with me and tonight I know exactly what he means. It must be great to be a part of all this back in Ireland. When we qualified for the second phase on Tuesday night, I did admit that part of me wanted to fly back to Dublin for the night and soak up the atmosphere. The tapes have given us a flavour of the scenes we are missing back home but they also reinforce our determination to keep this party on the road. We can now see for ourselves what it means to the people of Ireland. They are still on our side, they are right behind us, and they definitely want us to beat the Spanish on Sunday.

We will do our best. At least, we are still in the competition. Joao and his golfing friends must be pulling their hair out as Portugal lose to the Koreans in a game they should have won.

Losers go home. So does my old friend Mr Oliveira, the Portuguese boss. Shame that!

SATURDAY 15th JUNE

Technology is a wonderful thing. I wake this morning, 7,000 miles away, to find a fax under my door from home.

Peter Keeper is a member of Sundridge Park, my local golf club just outside Bromley in Kent. He is also a very realistic man who has a habit of putting things into perspective. The gist of his fax is simple. He reminds me that two years ago we were given no chance of emerging from the Group of Death alongside Holland and Portugal. Just six months ago, some doubted our ability to get past Iran in the play-offs. Then we lost our star player in Saipan and the pundits felt that would kill our World Cup hopes. Many, Peter reminds me, seriously doubted that we could ease past Germany, Cameroon and Saudi Arabia in the group stages in Japan. Now we are up against Spain and again they will give us no chance. We will have to win the World Cup, he reckons, before we get the credit we deserve.

His fax sums up the way people think about us. There is little I can do about that. I am happy to let the performances and the results speak for themselves and so far we are doing quite nicely on both fronts, thank you.

The last sixteen is a great achievement but I emphasise to the team again this morning that we cannot afford to rest on our laurels now. If we do, we will regret it to the end of our days. We must give it our best shot. We did not come all this way to roll over now and have our bellies rubbed by the Spaniards, say 'thanks lads' and go home. We have our pride to play for and we have those fans to repay for their faith.

I remind the players that there is no bigger party to spoil right now than the Spaniards'. They are in the same boat as the Italians back in 1990, they have everything to lose and we have everything to gain. The pressure is all on Spain.

When we train later at the match stadium, I tell Duffer and Robbie that they are to stay forward at all times tomorrow night. In previous games, the Spanish have been content to leave Fernando Hierro and Miguel Angel Nadal at the back and push everyone else up. Like Brazil, their tendency to attack en masse can leave them vulnerable on the break. If Camacho is half the coach I think he is then I reckon he will not leave his team open to such problems against Ireland. He will have noted the natural pace that Robbie and Duffer possess. If he leaves just two men to watch them, he will play right into our hands.

People talk about a lack of pace in their central defence but I have never been one to worry about speed at the back, for obvious reasons. Kevin Moran and I were never the fastest players off the blocks but what we lacked in speed we made up for in guile and cunning. Nadal and Hierro are the same, two very clever players who read the game exceptionally well and foresee danger. They don't get tight on strikers, they don't get sucked up to halfway and they seldom get turned. Still, Spain play a dangerous game with just those two left to man the defences and I wonder if Camacho will change his options tomorrow night.

Yes, the Spanish will create chances but they will also give us ample opportunity to get men forward in support of the front two. How they deal with Duffer and Robbie may be as crucial as the way we handle Morientes and Raul. I am not going to man-mark them. When you start to change the way you play to cater for the opposition, it creates more confusion than it is worth. We never man-marked the likes of Hagi or Figo in the past, so I have no intention of starting to do it now.

Spain's attacking flair is their prime asset and I've asked Ian Rogers to help me analyse it. Ian, a video expert, has been working with us since I was first introduced to him by Sky Sports' Rob McCaffrey some while back. He has this amazing computer technology that can break any game down into sections for analysis. We use it to video our own training sessions and games, but also to look at the opposition. Ian can isolate any aspect of the Spanish play for me before tomorrow night's game. I can see their patterns on corners, free-kicks, throw-ins, even their kick-outs. He can show me how Raul runs on and off the ball, how Morientes reacts when his strike partner is on the ball. It is a fascinating tool and one that is so useful when you are up against players of the skill and ability of the Spanish strikeforce.

Spain will present our defence with its toughest task yet, by a distance. The Germans were so strong at the back but the Spanish are the best side we have played out here in terms of forward power and pace. Still, Stan's partnership with Breeny has been cemented through this World Cup campaign and I have every faith in our back four.

There is a great buzz about the training session today. The lads are fired up for this one and, if anything, I need to calm them down. The practice game at the end of the night highlights their enthusiasm. We play old against young with the manager joining the veterans to try and knock some cheekiness out of the kids. It is a serious game that drags on and on and on. Next goal wins but there is no sign of it coming. The lads are going at full pelt and I am worried that they will leave too much behind them in the stadium tonight.

Eventually I tell Taff to call a halt, blow the final whistle and get them off before they run themselves into the ground. Instead of a golden goal, we decide the game on a penalty shoot-out in the goal to the left of the dug-outs. That goes to the wire as well with the lads firing penalties home until Kenny Cunningham misses one and the oldies lose the match. We are livid but the spirit is good.

Back at the hotel, I pull Ian Harte for a chat. Again today the press have been beating about the bush and asking me if I will surprise them with my team selection. The inference is that Hartey should be dropped.

Ian is still my best left-back and having played as well as he has done in the past for Ireland, he deserves my support now. He just needs to believe in himself and get back to the player he was when his fellow pros named him on their team of the season two years ago. Hartey is aggressive in the tackle and in the air. He can stop wingers in their tracks, he can ping great balls forward for Robbie and Duffer and he can cause havoc with free-kicks and corners. Perhaps some have forgotten how he dealt with Figo, Conceicao, Zenden and Overmars in the qualifiers.

Hartey has set himself high standards that he has yet to reach at this World Cup. He knows it as well as anyone. Players are not stupid, he is aware of the criticism and he knows where it is coming from. He knows it is time to get his act together. Maybe it's nerves, maybe the foot injury he brought to the World Cup is causing more concern than we know about. Whatever, I reassure him tonight that he is my first choice at left-back, that I rate him as highly as any left-sided player in this tournament.

I have picked the side that is best suited to Ireland's needs and he is a part of that team. I tell him again that I have no worries about his ability at all and no reason to drop him, no matter what anyone else has to say on the subject. I just want him to play to the standard he set himself a couple of years back. Only he can put it right. He is more than capable of that and he promises to deliver tomorrow night.

We need Hartey on top form. Tonight is England night. Katie has arrived back from London after a quick flight home for some exams and the family dine together in O'Kims as Sven's team knock the stuffing out of Denmark. England look good and I am delighted for them. I have seen so many England fans backing Ireland at games out here, with green hats and white shirts, and that's the way it should be. I know it is hard for our supporters when the boot is on the other foot but I am genuinely pleased for England and the English game tonight. I hope more Irish fans feel that way now as well. Maybe this World Cup can bring us closer as footballing nations. Our players earn their living over there so anything that is good for their game is good for our players. They looked comfortable and composed tonight and long may it continue.

SUNDAY 16th JUNE

World Cup Second Round

Republic of Ireland v Spain

It is time to be single-minded. It is a time to be positive. We can win this one. The Spanish can be brittle, we can get at them, we can score against them. We can beat them.

Late last night, as we signed shirts and balls and even World Cup lampshades in the team room at the Westin Hotel, I told the lads to dismiss the notion that this is the end of the road. Yes, we were all signing autographs like there's no tomorrow but there is no reason why we can't be sitting in Korea this time next week, looking forward to the semi-finals of the World Cup. When we left Japan last Wednesday, I was asked if I had any message for the host nation. My only response was to say 'See you soon'. We can go back and play on Japanese soil again if we work our socks off against Spain and anyone else awaiting us here in Korea.

Why not? This World Cup has been the great leveller, it has allowed nations like Ireland to rise to a new level and compete with the so-called footballing superpowers. South Korea and Japan are in the last sixteen with us and they too will fancy their chances against all comers.

Match day can drag when you're playing in the evening but today is busy. The players are relaxed, their minds focused. There is pressure, of course there is pressure, but nothing above the norm.

The Irish are out in huge numbers again, they wave us off from the hotel, their enthusiasm infectious. We leave early enough for the ground, an hour or so down the motorway from a busy Korean capital. Even on a Sunday the traffic is out in force, just like back home, and we have a narrow escape on our way to Suwon. Midway through the journey a car pulls across one of our police escort riders and our driver swerves to avoid them. He misses but the bike rider isn't so lucky, hits the car and loses a finger.

In the old days we were handed our shirts on the way to the ground, but that was something I changed when I became manager. Now they are laid out for the players, and each shirt has the name of the opposition and the date of the game embroidered on the centre of the chest, proof positive that you have played in that game for your country. You cannot buy those shirts. Only those fortunate enough to play for Ireland get to wear them and to keep them, or swap them if they wish to. I have so many shirts at home with no idea what game they came from. Now the players have a permanent reminder of their international careers.

Today, Taff decides to take advantage of the fact that the dressing-room is split in two. He winds the lads up by putting the team into one room and the subs into another with some of the staff. The bait isn't out for long. Dean Kiely bites and asks Taff if he is taking the mick. Taff replies that he knew someone would have a go at him just because he tried to give them all some space. The banter is good as the lads decide which room they're going into and then head out onto the pitch.

The Spanish are already out there, looking pretty in their blazers, polo shirts and slacks. They have a good look at us, anxious no doubt to know who is in and who is out of the Ireland team. I have told the players but no one else. We start with the same team again. Hartey is at left-back, Jason still on the bench. Once again, I am not going to change for the sake of it.

Spain take a different approach. The players are out doing their warm-up and I am sat back in the dressing-room when their team comes through. Camacho has responded to our front two, as I suspected he would. There is no Nadal, instead they go with the Real

Madrid pairing of Hierro and Ivan Helguera at centre-back. He has just paid Ireland the highest compliment possible, he has changed his team to cope with the pace of Damien Duff and Robbie Keane. How the times are changing.

His tactics will reflect this switch as well, I have no doubt about that. Against the South Africans, the full-backs were constantly urged to get forward but today will be different. His decision to recognise the threat posed by Duffer and Robbie makes me believe he will keep Carles Puyol and Juanfran pushed in alongside Hierro and Helguera at all times.

My thinking doesn't change. I am not going to worry about their pace and creativity upfront just because he is cautious about the speed of our front two. We will spring the offside on Raul and Morientes and see how they cope with that and we will leave Duffer and Robbie upfront at all times. I believe we have more to worry them than vice versa.

The game starts as expected. Spain sit with four across the back, the full-backs barely crossing the halfway line in the opening five minutes. They are being cagey, giving respect to Duffer and Robbie, who almost makes them pay with a third-minute shot from the edge of the box that whistles past the post.

I like our start but any smugness is soon wiped off my face. The game is only seven minutes old when Spain win a throw-in away to my right, deep in our half of the field. Before the match, I had emphasised to the defenders to be aware of the long throw threat from Puyol and Francisco de Pedro. We had picked that up on the videos and we even had it on the notice board back in the dressing-room. Now they shape for a long throw and we fall for the trap, setting up to defend a long ball into the box. Instead Puyol throws it short to Ruben Baraja, gets the return and floats in a brilliant cross to the near post. Morientes slips in ahead of Gary Breen and the ball is in the back of the net before we realise what is going on.

Sod it. Another game, another poor start and another early goal conceded. It is time to sink or swim now. The message from the bench is to keep our heads, keep our shape and carry on with the game plan.

Spain leave their four at the back and are content to hit us on the break but the shape of the game changes. We begin to win the midfield battles as Mattie and Kinse snap away at their opponents. Stan and Breeny are now playing a blinder at the back and end up catching Morientes, Raul and co offside no fewer than nine times in the first half.

Our best chance of the half falls to Robbie, just two minutes before the break. Mattie Holland plays him through but the ball bounces awkwardly and Robbie has to swivel before his flick goes over the bar. So near and yet so far.

Still, I am happy enough as we head for the dressing-room. The Spanish have scored a great goal but we have responded with character and determination once again. We are not being over-run, we are not being outplayed. They may have all the stars but they know they are in a game here.

Again, I have a plan B in mind. Just as in the game against Germany, I am concerned about where our goal is going to come from so I pull Duffer at the break and ask him if he is happy to play out wide on the right if I throw Quinny alongside Robbie. Duffer has no problem with the proposal. Kevin Kilbane is playing well and gives me options from deep so Kells will be the one to lose out if we need to change it.

Spain take the initiative again on the resumption. Raul sets up Morientes but he shoots at Shay from fifteen yards. We get a break five minutes later when their 'keeper Iker Casillas fails to control a high ball but Killer's effort is cleared off the line by Hierro.

Then the first potential disaster of the night befalls us. Stan is forced out with a hamstring injury picked up late in the first-half. Kenny Cunningham gets his chance as Breeny's new partner. He takes to the job like a duck to water and we barely notice the difference.

I am still thinking of the change discussed at the break but, of course, Gary starts the second-half like a man possessed. He makes one great burst forward then gets back to deny Raul any room to manoeuvre at the other end. However, I have to do something to unlock this rigid Spanish defence. Kells gets the hook in the fifty-fifth minute and he is none too pleased. He kicks a water bottle in anger on his way off but I can understand his frustrations.

Quinny is in and Duffer is out wide on the right. His wizardry on the ball causes Spain all sorts of problems and eventually he is blatantly pulled down by Juanfran for a sixty-third-minute penalty. The breakthrough has arrived. Ian Harte, our regular penalty taker, steps up to collect the ball from the referee. I am confident he will bury it as usual but I can barely watch as he steps back.

Hartey moves forward, kicks it to his left instead of the right as he normally does and Casillas is across in time to block it. The ball falls at the feet of Kevin Kilbane – and ricochets off his shin and past the post.

We are down but we are not out yet, not by a long shot. Quinny has made a difference, so has Duffer down the right. Again I urge the lads to keep their heads and their shape. This game is still alive for us if we show faith now.

Raul forces another save from Shay before Duffer inches one just wide in the eightieth minute. We are in the game, we are competing and creating chances but the ball is not going in. Just like the German game really.

The Spanish look increasingly desperate as the game goes on and the pace wears them down. Gaizka Mendieta replaces de Pedro and almost does a man-marking job on Duffer. Morientes is surprisingly replaced by David Albeda on seventy-two minutes and then Raul limps out of the action and our offside trap in the eighty-second minute.

It is time for me to make a change as well. Duffer has just clipped the outside of the post but there is still little sign of an Irish equaliser. We might as well throw caution to the wind now and go for it. We have nothing to lose by throwing an extra front player on for the final ten minutes or so. The choice is Clinton Morrison or David Connolly. Nobody has trained better than David over the past month, nobody has finished with more precision and accuracy in training. I go with the man of the moment and throw David in for Ian Harte.

We play three at the back again and after another eight minutes of torture – which includes a brave save by Casillas from Robbie – it pays off. Time is all but up when the Swedish referee Anders Frisk makes one of the great calls of the World Cup finals. He spots Hierro pulling Niall Quinn's jersey all over the shop as they contest a ninetieth-minute cross from Stevie Finnan. Frisk points to the spot straight away. I can barely believe my eyes. I still don't know what Hierro thought he was doing. The Spanish are distraught but the decision is entirely justified. They are still arguing with the referee as Robbie picks the ball up and places it gently on the spot.

What a kid. Imagine the emotions going through his head as he waits for the fuss to die down. We are seconds away from a World Cup exit and he is about to take the biggest penalty of his life. He is ice cool as he sends Casillas the wrong way. We have survived, we are into extra-time. The dream lives on.

I have five minutes now to get the show back on the road. My players are pumping with adrenaline, while the Spanish are at sixes and sevens. Camacho spends more time talking to Frisk than he does to his players. Half his team are sitting in the dug-out, resting their weary bones, as the reality of it all comes home to roost. They look in rag order, in total disarray.

I tell my players to stay on their feet, to show the Spaniards that we are still fit, still ready and hungry for action. We look like the team in the ascendancy and that is the way I want to keep it. The game is there for us now. Spain are down to ten men because Albeda has gone off with an injury and they are in trouble. We have to keep going forward and take the game to Spain. We have to believe we can win. We are not going to let our World Cup peter out. All we need is another goal, that's all.

Spain go on the defensive as soon as extra-time begins and the threat of the golden goal looms. Aside from one close call, thanks to Mendieta five minutes after the restart, we are in total control. We bombard them but their defence holds firm. They seem content to play for penalties now, we must continue to surge forward in the belief that a goal will come.

Robbie almost sneaks one with a volley after 108 minutes and moments later David Connolly goes within inches of folklore as he flashes a twenty-five-yard shot just wide. It is not to be. There is no golden goal, no last minute reprieve this time. Instead, we head for the lottery that is the penalty shoot-out. It is time to be big and brave.

I gather the lads in the centre of the pitch and call for calm. No matter what happens now, they have so much to be proud of. They have given their all in the last sixteen of the World Cup and the country, I know, is proud of them. They have lived up to that notice on the board inside the dressing-room. No matter what, we leave here tonight with no regrets.

Now, who wants to take a penalty? Hartey, Kells and Stan have all departed the action so they're ruled out straight away. Robbie, so confident from the spot half an hour earlier, puts his hand up straight away. So does Mattie, David Connolly and Kevin Kilbane, followed by Stevie Finnan. They are up for it in the heat of the moment. They feel confident that they can handle the pressure in this cauldron of emotion and that is fine by me. Every one of them knows what is needed now.

David reminds me that the psychologists say that the last man to volunteer should be the first man to take a penalty. Stevie was last in but he is fine about taking one so we will go with Robbie, Matt, David, Kevin and Stevie in that order.

We stand on the side of the pitch, put our hands together and repeat the 'no regrets' mantra as the drama begins again.

Spain win the toss and we are on first, in the same goal that we used for the penalty shoot-out after last night's training session.

Robbie hits his well and scores. 1–0. Hierro beats Shay with their first. 1–1.

Mattie is next. He hits the ball sweetly, so sweetly, but it cannons off the outside of the crossbar and wide. He is distraught as he makes his way back to the centre circle. 1–1. Baraja scores. 1–2.

David Connolly is next. His shot is straight at the 'keeper and Casillas saves. 1–2. We need Shay to do something big now. He doesn't have to, Juanfran hits it wide and we are still alive. 1–2.

Now Kevin Kilbane steps up to the plate. He has been taking

money off Quinny in training but this one doesn't fly right and Casillas saves again. It's getting too close for comfort now as Valeron steps up for the penalty that can win the tie for Spain. He misses. It's still 1–2.

Steve Finnan is next for Ireland. His head is as calm as can be as he strikes the perfect penalty past the Spanish 'keeper. It's 2–2 and just one spot kick left for the Spaniards.

Mendieta, a man I once voted for in the European Player of the Year awards, does a Tony Cascarino on it, stubbing the ground as he connects with the ball, just like Cas did in Genoa. The connection is not perfect but it beats Shay and we are out. The World Cup is over. Five penalties each and we are beaten, 3–2.

There are plenty of tears as we salute the fans on our final lap of honour of this World Cup finals. They are as distraught as the players collapsing in front of them.

I try to pick up the pieces, difficult as it is as my own emotions bring me close to tears. I tell David Connolly to always remember that he was brave enough to take that penalty, he could have been a hero. The same applies to Kevin. There can be no recriminations against him, his World Cup cannot be remembered for one penalty miss. Mattie Holland has had a great tournament. He has been one of the stars of the show so forget about this and remember only the good times. This World Cup, all five weeks and four games of it, should not be remembered for three penalty misses.

There are no regrets as we leave this field today, no regrets at all. We gave it our best shot. No one can ask for any more than that.

The dressing-room is not for the faint-hearted. Grown men are in tears. The World Cup is over. We are going home. I tell the players to be proud, to accept that they gave everything out there and came so close to the quarter-finals. They are down now, we are all down, but we will be back.

The rest of the night is a blur. As we leave through the mixed zone, some players stop to talk, others ask to be left alone with their disappointment. A meal awaits at the hotel and then the players drift into the Seoul night, finally free to let their hair down. I tell them to celebrate. This is a time for celebration, not recrimination.

I sit with family and close friends and I wonder what might have been.

Republic of Ireland 1, Spain 1
(*After extra time Spain win 3–2 on penalties*)

MONDAY 17th JUNE

It's the finality of it all that hurts. Football will carry on for another fortnight in Japan and Korea but the World Cup is over now for Ireland, the dream is dead. This morning I wake up with just one certainty in my mind. We are going home to Dublin tomorrow, back to normality.

Yet in some senses life will never be the same again for any of us. As a manager, I have changed over the last five weeks. I could not have ridden the rollercoaster of emotions that I've been on since Saipan and not change. Too much was thrown at me, too many questions were asked of me not to have had a profound effect on the way I do my job. I will never make a harder decision. I will never be caught by such a surprise again. I will never experience a tougher or a lonelier time in football. I can never again come under the same pressure. Nothing can ever arise that will have the same effect or the same potential for destruction as the events in Saipan and Izumo. I will certainly never make the front page of the *Calcutta Times* again.

Has it strengthened my resolve? I believe so. I was tested to the limit in the course of this World Cup and I came through, my team came through. I defy anyone to look at the action on the field over the last fortnight and accuse Ireland of failure. We battled against the odds and we ended the World Cup finals unbeaten in normal play, only a penalty kick away from the quarter-finals. I am proud of that achievement, satisfied with the way we all conducted ourselves under such pressure and thrilled with the way we played and performed in this tournament.

I believe that we have redeemed this team's reputation in the wake of very trying circumstances. It could all have been so different if results had gone any other way. We skated on very thin ice and I did fear for the outcome early on but those players stood up to be counted and proved, once and for all, that the team is all important. The team will be here long after Mick McCarthy and Roy Keane have been forgotten about, we should never forget that. The team will move on now and progress on and off the pitch with this World Cup experience behind them. It will make them better players at club level and, I believe, a better team on the international stage.

I start all over again this morning. The World Cup is already history as far as Mick McCarthy, Ireland manager, is concerned. On the back of this success in Japan, the nation will expect us to qualify for the 2004 European Championship finals in Portugal. Not just that, they will expect us to compete with the big guns in two year's time and make a real impact on the Euro stage. The days of heroic failure are over. It will no longer be enough to qualify, Ireland teams must compete in future.

There are, of course, no guarantees. Last time out I deliberately picked Holland away first because I knew they would be coming down from the high of Euro 2000 and vulnerable. This time we have to bounce straight back to competitive action after a World Cup finals. That will not be easy. I always remember the Celtic manager Billy McNeill complaining that he sent three Irish players to Euro '88 and didn't get any back for months after the start of the Scottish season. Packie, Chris Morris and I were exhausted after that tournament and I even lost my place in the Celts defence when I went back to club football. My players face that same challenge now. Some will move up a gear in light of their World Cup experience, others will face challenges from the youngsters coming through.

There are so many questions looming on the horizon now. Will my first-choice players taste regular first-team football with their clubs this season? Will Richard Sadlier come through as a real alternative to Niall Quinn? Will Clinton Morrison or David Connolly become the goalscorer we need to take the pressure off Robbie and Duffer? What about Stan's replacement at centre-back? Will Kenny, Andy O'Brien, Richard Dunne or John O'Shea stake their claim?

Can Colin Healy and Stephen McPhail deliver on their promise now, can Mark Kennedy offer a real challenge to Kevin on the left?

We need new faces now as well. Last night I stood up at the front of the bus and publicly thanked Niall Quinn and Steve Staunton for their years of service to the Irish shirt. Quinny told me to thank Alan Kelly as well, letting the cat out of the bag about Kells' retirement. They will be missed but, like me, they move on.

I have two years left with Ireland now. I finally signed that contract on the night before the Spanish game and my future has been settled for a while at least. People are talking about deals until 2006 and even 2008 but that is all rubbish. If we don't qualify for Euro 2004, I will be gone, out of here, end of story.

If I sign a six-year deal now, do the FAI have the money to pay me up if it doesn't work out and they want to sack me? No. I have always worked on two-year deals with the Association. That was wrong back in 1996 but now it suits me as well. A part of me wants to go back to the asylum, wants to manage in the Premiership. If that chance comes after Portugal then I feel I should be free to take up any offers.

There were times during this World Cup when I wondered if I should even carry on for the next two years. Those thoughts have been put to bed now. The performances and the way the players responded to me on the pitch at this World Cup have left me in no doubt that we are on the right road.

We can go to Portugal in two years' time. We can bring 40,000 fans to the Algarve with us. And I make just one promise as I look to the future – there will be no regrets.

Afterword

The reaction to Ireland's World Cup adventure has been nothing short of astonishing, nothing less than humbling. A hundred thousand people made the effort to turn out in the Phoenix Park and welcome us home from the Far East. Their response, more than anything else, proved to us all how much the Irish football team achieved this summer. Since then, the feedback has been so warm, so positive.

At times during the World Cup I did wonder what the Irish people thought of me, how they felt about the manager who sent their best player home. I was under so much pressure during those weeks that I was conscious mostly of the negative stuff coming my way, the attacks and the criticism. It felt, at times, as if the world was against me. Since I've been back, I've realised that feeling was unfair to the many who have given me nothing but support and appreciation.

I have received standing ovations in restaurants in Naas, rounds of applause in my favourite curry house in Bromley, the Papadom, free drinks in my local. The English journalists who covered the World Cup finals sent me a fax offering their congratulations for the way the Ireland World Cup party played and conducted ourselves. Everyone from President Mary McAleese to Tony Blair to Bono to hundreds of ordinary men and women sent me thank you cards and faxes and I am grateful to all of them.

I am also realistic enough to know that their praise is all thanks to the performances of the team of the Republic of Ireland, my country, at the World Cup finals. The Irish players touched so many with their achievements on and off the park in the Far East. The pride they have given me over the last three months is immense, greater than anyone can ever know.

I am not comfortable with the fame game. I all but blush when plaudits come my way. I would prefer the credit to be passed on to every one of the twenty-two players who were with me in Japan and Korea and were involved in those games against Cameroon, Germany, Saudi Arabia and Spain. Unfortunately, all the congratulations justly given to those players and the backroom team who flew the flag for Ireland have been overshadowed by the aftermath of the night when Roy Keane left me with no option but to send him home from Saipan.

Keane's expulsion took much of the pleasure of the World Cup finals away from me and that is something I will always regret. Perhaps I was naive to believe managing your country at the World Cup finals could be one hundred per cent pleasurable and positive. Maybe I was wrong to hope that Ireland's third World Cup finals could be a success and a pleasure for all of us from start to finish. That was all I wanted going to Japan, to take pleasure in doing my best for my country. Instead, I got dragged into a war I never wanted to fight, a war that is still going on.

Keane has stoked the fires of controversy ever since his return. As I sit in Helsinki after a 3–0 win over Finland, I should be looking forward to a future that is full of possibilities for the Irish team as we look to build on the World Cup and not just qualify but compete at the 2004 European Championship. Instead, I am forced to look back once again to events in the recent past.

I wish the Roy Keane incident had never happened. I have nothing but the utmost respect for Roy Keane the footballer and I have been nothing but supportive of him in the six years I have been in charge of this team. I stood by him when people booed him, I harangued his biggest critics, I made exceptions for him when the need arose.

Despite all that, ten years of anger towards me, seemingly fuelled by events in Boston back in 1992, exploded from Roy Keane on that fateful night in Saipan. I did not see it coming, the ill-feeling that he clearly has towards me was never evident in all the times I have worked with Roy Keane since I was appointed Irish boss in 1996. I still cannot believe that I ever did anything to Roy Keane that could not have been sorted out. I would have tried to resolve it if I had known how deeply he hated me, how much he resented what happened in Boston. Perhaps the saddest thing in all this is that he couldn't overcome his feelings towards me, or at least bury his anger for another few weeks to play for his country in the World Cup finals, not for Mick McCarthy, but for Ireland.

Could I have handled him differently? I don't think so. Do I regret giving him a room on his own after Denis Irwin retired in 2000? No. He didn't want to share with anyone anyway and I'd have done the same for any other player if they had asked. I am not a dictator, I let players make up their minds and I respect their wishes within reason, so long as they do the business for Ireland on the field. Roy Keane never let me down in that regard.

From what Roy Keane has said, it seems clear that he sees no chance of reconciliation between us. It is obvious to me now that he hates me with a vengeance but that doesn't bother me in the slightest. I actually feel sorry that he could carry that sort of anger against me around with him for such a long time.

More than anything else I feel sad when I look at the Roy Keane situation right now. Part of me says there is no way back for him, that I could never work with him again after the things he said to me in that hotel room all those weeks ago, and the things he has said since. But I am not a vindictive person, I am not someone who likes to hold grudges and bear malice. I do not want to sit here and answer any of the criticisms that he has thrown at me since Saipan. I know better than most that a failure to move on any issue, a failure to forgive, a failure to agree to dialogue causes anger and resentment.

Despite everything that has been said, despite all the hurtful comments thrown at me, I would still talk to Roy Keane if he rings me. Only one man denied his country his services at the World Cup finals. Only one man can end all this. The national team is bigger than Roy Keane or Mick McCarthy, and I know that better than anyone.

All I am interested in now is the future, and moving on. We have a European Championships to qualify for and I hope to see you all in Portugal in 2004.

Mick McCarthy
August 2002

Appendix

IRELAND WORLD CUP TEAMS

Group Two qualifiers

September 2nd 2000 – Amsterdam Arena
Holland 2 (Talan 71 mins, Van Bronckhorst 84 mins)
Republic of Ireland 2 (Robbie Keane 21 mins, McAteer 65 mins)

Holland: Van der Sar; Reiziger (Seedorf 46 mins), Konterman (Talan 65 mins), F. de Boer, Van Bronckhorst, Bosvelt, R. de Boer, Witschge (Bruggink 61 mins), Kluivert, Cocu, Bouma.
Republic of Ireland: A. Kelly; Carr, Harte, Dunne, Breen, Roy Keane, McAteer (G. Kelly 75 mins), Kinsella, Quinn (Connolly 72 mins), Robbie Keane, Kilbane (Staunton 80 mins).

October 7th 2000 – Stadium of Light, Lisbon
Portugal 1 (Conceicao 57 mins)
Republic of Ireland 1 (Holland 73 mins)

Portugal: Quim; Jorge Costa, Dimas (Capucho 88 mins), Beto, Couto, Vidigal, Figo, Joao Pinto (Simao 77 mins), Sa Pinto (Pauleta 77 mins), Rui Costa, Conceicao.
Republic of Ireland: A. Kelly; Carr, Harte, Dunne, Breen, Roy Keane, McAteer (Duff 69 mins), Kinsella, Quinn (Holland 46 mins), Robbie Keane (Finnan 84 mins), Kilbane.

October 11th 2000 – Lansdowne Road
Republic of Ireland 2 (Kinsella 25 mins, Dunne 51 mins)
Estonia 0

Republic of Ireland: A. Kelly; Carr, Harte, Dunne, Breen, Roy Keane, McAteer (Duff 46 mins), Kinsella, Quinn, Robbie Keane (Foley 88 mins), Kilbane (Finnan 88 mins).
Estonia: Poom; Lemsalu, Stepanov, Allas, Saviauk, Vilkmae (Haavistu 79 mins), Terekhov, Oper, Anniste, Reim, Zelinski (Ustritski 79 mins).

March 24th 2001 – GSP Stadium, Nicosia
Cyprus 0
Republic of Ireland 4 (Roy Keane 32 mins, Harte 42 mins, G. Kelly 80 mins, Roy Keane 88 mins)

Cyprus: Panayiotou; Konnafi, Melanarkitis (Filippou 53 mins), Ioakim, Charalambous, Pounas (Malekkos 41 mins), Theodotou, Spoljaric, Okkas (Agathokleous 70 mins), Christodoulou, Constantinou.
Republic of Ireland: Given; G. Kelly, Harte, Cunningham, Breen, Roy Keane, McAteer (Holland 77 mins), Kinsella, Connolly, Robbie Keane (Doherty 87 mins), Kilbane (Duff 81 mins).

March 28th 2001 – Mini-Estadi, Barcelona
Andorra 0
Republic of Ireland 3 (Harte pen 33 mins, Kilbane 76 mins, Holland 80 mins)

Andorra: A. Sanchez; Pol, Lucendo, Alonso (Soria 90 mins), T. Lima, S. Lima, Sonejee, Garcia, Gonzalez (Escura 82 mins), S. Sanchez (Jimenez 88 mins), Ruiz.
Republic of Ireland: Given; G. Kelly, Harte, Cunningham, Breen, Roy Keane, Duff, Holland, Connolly (Doherty 26 mins), Robbie Keane, Kilbane (Finnan 85 mins).

April 25th 2001 – Lansdowne Road, Dublin
Republic of Ireland 3 (Kilbane 33 mins, Kinsella 36 mins, Breen 73 mins)
Andorra 1 (Lima 31 mins)

Republic of Ireland: Given; G. Kelly, Harte, Dunne, Breen (Staunton 82 mins), Kinsella (Finnan 77 mins), Holland, Kennedy (Carr 64 mins), Connolly, Doherty, Kilbane.
Andorra: A. Sanchez; Escura, Garcia, Alonso, S. Lima, T. Lima, Gonzalez (Soria 84 mins), Jimenez (Pujol 78 mins), Sonejee, S. Sanchez (Fernandez 90 mins), Ruiz.

June 2nd 2001 – Lansdowne Road, Dublin
Republic of Ireland 1 (Roy Keane 68 mins)
Portugal 1 (Figo 78 mins)

Republic of Ireland: Given; Carr, Harte, Dunne, Staunton, G. Kelly, Kinsella (McAteer 80 mins), Roy Keane, Kilbane, Quinn (Holland 78 mins), Robbie Keane (Duff 61 mins).
Portugal: Ricardo; Jorge Costa, Rui Jorge (Joao Pinto 68 mins), Beto, Litos (Pereira 88 mins), Frechaut, Figo, Barbosa (Capucho 67 mins), Pauleta, Rui Costa, Petit.

June 6th 2001 – Lillekula Stadium, Tallinn
Estonia 0
Republic of Ireland 2 (Dunne 8 mins, Holland 38 mins)

Estonia: Kaalma; Saviauk, Stepanov, Piiroja, Rooba (Allas 69 mins), Reim, Haavistu (Terekhov 59 mins), Novikov (Ustritski 72 mins), Zelinksi, Kristal, Oper.
Republic of Ireland: Given; Carr, Harte, Dunne, Staunton, G. Kelly, Holland, Kinsella, Kilbane, Duff (O'Brien 88 mins), Quinn (Doherty 36 mins).

September 1st, 2001 – Lansdowne Road, Dublin
Republic of Ireland 1 (McAteer 68 mins)
Holland 0

Republic of Ireland: Given; G. Kelly, Harte (Quinn 87 mins), Staunton, Dunne, McAteer (O'Brien 90 mins), Roy Keane, Holland, Kilbane, Duff, Robbie Keane (Finnan 60 mins).
Holland: Van Der Sar; Melchiot, Stam, Hofland, Numan (Van Hooijdonk 63 mins), Van Bommel, Zenden (Hasselbaink 55 mins), Cocu, Van Nistelrooy, Kluivert, Overmars (Van Bronckhurst 71 mins).

October 6th 2001 – Lansdowne Road, Dublin
Republic of Ireland 4 (Harte 3 mins, Quinn 11 mins, Connolly 63 mins, Roy Keane 67 mins)
Cyprus 0

Republic of Ireland: Given; Finnan, Harte, Breen, Staunton, Roy Keane, Kennedy (Carlsey 63 mins), Holland, Quinn (Morrison 68 mins), Connolly, Kilbane (McPhail 83 mins).
Cyprus: Panayiotou; Konnafi (Louka 68 mins), Kotsonis, Daskalakis, Nicolaou, Melanarkitis, Theodotou, Satsias, Okkas (Themistokleous 83 mins), Christodoulou, Yiasoumi (Kontolefterou 86 mins).

WORLD CUP PLAY-OFFS

November 11th 2001
Republic of Ireland 2 (Harte pen 44 mins, Robbie Keane 50 mins)
Iran 0

Republic of Ireland: Given; Finnan, Harte, Breen, Staunton (Cunningham 75 mins), McAteer (G. Kelly 83 mins), Roy Keane, Holland, Kilbane, Quinn, Robbie Keane.

Iran: Mirzapour; Mahdavikia, Minavand, Peyrovani, Bagheri, Karimi, Karianpour, Ali Daei, Vahedinikbakht (Khaziravi 45 mins), Golmohammadi, Rezaei.

November 15th 2001 – Azadi Stadium, Tehran
Iran 1 (Golmohammadi 91 mins)
Republic of Ireland 0
(*Ireland win 2–1 on aggregate*)

Iran: Mirzapour; Mahdavikia; Minavand, Peyrovani, Bagheri, Karimi, Karianpour, Ali Daei, Vahedinikbakht, Golmohammadi, Rezaei.
Republic of Ireland: Given; Finnan, Harte, Breen, Staunton, McAteer, Kinsella, Holland, Kilbane (G. Kelly 85 mins), Connolly, Robbie Keane (Morrison 75 mins).

WORLD CUP FINALS
GROUP E

June 1st 2002 – Big Swan Stadium, Niigata
Republic of Ireland 1 (Holland 52 mins)
Cameroon 1 (Mboma 39 mins)

Republic of Ireland: Given; G. Kelly, Breen, Staunton, Harte (Reid 75 mins), McAteer (Finnan 46 mins), Kinsella, Holland, Kilbane, Robbie Keane, Duff.
Cameroon: Alioum; Tchato, Wome, Song, Kalla, Geremi, Lauren, Foe, Oliembe, Mboma (Suffo 69 mins), Eto'o.

June 5th 2002 – Kashima Stadium, Ibaraki
Republic of Ireland 1 (Keane 92 mins)
Germany 1 (Klose 19 mins)

Republic of Ireland: Given; Finnan, Harte (Quinn 70 mins), Breen, Staunton (Cunningham 87 mins), G. Kelly (Reid 70 mins), Kinsella, Holland, Kilbane, Keane, Duff.
Germany: Khan; Linke, Ramelow, Ziege, Hamann, Jancker (Bierhoff 75 mins), Klose (Bode 85 mins), Ballack, Schneider (Jeremies 89 mins), Metzelder, Frings.

June 11th 2002 – International Stadium, Yokohama
Republic of Ireland 3 (Keane 7 mins, Breen 61 mins, Duff 87 mins)
Saudi Arabia 0

Republic of Ireland: Given; Finnan, Breen, Staunton, Harte (Quinn 46 mins), G. Kelly (McAteer 80 mins), Kinsella (Carsley 89 mins), Holland, Kilbane, Keane, Duff.
Saudi Arabia: Al Deayea; Al Jahani (Al Dosari 79 mins), Tukar, Zubromawi (Al Dosary 68 mins), Al Shehri, Al Shahrani, Sulimani, Khathran (Al Shlhoub 67 mins), Al Dossari, Al Temyat, Al Yami.

ROUND OF 16

June 16th 2002 – World Cup Stadium, Suwon
Republic of Ireland 1 (Keane 90 mins pen)
Spain 1 (Morientes 8 mins)
(*After extra time – Spain win 3–2 on penalties*)

Republic of Ireland: Given; Finnan, Breen, Staunton (Cunningham 50 mins), Harte (Connolly 82 mins), G. Kelly (Quinn 55 mins), Kinsella, Holland, Kilbane, Keane, Duff.
Spain: Casillas; Juanfran, Helguera, Puyol, Hierro, Raul (Luque 80 mins), Baraja, Morientes (Albelda 72 mins), De Pedro (Mendieta 66 mins), Valeron, Luis Enrique.